Real-Resumes for Restaurant, Food Service & Hotel Jobs...
including real resumes used to change careers
and transfer skills to other industries

Anne McKinney, Editor

PREP PUBLISHING

FAYETTEVILLE, NC

PREP Publishing

1110½ Hay Street
Fayetteville, NC 28305
(910) 483-6611

Library of Congress Cataloging-in-Publication Data

Real-resumes for restaurant food service & hotel jobs :--including real resumes used to change careers and transfer skills to other industries / Anne McKinney, editor.
     p. cm. -- (Real-resumes series)
   ISBN 1-885288-28-X (trade pbk.)
   1. Résumés (Employment) 2. Restaurants--Employees. 3. Food service employees. 4. Hotels--Employees. I. McKinney, Anne, 1948- II. Series.

   HF5383 .R39589 2002
   650.14'2--dc21
                                     2002027089
                                            CIP

Printed in the United States of America

By PREP Publishing

Table of Contents

Real-Resumes for Restaurant, Food Service & Hotel Jobs..
including real resumes used to change careers
and transfer skills to other industries

Anne McKinney, Editor

Welcome to the Real-Resumes Series. The Real-Resumes Series is a series of books which have been developed based on the experiences of real job hunters and which target specialized fields or types of resumes. As the editor of the series, I have carefully selected resumes and cover letters (with names and other key data disguised, of course) which have been used successfully in real job hunts. That's what we mean by "Real-Resumes." What you see in this book are *real* resumes and cover letters which helped real people get ahead in their careers.

The Real-Resumes Series is based on the work of the country's oldest resume-preparation company known as PREP Resumes. If you would like a free information packet describing the company's resume preparation services, call 910-483-6611 or write to PREP at 1110½ Hay Street, Fayetteville, NC 28305. If you have a job hunting experience you would like to share with our staff at the Real-Resumes Series, please contact us at preppub@aol.com or visit our website at http://www.prep-pub.com.

We hope the superior samples will help you manage your current job campaign and your career so that you will find work aligned to your career interests.

The resumes and cover letters in this book are designed to be of most value to people already in a job hunt or contemplating a career change. If we could give you one word of advice about your career, here's what we would say: Manage your career and don't stumble from job to job in an incoherent pattern. Try to find work that interests you, and then identify prosperous industries which need work performed of the type you want to do. Learn early in your working life that a great resume and cover letter can blow doors open for you and help you maximize your salary.

As the editor of this book, I would like to give you some tips on how to make the best use of the information you will find here. Because you are considering a career change, you already understand the concept of managing your career for maximum enjoyment and self-fulfillment. The purpose of this book is to provide expert tools and advice so that you *can* manage your career. Inside these pages you will find resumes and cover letters that will help you find not just a job but the type of work you want to do.

Overview of the Book

Every resume and cover letter in this book actually worked. And most of the resumes and cover letters have common features: most are one-page, most are in the chronological format, and most resumes are accompanied by a companion cover letter. In this section you will find helpful advice about job hunting. Step One begins with a discussion of why employers prefer the one-page, chronological resume. In Step Two you are introduced to the direct approach and to the proper format for a cover letter. In Step Three you learn the 14 main reasons why job hunters are not offered the jobs they want, and you learn the six key areas employers focus on when they interview you. Step Four gives nuts-and-bolts advice on how to handle the interview, send a follow-up letter after an interview, and negotiate your salary.

The cover letter plays such a critical role in a career change. You will learn from the experts how to format your cover letters and you will see suggested language to use in particular career-change situations. It has been said that "A picture is worth a thousand words" and, for that reason, you will see numerous examples of effective cover letters used by real individuals to change fields, functions, and industries.

The most important part of the book is the Real-Resumes section. Some of the individuals whose resumes and cover letters you see spent a lengthy career in an industry they loved. Then there are resumes and cover letters of people who wanted a change but who probably wanted to remain in their industry. Many of you will be especially interested by the resumes and cover letters of individuals who knew they definitely wanted a career change but had no idea what they wanted to do next. Other resumes and cover letters show individuals who knew they wanted to change fields and had a pretty good idea of what they wanted to do next.

Whatever your field, and whatever your circumstances, you'll find resumes and cover letters that will "show you the ropes" in terms of successfully changing jobs and switching careers.

Before you proceed further, think about why you picked up this book.
- Are you dissatisfied with the type of work you are now doing?
- Would you like to change careers, change companies, or change industries?
- Are you satisfied with your industry but not with your niche or function within it?
- Do you want to transfer your skills to a new product or service?
- Even if you have excelled in your field, have you "had enough"? Would you like the stimulation of a new challenge?
- Are you aware of the importance of a great cover letter but unsure of how to write one?
- Are you preparing to launch a second career after retirement?
- Have you been downsized, or do you anticipate becoming a victim of downsizing?
- Do you need expert advice on how to plan and implement a job campaign that will open the maximum number of doors?
- Do you want to make sure you handle an interview to your maximum advantage?

- Would you like to master the techniques of negotiating salary and benefits?
- Do you want to learn the secrets and shortcuts of professional resume writers?

Using the Direct Approach

As you consider the possibility of a job hunt or career change, you need to be aware that most people end up having at least three distinctly different careers in their working lifetimes, and often those careers are different from each other. Yet people usually stumble through each job campaign, unsure of what they should be doing. Whether you find yourself voluntarily or unexpectedly in a job hunt, the direct approach is the job hunting strategy most likely to yield a full-time permanent job. The direct approach is an active, take-the-initiative style of job hunting in which you choose your next employer rather than relying on responding to ads, using employment agencies, or depending on other methods of finding jobs. You will learn how to use the direct approach in this book, and you will see that an effective cover letter is a critical ingredient in using the direct approach.

Lack of Industry Experience Not a Major Barrier to Entering New Field

"Lack of experience" is often the last reason people are not offered jobs, according to the companies who do the hiring. If you are changing careers, you will be glad to learn that experienced professionals often are selling "potential" rather than experience in a job hunt. Companies look for personal qualities that they know tend to be present in their most effective professionals, such as communication skills, initiative, persistence, organizational and time management skills, and creativity. Frequently companies are trying to discover "personality type," "talent," "ability," "aptitude," and "potential" rather than seeking actual hands-on experience, so your resume should be designed to aggressively present your accomplishments. Attitude, enthusiasm, personality, and a track record of achievements in any type of work are the primary "indicators of success" which employers are seeking, and you will see numerous examples in this book of resumes written in an all-purpose fashion so that the professional can approach various industries and companies.

The Art of Using References in a Job Hunt

You probably already know that you need to provide references during a job hunt, but you may not be sure of how and when to use references for maximum advantage. You can use references very creatively during a job hunt to call attention to your strengths and make yourself "stand out." Your references will rarely get you a job, no matter how impressive the names, but the way you use references can boost the employer's confidence in you and lead to a job offer in the least time.

You should ask from three to five people, including people who have supervised you, if you can use them as a reference during your job hunt. You may not be able to ask your current boss since your job hunt is probably confidential.

A common question in resume preparation is: "Do I need to put my references on my resume?" No, you don't. Even if you create a references page at the same time you prepare your resume, you don't need to mail, e-mail, or fax your references page with the resume and cover letter. Usually the potential employer is not interested in references until he meets you, so the earliest you need to have references ready is at the first interview. Obviously there are exceptions to this standard rule of thumb; sometimes an ad will ask you to send references with your first response. Wait until the employer requests references before providing them.

The "direct approach" is the style of job hunting most likely to yield the maximum number of job interviews.

Using references in a skillful fashion in your job hunt will inspire confidence in prospective employers and help you "close the sale" after interviews.

An excellent attention-getting technique is to take to the first interview not just a page of references (giving names, addresses, and telephone numbers) but an actual letter of reference written by someone who knows you well and who preferably has supervised or employed you. A professional way to close the first interview is to thank the interviewer, shake his or her hand, and then say you'd like to give him or her a copy of a letter of reference from a previous employer. Hopefully you already made a good impression during the interview, but you'll "close the sale" in a dynamic fashion if you leave a letter praising you and your accomplishments. For that reason, it's a good idea to ask supervisors during your final weeks in a job if they will provide you with a written letter of recommendation which you can use in future job hunts. Most employers will oblige, and you will have a letter that has a useful "shelf life" of many years. Such a letter often gives the prospective employer enough confidence in his opinion of you that he may forego checking out other references and decide to offer you the job on the spot or in the next few days.

With regard to references, it's best to provide the names and addresses of people who have supervised you or observed you in a work situation.

Whom should you ask to serve as references? References should be people who have known or supervised you in a professional, academic, or work situation. References with big titles, like school superintendent or congressman, are fine, but remind busy people when you get to the interview stage that they may be contacted soon. Make sure the busy official recognizes your name and has instant positive recall of you! If you're asked to provide references on a formal company application, you can simply transcribe names from your references list. In summary, follow this rule in using references: If you've got them, flaunt them! If you've obtained well-written letters of reference, make sure you find a polite way to push those references under the nose of the interviewer so he or she can hear someone other than you describing your strengths. Your references probably won't ever get you a job, but glowing letters of reference can give you credibility and visibility that can make you stand out among candidates with similar credentials and potential!

The approach taken by this book is to (1) help you master the proven best techniques of conducting a job hunt and (2) show you how to stand out in a job hunt through your resume, cover letter, interviewing skills, as well as the way in which you present your references and follow up on interviews. Now, the best way to "get in the mood" for writing your own resume and cover letter is to select samples from the Table of Contents that interest you and then read them. A great resume is a "photograph," usually on one page, of an individual. If you wish to seek professional advice in preparing your resume, you may contact one of the professional writers at Professional Resume & Employment Publishing (PREP) for a brief free consultation by calling 1-910-483-6611.

Part One: Some Advice About Your Job Hunt

What if you don't know what you want to do?

Your job hunt will be more comfortable if you can figure out what type of work you want to do. But you are not alone if you have no idea what you want to do next! You may have knowledge and skills in certain areas but want to get into another type of work. What *The Wall Street Journal* has discovered in its research on careers is that most of us end up having at least three distinctly different careers in our working lives; it seems that, even if we really like a particular kind of activity, twenty years of doing it is enough for most of us and we want to move on to something else!

That's why we strongly believe that you need to spend some time figuring out *what interests you* rather than taking an inventory of the skills you have. You may have skills that you simply don't want to use, but if you can build your career on the things that interest you, you will be more likely to be happy and satisfied in your job. Realize, too, that interests can change over time; the activities that interest you now may not be the ones that interested you years ago. For example, some professionals may decide that they've had enough of retail sales and want a job selling another product or service, even though they have earned a reputation for being an excellent retail manager. We strongly believe that interests rather than skills should be the determining factor in deciding what types of jobs you want to apply for and what directions you explore in your job hunt. Obviously one cannot be a lawyer without a law degree or a secretary without secretarial skills; but a professional can embark on a next career as a financial consultant, property manager, plant manager, production supervisor, retail manager, or other occupation if he/she has a strong interest in that type of work and can provide a resume that clearly demonstrates past excellent performance in *any* field and *potential* to excel in another field. As you will see later in this book, "lack of exact experience" is the last reason why people are turned down for the jobs they apply for.

> Figure out what interests you and you will hold the key to a successful job hunt and working career. (And be prepared for your interests to change over time!)

How can you have a resume prepared if you don't know what you want to do?

You may be wondering how you can have a resume prepared if you don't know what you want to do next. The approach to resume writing which PREP, the country's oldest resume-preparation company, has used successfully for many years is to develop an "all-purpose" resume that translates your skills, experience, and accomplishments into language employers can understand. What most people need in a job hunt is a versatile resume that will allow them to apply for numerous types of jobs. For example, you may want to apply for a job in pharmaceutical sales but you may also want to have a resume that will be versatile enough for you to apply for jobs in the construction, financial services, or automotive industries.

> "Lack of exact experience" is the last reason people are turned down for the jobs for which they apply.

Based on more than 20 years of serving job hunters, we at PREP have found that your best approach to job hunting is **an all-purpose resume** and **specific cover letters tailored to specific fields** rather than using the approach of trying to create different resumes for every job. If you are remaining in your field, you may not even need more than one "all-purpose" cover letter, although the cover letter rather than the resume is the place to communicate your interest in a narrow or specific field. An all-purpose resume and cover letter that translate your experience and accomplishments into plain English are the tools that will maximize the number of doors which open for you while permitting you to "fish" in the widest range of job areas.

Your resume will provide the script for your job interview.
When you get down to it, your resume has a simple job to do: Its purpose is to blow as many doors open as possible and to make as many people as possible want to meet you. So a well-written resume that really "sells" you is a key that will create opportunities for you in a job hunt.

This statistic explains why: The typical newspaper advertisement for a job opening receives more than 245 replies. And normally only 10 or 12 will be invited to an interview.

But here's another purpose of the resume: it provides the "script" the employer uses when he interviews you. If your resume has been written in such a way that your strengths and achievements are revealed, that's what you'll end up talking about at the job interview. Since the resume will govern what you get asked about at your interviews, you can't overestimate the importance of making sure your resume makes you look and sound as good as you are.

Your resume is the "script" for your job interviews. Make sure you put on your resume what you want to talk about or be asked about at the job interview.

So what is a "good" resume?
Very literally, your resume should motivate the person reading it to dial the phone number or e-mail the screen name you have put on the resume. When you are relocating, you should put a local phone number on your resume if your physical address is several states away; employers are more likely to dial a local telephone number than a long-distance number when they're looking for potential employees.

If you have a resume already, look at it objectively. Is it a limp, colorless "laundry list" of your job titles and duties? Or does it "paint a picture" of your skills, abilities, and accomplishments in a way that would make someone want to meet you? Can people understand what you're saying? If you are attempting to change fields or industries, can potential employers see that your skills and knowledge are transferable to other environments? For example, have you described accomplishments which reveal your problem-solving abilities or communication skills?

The one-page resume in chronological format is the format preferred by most employers.

How long should your resume be?
One page, maybe two. Usually only people in the academic community have a resume (which they usually call a *curriculum vitae*) longer than one or two pages. Remember that your resume is almost always accompanied by a cover letter, and a potential employer does not want to read more than two or three pages about a total stranger in order to decide if he wants to meet that person! Besides, don't forget that the more you tell someone about yourself, the more opportunity you are providing for the employer to screen you out at the "first-cut" stage. A resume should be concise and exciting and designed to make the reader want to meet you in person!

Should resumes be functional or chronological?
Employers almost always prefer a chronological resume; in other words, an employer will find a resume easier to read if it is immediately apparent what your current or most recent job is, what you did before that, and so forth, in reverse chronological order. A resume that goes back in detail for the last ten years of employment will generally satisfy the employer's curiosity about your background. Employment more than ten years old can be shown even more briefly in an "Other Experience" section at the end of your "Experience" section. Remember that your intention is not to tell everything you've done but to "hit the high points" and especially impress the employer with what you learned, contributed, or accomplished in each job you describe.

Once you get your resume, what do you do with it?

You will be using your resume to answer ads, as a tool to use in talking with friends and relatives about your job search, and, most importantly, in using the "direct approach" described in this book.

When you mail your resume, always send a "cover letter."

A "cover letter," sometimes called a "resume letter" or "letter of interest," is a letter that accompanies and introduces your resume. Your cover letter is a way of personalizing the resume by sending it to the specific person you think you might want to work for at each company. Your cover letter should contain a few highlights from your resume—just enough to make someone want to meet you. Cover letters should always be typed or word processed on a computer—never handwritten.

Never mail or fax your resume without a cover letter.

1. Learn the art of answering ads.

There is an "art," part of which can be learned, in using your "bestselling" resume to reply to advertisements.

Sometimes an exciting job lurks behind a boring ad that someone dictated in a hurry, so reply to any ad that interests you. Don't worry that you aren't "25 years old with an MBA" like the ad asks for. Employers will always make compromises in their requirements if they think you're the "best fit" overall.

What about ads that ask for "salary requirements?"

What if the ad you're answering asks for "salary requirements?" The first rule is to avoid committing yourself in writing at that point to a specific salary. You don't want to "lock yourself in."

What if the ad asks for your "salary requirements?"

There are two ways to handle the ad that asks for "salary requirements."

First, you can ignore that part of the ad and accompany your resume with a cover letter that focuses on "selling" you, your abilities, and even some of your philosophy about work or your field. You may include a sentence in your cover letter like this: "I can provide excellent personal and professional references at your request, and I would be delighted to share the private details of my salary history with you in person."

Second, if you feel you must give some kind of number, just state a range in your cover letter that includes your medical, dental, other benefits, and expected bonuses. You might state, for example, "My current compensation, including benefits and bonuses, is in the range of $30,000-$40,000."

Analyze the ad and "tailor" yourself to it.

When you're replying to ads, a finely tailored cover letter is an important tool in getting your resume noticed and read. On the next page is a cover letter which has been "tailored to fit" a specific ad. Notice the "art" used by PREP writers of analyzing the ad's main requirements and then writing the letter so that the person's background, work habits, and interests seem "tailor-made" to the company's needs. Use this cover letter as a model when you prepare your own reply to ads.

Date

Mr. Arthur Wise
PYA Monarch.
9439 Goshen Lane
Dallas, TX 22105

Dear Mr. Wise:

I would appreciate an opportunity to show you in person, soon, that I am the energetic, dynamic individual you are looking for as your Sales Representative and Food Broker for PYA Monarch in the Dallas area.

Here are just three reasons why I believe I am the effective young professional you seek:

- *I am a proven salesperson* with a demonstrated ability to "prospect" and produce sales. In my current job as a sales representative, I contact more than 150 business professionals per week and won my company's annual award for outstanding sales performance.

- *I enjoy traveling and am eager to assist in the growth of your business.* I am fortunate to have the natural energy, industry, and enthusiasm required to put in the long hours necessary for effective sales performance.

- *I understand the food brokerage business and my lifestyle is suited to the long hours and weekend work.* I am single and available to meet customers at their convenience.

I am fortunate to have the natural energy, industry, and enthusiasm required to put in the long hours necessary for effective sales performance. You will find me, I am certain, a friendly, good-natured person whom you would be proud to call part of your "team." I would enjoy the opportunity to share my proven sales techniques and extensive knowledge with other junior sales professionals in a management and development position.

I hope you will call or write me soon to suggest a convenient time when we might meet to discuss your needs further and how I might serve them.

Yours sincerely,

Your Name

Employers are trying to identify the individual who wants the job they are filling. Don't be afraid to express your enthusiasm in the cover letter!

2. Talk to friends and relatives.

Don't be shy about telling your friends and relatives the kind of job you're looking for. Looking for the job you want involves using your network of contacts, so tell people what you're looking for. They may be able to make introductions and help set up interviews.

About 25% of all interviews are set up through "who you know," so don't ignore this approach.

3. Finally, and most importantly, use the "direct approach."

The "direct approach" is a strategy in which you choose your next employer.

More than 50% of all job interviews are set up by the "direct approach." That means you actually mail, e-mail, or fax a resume and a cover letter to a company you think might be interesting to work for.

To whom do you write?

In general, you should write directly to the *exact name* of the person who would be hiring you: say, the vice-president of marketing or data processing. If you're in doubt about to whom to address the letter, address it to the president by name and he or she will make sure it gets forwarded to the right person within the company who has hiring authority in your area.

How do you find the names of potential employers?

You're not alone if you feel that the biggest problem in your job search is finding the right names at the companies you want to contact. But you can usually figure out the names of companies you want to approach by deciding first if your job hunt is primarily geography-driven or industry-driven.

In a **geography-driven job hunt,** you could select a list of, say, 50 companies you want to contact **by location** from the lists that the U.S. Chambers of Commerce publish yearly of their "major area employers." There are hundreds of local Chambers of Commerce across America, and most of them will have an 800 number which you can find through 1-800-555-1212. If you and your family think Atlanta, Dallas, Ft. Lauderdale, and Virginia Beach might be nice places to live, for example, you could contact the Chamber of Commerce in those cities and ask how you can obtain a copy of their list of major employers. Your nearest library will have the book which lists the addresses of all chambers.

In an **industry-driven job hunt,** and if you are willing to relocate, you will be identifying the companies which you find most attractive in the industry in which you want to work. When you select a list of companies to contact **by industry,** you can find the right person to write and the address of firms by industrial category in *Standard and Poor's, Moody's,* and other excellent books in public libraries. Many Web sites also provide contact information.

Many people feel it's a good investment to actually call the company to either find out or double-check the name of the person to whom they want to send a resume and cover letter. It's important to do as much as you feasibly can to assure that the letter gets to the right person in the company.

On-line research will be the best way for many people to locate organizations to which they wish to send their resume. It is outside the scope of this book to teach Internet research skills, but librarians are often useful in this area.

What's the correct way to follow up on a resume you send?
There is a polite way to be aggressively interested in a company during your job hunt. It is ideal to end the cover letter accompanying your resume by saying, "I hope you'll welcome my call next week when I try to arrange a brief meeting at your convenience to discuss your current and future needs and how I might serve them." Keep it low key, and just ask for a "brief meeting," not an interview. Employers want people who show a determined interest in working with them, so don't be shy about following up on the resume and cover letter you've mailed.

It pays to be aware of the 14 most common pitfalls for job hunters.

STEP THREE: Preparing for Interviews

But a resume and cover letter by themselves can't get you the job you want. You need to "prep" yourself before the interview. Step Three in your job campaign is "Preparing for Interviews." First, let's look at interviewing from the hiring organization's point of view.

What are the biggest "turnoffs" for potential employers?
One of the ways to help yourself perform well at an interview is to look at the main reasons why organizations *don't* hire the people they interview, according to those who do the interviewing.

Notice that "lack of appropriate background" (or lack of experience) is the *last* reason for not being offered the job.

The 14 Most Common Reasons Job Hunters Are Not Offered Jobs (according to the companies who do the interviewing and hiring):

1. Low level of accomplishment
2. Poor attitude, lack of self-confidence
3. Lack of goals/objectives
4. Lack of enthusiasm
5. Lack of interest in the company's business
6. Inability to sell or express yourself
7. Unrealistic salary demands
8. Poor appearance
9. Lack of maturity, no leadership potential
10. Lack of extracurricular activities
11. Lack of preparation for the interview, no knowledge about company
12. Objecting to travel
13. Excessive interest in security and benefits
14. Inappropriate background

Department of Labor studies have proven that smart, "prepared" job hunters can increase their beginning salary while getting a job in *half* the time it normally takes. (4½ months is the average national length of a job search.) Here, from PREP, are some questions that can prepare you to find a job faster.

Are you in the "right" frame of mind?
It seems unfair that we have to look for a job just when we're lowest in morale. Don't worry *too* much if you're nervous before interviews. You're supposed to be a little nervous, especially if the job means a lot to you. But the best way to kill unnecessary

fears about job hunting is through 1) making sure you have a great resume and 2) preparing yourself for the interview. Here are three main areas you need to think about before each interview.

Do you know what the company does?

Don't walk into an interview giving the impression that, "If this is Tuesday, this must be General Motors."

Find out before the interview what the company's main product or service is. Where is the company heading? Is it in a "growth" or declining industry? (Answers to these questions may influence whether or not you want to work there!)

Information about what the company does is in annual reports, in newspaper and magazine articles, and on the Internet. If you're not yet skilled at Internet research, just visit your nearest library and ask the reference librarian to guide you to printed materials on the company.

Do you know what you want to do for the company?

Before the interview, try to decide how you see yourself fitting into the company. Remember, "lack of exact background" the company wants is usually the last reason people are not offered jobs.

Understand before you go to each interview that the burden will be on you to "sell" the interviewer on why you're the best person for the job and the company.

How will you answer the critical interview questions?

Put yourself in the interviewer's position and think about the questions you're most likely to be asked. Here are some of the most commonly asked interview questions:

Q: "What are your greatest strengths?"
A: Don't say you've never thought about it! Go into an interview knowing the three main impressions you want to leave about yourself, such as "I'm hard-working, loyal, and an imaginative cost-cutter."

Q: "What are your greatest weaknesses?"
A: Don't confess that you're lazy or have trouble meeting deadlines! Confessing that you tend to be a "workaholic" or "tend to be a perfectionist and sometimes get frustrated when others don't share my high standards" will make your prospective employer see a "weakness" that he likes. Name a weakness that your interviewer will perceive as a strength.

Q: "What are your long-range goals?"
A: If you're interviewing with Microsoft, don't say you want to work for IBM in five years! Say your long-range goal is to be *with* the company, contributing to its goals and success.

Q: "What motivates you to do your best work?"
A: Don't get dollar signs in your eyes here! "A challenge" is not a bad answer, but it's a little cliched. Saying something like "troubleshooting" or "solving a tough problem" is more interesting and specific. Give an example if you can.

Research the company before you go to interviews.

Anticipate the questions you will be asked at the interview, and prepare your responses in advance.

Q: "What do you know about this organization?"

A: Don't say you never heard of it until they asked you to the interview! Name an interesting, positive thing you learned about the company recently from your research. Remember, company executives can sometimes feel rather "maternal" about the company they serve. Don't get onto a negative area of the company if you can think of positive facts you can bring up. Of course, if you learned in your research that the company's sales seem to be taking a nose-dive, or that the company president is being prosecuted for taking bribes, you might politely ask your interviewer to tell you something that could help you better understand what you've been reading. Those are the kinds of company facts that can help you determine whether or not you want to work there.

Go to an interview prepared to tell the company why it should hire you.

Q: "Why should I hire you?"

A: "I'm unemployed and available" is the wrong answer here! Get back to your strengths and say that you believe the organization could benefit by a loyal, hard-working cost-cutter like yourself.

In conclusion, you should decide in advance, before you go to the interview, how you will answer each of these commonly asked questions. Have some practice interviews with a friend to role-play and build your confidence.

STEP FOUR: Handling the Interview and Negotiating Salary

Now you're ready for Step Four: actually handling the interview successfully and effectively. Remember, the purpose of an interview is to get a job offer.

A smile at an interview makes the employer perceive of you as intelligent!

Eight "do's" for the interview

According to leading U.S. companies, there are eight key areas in interviewing success. You can fail at an interview if you mishandle just one area.

1. **Do wear appropriate clothes.**

You can never go wrong by wearing a suit to an interview.

2. **Do be well groomed.**

Don't overlook the obvious things like having clean hair, clothes, and fingernails for the interview.

3. **Do give a firm handshake.**

You'll have to shake hands twice in most interviews: first, before you sit down, and second, when you leave the interview. Limp handshakes turn most people off.

4. **Do smile and show a sense of humor.**

Interviewers are looking for people who would be nice to work with, so don't be so somber that you don't smile. In fact, research shows that people who smile at interviews are perceived as more intelligent. So, smile!

5. **Do be enthusiastic.**

Employers say they are "turned off" by lifeless, unenthusiastic job hunters who show no special interest in that company. The best way to show some enthusiasm for the employer's operation is to find out about the business beforehand.

6. Do show you are flexible and adaptable.

An employer is looking for someone who can contribute to his organization in a flexible, adaptable way. No matter what skills and training you have, employers know every new employee must go through initiation and training on the company's turf. Certainly show pride in your past accomplishments in a specific, factual way ("I saved my last employer $50.00 a week by a new cost-cutting measure I developed"). But don't come across as though there's nothing about the job you couldn't easily handle.

7. Do ask intelligent questions about the employer's business.

An employer is hiring someone because of certain business needs. Show interest in those needs. Asking questions to get a better idea of the employer's needs will help you "stand out" from other candidates interviewing for the job.

8. Do "take charge" when the interviewer "falls down" on the job.

Employers are seeking people with good attitudes whom they can train and coach to do things their way.

Go into every interview knowing the three or four points about yourself you want the interviewer to remember. And be prepared to take an active part in leading the discussion if the interviewer's "canned approach" does not permit you to display your "strong suit." You can't always depend on the interviewer's asking you the "right" questions so you can stress your strengths and accomplishments.

An important "don't": Don't ask questions about salary or benefits at the first interview. Employers don't take warmly to people who look at their organization as just a place to satisfy salary and benefit needs. Don't risk making a negative impression by appearing greedy or self-serving. The place to discuss salary and benefits is normally at the second interview, and the employer will bring it up. Then you can ask questions without appearing excessively interested in what the organization can do for you.

Now...negotiating your salary

Even if an ad requests that you communicate your "salary requirement" or "salary history," you should avoid providing those numbers in your initial cover letter. You can usually say something like this: "I would be delighted to discuss the private details of my salary history with you in person."

Once you're at the interview, you must avoid even appearing *interested* in salary before you are offered the job. Make sure you've "sold" yourself before talking salary. First show you're the "best fit" for the employer and then you'll be in a stronger position from which to negotiate salary. **Never** bring up the subject of salary yourself. Employers say there's no way you can avoid looking greedy if you bring up the issue of salary and benefits before the company has identified you as its "best fit."

Don't appear excessively interested in salary and benefits at the interview.

Interviewers sometimes throw out a salary figure at the first interview to see if you'll accept it. You may not want to commit yourself if you think you will be able to negotiate a better deal later on. Get back to finding out more about the job. This lets the interviewer know you're interested primarily in the job and not the salary.

When the organization brings up salary, it may say something like this: "Well, Mary, we think you'd make a good candidate for this job. What kind of salary are we talking about?" You may not want to name a number here, either. Give the ball back to the interviewer. Act as though you hadn't given the subject of salary much thought and respond something like this: "Ah, Mr. Jones, I wonder if you'd be kind enough to tell me what salary you had in mind when you advertised the job?" Or ... "What is the range you have in mind?"

Don't worry, if the interviewer names a figure that you think is too low, you can say so without turning down the job or locking yourself into a rigid position. The point here is to negotiate for yourself as well as you can. You might reply to a number named by the interviewer that you think is low by saying something like this: "Well, Mr. Lee, the job interests me very much, and I think I'd certainly enjoy working with you. But, frankly, I was thinking of something a little higher than that." That leaves the ball in your interviewer's court again, and you haven't turned down the job either, in case it turns out that the interviewer can't increase the offer and you still want the job.

Salary negotiation can be tricky.

Last, send a follow-up letter.

Mail, e-mail, or fax a letter right after the interview telling your interviewer you enjoyed the meeting and are certain (if you are) that you are the "best fit" for the job. The people interviewing you will probably have an attitude described as either "professionally loyal" to their companies, or "maternal and proprietary" if the interviewer also owns the company. In either case, they are looking for people who want to work for *that* company in particular. The follow-up letter you send might be just the deciding factor in your favor if the employer is trying to choose between you and someone else. You will see an example of a follow-up letter on page 16.

A follow-up letter can help the employer choose between you and another qualified candidate.

A cover letter is an essential part of a job hunt or career change.

Many people are aware of the importance of having a great resume, but most people in a job hunt don't realize just how important a cover letter can be. The purpose of the cover letter, sometimes called a **"letter of interest,"** is to introduce your resume to prospective employers. The cover letter is often the critical ingredient in a job hunt because the cover letter allows you to say a lot of things that just don't "fit" on the resume. For example, you can emphasize your commitment to a new field and stress your related talents. The cover letter also gives you a chance to stress outstanding character and personal values. On the next two pages you will see examples of very effective cover letters.

A cover letter is an essential part of a career change.

Please do not attempt to implement a career change without a cover letter. A cover letter is the first impression of you, and you can influence the way an employer views you by the language and style of your letter.

Special help for those in career change

We want to emphasize again that, especially in a career change, the cover letter is very important and can help you "build a bridge" to a new career. A creative and appealing cover letter can begin the process of encouraging the potential employer to imagine you in an industry other than the one in which you have worked.

As a special help to those in career change, there are resumes and cover letters included in this book which show valuable techniques and tips you should use when changing fields or industries. The resumes and cover letters of career changers are identified in the table of contents as "Career Change" and you will see the "Career Change" label on cover letters in Part Two where the individuals are changing careers.

Date

Addressing the Cover Letter: Get the exact name of the person to whom you are writing. This makes your approach personal.

Exact Name of Person
Exact Title of Person
Company Name
Address
City, State Zip

Dear Sir or Madam:

First Paragraph: This explains why you are writing.

With the enclosed resume, I would like to make you aware of my strong desire to become a part of your organization's management trainee program.

Second Paragraph: You have a chance to talk about whatever you feel is your most distinguishing feature.

As you will see from my resume, I recently earned my Bachelor of Science in Hotel Management degree at Cornell University. Since it has always been my childhood dream to become a General Manager for a hospitality industry firm, my college graduation was an especially meaningful event in my life. My parents operated a "mom-and-pop" restaurant throughout my youth, and a love for the industry "got in my blood."

Third Paragraph: You bring up your next most distinguishing qualities and try to sell yourself.

While earning my college degree, I recently completed internships with major hospitality industry firms, and I successfully assumed all the duties of an assistant catering manager. During those internships, under the guidance of experienced restaurant and hotel professionals, I wrote a project development plan, and I also developed a new vegetarian menu for an established restaurant. The menu has been test marketed in five select cities, and the preliminary results indicate that the menu will be adopted nationally.

Fourth Paragraph: Here you have another opportunity to reveal qualities or achievements which will impress your future employer.

In summer jobs while earning my college degree, I worked in all aspects of the hospitality industry as I held part-time jobs as a waitress and hostess. I am highly skilled at working as part of team on restaurant crews, and I am dedicated to the highest standards of profitability and customer service.

Final Paragraph: She asks the employer to contact her. Make sure your reader knows what the "next step" is.

If you can use a highly motivated young professional with unlimited personal initiative as well as strong personal qualities of dependability and trustworthiness, I hope you will contact me to suggest a time when we might meet to discuss your needs. I can provide excellent personal and professional references, and I am eager to apply my natural creativity and industry knowledge to benefit a hospitality industry firm.

Sincerely,

Alternate Final Paragraph: It's more aggressive (but not too aggressive) to let the employer know that you will be calling him or her. Don't be afraid to be persistent. Employers are looking for people who know what they want to do.

Melanie Thompson

Alternate final paragraph:
I hope you will welcome my call soon when I contact you to try to arrange a brief meeting to discuss your needs and how my talents might help you. I appreciate whatever time you could give me in the process of exploring your needs.

Date

Exact Name of Person
Title or Position
Name of Company
Address (number and street)
Address (city, state, and zip)

Dear Exact Name of Person: (or Dear Sir or Madam if answering a blind ad)

I would appreciate an opportunity to talk with you soon about how I could contribute to your organization through my experience as a Waitress and Hostess along with my knowledge of the restaurant business. Mr. Thomas Crane, a General Manager with the Princess Cruise Lines, recently made me aware of the career opportunities available within your organization, and he strongly encouraged me to approach you. I am interested in discussing employment opportunities with you.

You will see from my resume that I began working when I was 16 years old while I was in high school. I have become a skilled waitress while working in various restaurants, and I had an opportunity to learn from veteran industry professionals.

Most recently I have worked as a Hostess for an upscale restaurant, and I am respected for my gracious style of interacting with the public. I have become skilled at hiring, training, and supervising restaurant personnel, including waitstaff and kitchen prep workers.

Although I am held in the highest regard by my current employer, I have decided to explore career opportunities outside my current firm. I am seeking an employer who can use a highly motivated individual with strong communication skills and an outstanding employment record. I am aware that becoming a part of a cruise line would involve extensive travel, and I am ready for that challenge. I am single and available for frequent and extended travel as your needs require.

If you can use a self-starter who could rapidly become a valuable part of your organization, I hope you will contact me to suggest a time when we might meet to discuss your needs and how I might serve them. I can provide outstanding references.

Sincerely,

Lonnie Patton

cc: Thomas Crane

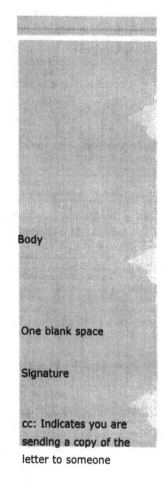

Semi-blocked Letter

Date
Three blank spaces

Address

Salutation
One blank space

Body

One blank space

Signature

cc: Indicates you are
sending a copy of the
letter to someone

Exact Name of Person
Title or Position
Name of Company
Address (number and street)
Address (city, state, and zip)

Follow-up Letter

A great follow-up letter
can motivate the
employer
to make the job offer,
and the salary offer may
be influenced by the
style and tone of your
follow-up
letter, too!

Dear Exact Name:

I am writing to express my appreciation for the time you spent with me on 9 December, and I want to let you know that I am sincerely interested in the position of Controller which we discussed.

I feel confident that I could skillfully interact with your 60-person work force, and I would cheerfully travel as your needs require. I want you to know, too, that I would not consider relocating to Salt Lake City to be a hardship! It is certainly one of the most beautiful areas I have ever seen.

As you described to me what you are looking for in the person who fills this position, I had a sense of "déjà vu" because my current boss was in a similar position when I went to work for him. He needed someone to come in and be his "right arm" and take on an increasing amount of his management responsibilities so that he could be freed up to do other things. I have played a key role in the growth and profitability of his multiunit business, and he has come to depend on my sound financial and business advice as much as my day-to-day management skills. Since Christmas is the busiest time of the year in the restaurant business, I feel that I could not leave him during that time. I could certainly make myself available by mid-January.

It would be a pleasure to work for a successful individual such as yourself, and I feel I could contribute significantly to your hotel chain not only through my accounting and business background but also through my strong qualities of loyalty, reliability, and trustworthiness. I am confident that I could learn Quick Books rapidly, and I would welcome being trained to do things your way.

Yours sincerely,

Jacob Evangelisto

In this section, you will find resumes and cover letters of restaurant, food service, and hotel professionals—and of people who want to work in those fields. How do they differ from other job hunters? Why should there be a book dedicated to people seeking jobs in these areas? Based on more than 20 years of experience in working with job hunters, this editor is convinced that resumes and cover letters which "speak the lingo" of the field you wish to enter will communicate more effectively than language which is not industry specific. This book is designed to help people (1) who are seeking to prepare their own resumes and (2) who wish to use as models "real" resumes of individuals who have successfully launched careers in the restaurant, food service, or hotel field or who have advanced in the field. You will see a wide range of experience levels reflected in the resumes in this book. Some of the resumes and cover letters were used by individuals seeking to enter the field; others were used successfully by senior professionals to advance in the field.

Newcomers to an industry sometimes have advantages over more experienced professionals. In a job hunt, junior professionals can have an advantage over their more experienced counterparts. Prospective employers often view the less experienced workers as "more trainable" and "more coachable" than their seniors. This means that the mature professional who has already excelled in a first career can, with credibility, "change careers" and transfer skills to other industries.

Newcomers to the field may have disadvantages compared to their seniors. Almost by definition, the inexperienced professional—the young person who has recently earned a college degree, or the individual who has recently received certifications respected by the industry—is less tested and less experienced than senior managers, so the resume and cover letter of the inexperienced professional may often have to "sell" his or her potential to do something he or she has never done before. Lack of experience in the field she wants to enter can be a stumbling block to the junior manager, but remember that many employers believe that someone who has excelled in anything— academics, for example—can excel in many other fields.

Some advice to inexperienced professionals...
If senior professionals could give junior professionals a piece of advice about careers, here's what they would say: Manage your career and don't stumble from job to job in an incoherent pattern. Try to find work that interests you, and then identify prosperous industries which need work performed of the type you want to do. Learn early in your working life that a great resume and cover letter can blow doors open for you and help you maximize your salary.

Special help for career changers...
For those changing careers, you will find useful the resumes and cover letters marked "Career Change" on the following pages. Consult the Table of Contents for page numbers showing career changers.

Restaurant, food service, and hotel industry folks might be said to "talk funny." They talk in lingo specific to their field, and you will find helpful examples throughout this book.

Date

Exact Name of Person
Title or Position
Name of Company
Address (number and street)
Address (city, state, and ZIP)

ACCOUNT MANAGER
for a food services
contractor at a college

Dear Exact Name of Person: (or Dear Sir or Madam if answering a blind ad.)

Can you use an articulate, detail-oriented professional who offers outstanding abilities in the areas of sales program development and management, financial management, and the training and supervision of employees?

You will see by my enclosed resume that I have built a track record of accomplishments with Hughett Management Services where I am currently the Account Director at Mission College in Santa Clara, California. During my six years in this position I have reduced labor costs and increased auxiliary sales while overseeing a program with a $900,000 annual operating budget. I manage two supervisors and a 30-person staff which provides resident dining, catering, conference, and retail dining services on a private college campus.

In addition to my business, inventory control, personnel, and human resources management responsibilities, I am heavily involved in the development and management of promotional materials and programs. I have refined my natural verbal and written communication skills while acting as liaison between corporate headquarters and the university, training and dealing with employees, and handling customer service activities.

I believe that you would find me to be an articulate professional with the ability to learn quickly and apply my organizational skills and common sense approach.

I hope you will welcome my call soon to arrange a brief meeting at your convenience to discuss your current and future needs and how I might serve them. Thank you in advance for your time.

Sincerely yours.

John T. Stewart

Alternate last paragraph:
I hope you will call or write me soon to suggest a time convenient for us to meet and discuss your current and future needs and how I might serve them. Thank you in advance for your time.

JOHN THOMAS STEWART

1110½ Hay Street, Fayetteville, NC 28305   •   preppub@aol.com   •   (910) 483-6611

OBJECTIVE
To offer my expertise in reducing costs as well as increasing profits and customer satisfaction while displaying exceptional sales, leadership, and financial management abilities and refining organizational, training, and time management skills.

EXPERIENCE
Built a track record of accomplishments with Hughett Management Services at Mission College, Santa Clara, CA:

ACCOUNT DIRECTOR. (2003-present). Have reduced total labor costs more than $96,000 while overseeing all aspects of operating a $900,000 program which provides this college campus with resident dining, catering, conference, and retail dining services.

- Provide outstanding customer satisfaction in all areas of dining services with a staff of two supervisors and approximately 30 employees.
- Polished managerial abilities while developing budgets and business plans along with making revisions in procedures which led to increases in sales and production.
- Manage a procurement program for more than 1,000 line items.
- Reconcile profit and loss statements and balance sheet management.
- Supervise accounts payable and receivable, payroll, and weekly financial reports sent to the corporate office as well as acting as liaison between the corporation and client.
- Assist the regional sales director in the development of sales proposals by using sales and cost analysis modules.
- Use my communication skills to prepare brochures, calendars, and other promotional materials as well as in the development of a client communication manual.
- Increased Operating Profit Contributions (OPC) from $25,000 to $90,000 and auxiliary sales to more than $228,000 by identifying opportunities, developing strategy, and implementing new plans

FOOD SERVICE MANAGER. (2000-2003). Gained exposure to a wide range of day-to-day operational activities required to ensure the smooth operation of the campus dining, catering, and conference food services.

- Applied organizational skills overseeing fiscal areas of operations which included purchasing as well as inventory, labor cost, and cash-handling controls.
- Handled additional activities ranging from vendor specifications, to menu development and implementation, to promotions and marketing, to catering, to sanitation and safety. Updated the automated procedures which reduced unit labor costs.
- Implemented a computerized system used to handle payroll and accounts payable.

STUDENT MANAGER. Hughett Management Services, Northern Arizona University, Flagstaff, AZ (1997-1999). Hired by the corporation while attending the university, was in charge of food handling controls and supervised 10 part-time employees.

EDUCATION & TRAINING
B.A., Business Administration (minor in Marketing and Finance), Northern Arizona Univ., Flagstaff, AZ; May 1999.
Completed extensive corporate training programs in major areas of emphasis including:
    Total Quality Management 1 and II   diversity/sensitivity training
    Hazard Analysis Critical Control Points (HACCP)   food-borne illness

CERTIFICATIONS
Am a licensed food handler with certification in food-borne illness.

PERSONAL
Am a fast learner who is capable of easily adjusting to new environments. Enjoy using my well-developed communication skills to impact on productivity and customer satisfaction.

Exact Name of Person
Title or Position
Name of Company
Address (no., street)
Address (city, state, zip)

ASSISTANT MANAGER
for a popular restaurant

Dear Exact Name of Person: (or Dear Sir or Madam if answering a blind ad.)

Can you use a hardworking young professional who offers outstanding abilities in training and supervising employees, controlling inventory, handling customer relations, and increasing operational efficiency?

My experience, as you will see from my resume, has given me opportunities to excel in training and motivating employees to work together. I have consistently built productive teams, reduced employee turnover, and found ways to improve procedures.

I have had direct supervision over as many as 33 employees while also being involved in areas including conducting inventories, reorganizing storage facilities, preparing daily/weekly/monthly reports, and troubleshooting production and customer service difficulties.

I feel that I offer a mix of experience and skills which could be easily transferred to other businesses because of my adaptability and proven expertise in passing my knowledge on to others.

I hope you will welcome my call soon to arrange a brief meeting at your convenience to discuss your current and future needs and how I might serve them. Thank you in advance for your time.

Sincerely yours,

Donald J. Jeffries

Alternate last paragraph:
I hope you will call or write soon to suggest a time convenient for us to meet and discuss your current and future needs and how I might serve them. Thank you in advance for your time.

DONALD JOSEPH JEFFRIES ("Don")

1110½ Hay Street, Fayetteville, NC 28305   •   preppub@aol.com   •   (910) 483-6611

OBJECTIVE

To benefit an organization that can use my skills in training employees, building sales, and managing operations as well as my knowledge of inventory management and my proven expertise for increasing productivity/efficiency.

EXPERIENCE

Have been promoted in the following history of advancement by this regional restaurant chain, Frank 'N Stein:

2003-present: ASSISTANT MANAGER. Lander, WY. Was promoted from another location in the chain to oversee operations including controlling inventory, maintaining the building, making deposits, supervising employees, and handling store security.

- Have been successful in eliminating waste, increasing productivity, and reducing manhours.
- Reorganized storage space to make supplies easier to locate.

2002: SUPERVISORY FACILITY MANAGER. Jackson, WY. Managed operational areas including determining weekly supply orders, scheduling and supervising 10 employees, conducting regular inventories, and preparing closing reports.

- Implemented a system of assigning cashiers to their own registers which eliminated confusion and improved cashier efficiency.

2000-02: ASSISTANT KITCHEN MANAGER. Jackson, WY. Made decisions on what to serve for the daily food specials, set prices on special items, ordered around 30 pounds of seafood daily, and then prepared the items.

- Reduced the employee turnover rate to below 10%.

ADVANCED IN THE FOLLOWING "TRACK RECORD" WITH THE MCDONALD'S/ GTB CORPORATION:

TRAINING SPECIALIST and **SUPERVISOR**. Lincoln, NE (1998-2000). Interviewed, hired, trained, supervised, and scheduled up to 33 employees.

- Reduced employee turnover 40% my first six months on the job.
- Coordinated daily sales reports for three shifts.
- Processed invoices and bills for the home office.

ASSISTANT MANAGER. Omaha, NE (1998). Scheduled and supervised from 28 to 33 employees in addition to preparing stock orders, counseling employees, preparing bank deposits and ensuring change was available for cashiers, and making hourly and daily reports.

- Earned a 98% annual inspection rating—the highest score of 15 stores in the district.
- Excelled in training employees who went on to become effective managers.

ASSISTANT MANAGER. Jackson, WY (1996-97). Gained extensive experience in training employees and in troubleshooting production and customer service problems as "second-in-command" of a high-volume fast-food restaurant.

- Was credited with a 60% profit increase after proving an employee had stolen from the company and other employees saw that management was serious about finding ways to decrease employee theft.

EDUCATION

Completed one year of college course work in Business Management, University of Nebraska.

PERSONAL

Can use personal computers to prepare business reports and manage inventories. Am familiar with most types of commercial kitchen equipment. Excellent references on request.

Date

Exact Name of Person
Title or Position
Name of Company
Address (no., street)
Address (city, state, zip)

Dear Exact Name of Person: (or Dear Sir or Madam if answering a blind ad.)

With the enclosed resume, I would like to make you aware of my interest in pursuing management employment opportunities with the TGI Friday's organization.

As you will see from my resume, I have worked for Domino's Pizza Inc. for the past four years and have been promoted rapidly. Currently as an Assistant Manager, I handle a variety of financial, human resources, and customer service responsibilities. I am being groomed for further promotion to store management.

Although I am held in the highest regard by the Domino's Pizza organization, I am attracted to TGI Friday's because I have experienced its hospitality on many occasions. In comparison with other restaurants, I have always found the atmosphere at Friday's to be a happy, fun, and lively one, and I have been impressed with the smooth operations I have observed. I am confident that I could become an asset to the organization, and I am equally sure that I would thrive on the fast pace and challenges of Friday's.

If you can use an experienced food industry management professional, I hope you will consider me for current or future openings. I can provide outstanding personal and professional references.

Sincerely,

Heather Ann Ricardo

HEATHER ANN RICARDO

1110½ Hay Street, Fayetteville, NC 28305 • preppub@aol.com • (910) 483-6611

OBJECTIVE

To contribute to an organization that can use an experienced food service professional who can produce extraordinary "bottom-line" results through applying strong customer service and management skills.

EXPERIENCE

For the past five years, have excelled in a "track record" of promotion with Domino's Pizza Inc., a nationally known chain, which is grooming me for promotion to Store Manager:

2003-present: ASSISTANT MANAGER. Macon, GA. After relocating to Georgia, immediately sought employment with the Domino's chain; I was interviewed and hired within a 24-hour period based upon strong recommendations of my previous employers.

- **Personnel & Human Resources:** Interview, hire, fire, and evaluate employees. Prepare schedules for 40 people, including other managers, in this 7-day-a-week business.
- **Financial Management:** Am responsible for managing financial transactions at this store which produces weekly sales of $17,000 to $22,000; at the end of the day, I count the store down and make deposits. Count the money when I check a driver out.
- **Computer Operations:** Utilize computers to receive inventories, make deposit entries, and consult the make line procedures. Prepare employee reports using the computer.
- **Security:** Have access to all security and alarm codes. Am second on the list of people to call if the alarm goes off after operating hours.
- **Customer Service:** Have significantly improved customer satisfaction at this store. Am the "go-to" person if the store has a customer complaint, and I personally resolve the problem in a way that is financially responsible and responsive to customer needs. Am involved in special promotions with police stations, churches, and other organizations.
- **Highlights of accomplishments:** Have reduced labor costs to below targeted levels without compromising customer service. Have reduced food costs to its targeted level. Improved customer satisfaction by firing offensive employees who could not be retrained in proper Customer Service techniques. Continuously instill in employees the concept that a satisfied customer is the best advertising.

2002: MANAGER TRAINEE & SHIFT LEADER. Knoxville, TN. Upon relocating back to Knoxville, was immediately rehired as a Manager Trainee based on excellent job performance.
- As a Shift Leader, opened a new Knoxville store and handled bank deposits for an operation which generated $15,000 weekly in sales.
- Managed a team of 15-20 people who included drivers, cooks, insiders, and prep personnel.

1999-2001: COOK & "INSIDER." Bristol, TN. Began working at Domino's Pizza when I was 16 years old, my first job with the store included driving around in Bristol and surrounding areas hanging fliers for the business on residential doorknobs.
- Was promoted to "insider" which involved answering phones and cashing out customers.
- At the age of 18, was promoted to the "make line," as I was then legally old enough.
- Between the ages of 18 and 19, was trained by the general manager and assistant managers in managerial skills and Domino's procedures.

Other experience: Cook. Buckeye Grill. Worked full-time while in high school.

EDUCATION

Graduated from North Bristol High School, Bristol, TN 1999; graduated at age 16.

PERSONAL

In my spare time, coach ladies' tennis. Also enjoy singing and writing/performing songs. Have played flute for 11 years. Outstanding professional and personal references.

Exact Name of Person
Exact Title
Exact Name of Company
Address
City, State, Zip

ASSISTANT MANAGER
for a seafood chain

Dear Exact Name of Person (or Dear Sir or Madam if answering a blind ad):

I would appreciate an opportunity to talk with you soon about how I could contribute to your organization through my proven skills in management, marketing, and customer service.

As you will see from my enclosed resume, I was recruited by Landry Seafood and have worked in supervisory positions in various regional locations including Illinois, Indiana, and Michigan. In my current position, I schedule up to 100 people and directly supervise 20 individuals on my shift at a store which grosses $250,000 monthly. I am held accountable for controlling labor and food costs as a percentage of sales, and I have become well known for my creativity and resourcefulness in developing and implementing new merchandising ideas.

I am highly computer literate and utilize a computer daily for producing sales and inventory reports as well as for financial accounting and record keeping.

Although I am held in high regard by my current employer, I am selectively exploring opportunities in other companies where my management and communication skills could be of value. I can provide excellent references at the appropriate time.

If you can use a hard worker with strong personal initiative and outstanding customer service abilities, I hope you will contact me to suggest a time when we might meet in person to discuss your needs. I thank you in advance for your time.

Sincerely,

Marie Parkinson

MARIE PARKINSON

1110½ Hay Street, Fayetteville, NC 28305   •   preppub@aol.com   •   (910) 483-6611

OBJECTIVE

To contribute to an organization that can use a resourceful and highly motivated young manager with proven skills related to customer service, management, and sales.

EDUCATION

College: Completed 3 ½ years of college pursuing a business degree, Michigan State University, East Lansing, MI; am completing degree in my spare time.
Hold Associate of Liberal Arts degree in Human Resource Administration, Southeastern Illinois College, Harrisburg, IL, 1997.
Management: Completed extensive management and customer service training sponsored by Landry Seafood, 2001-present.
Food Service, Sanitation, and Quality Control: Extensive training in these areas.

COMPUTERS

Utilize computers on a daily basis and am proficient with Windows.

EXPERIENCE

ASSISTANT MANAGER. Joe's Crab Shack/Landry Seafood, East Lansing, MI and Indianapolis, IN (2002-present). Was recruited by Landry Seafood for its management training program, and excelled in its three-month training program in Chicago; have worked at stores in Illinois, Indiana, and Michigan.

- In my current job in East Lansing, am one of four assistant managers for a store which grosses more than $250,000 monthly.
- Schedule up to 100 employees and directly supervise 20 or more employees on my shift; develop crew schedules based on sales projections, and am held accountable for controlling labor and food costs as a percentage of sales.
- Utilize a computer daily to produce inventory and sales reports; handle daily financial accounting of all sales and purchases; assist in daily data collection of stock inventory.
- Well known for my creativity and resourcefulness, have excelled in taking on special projects related to maximizing merchandising effectiveness.
- Recruit, interview, and orient new hires; coach and train associates in job skills; played a key role in helping the store in Indianapolis, IN receive an A+ rating, become named Landry's only training store in Indiana, and receive the "Outstanding Facility" award.
- Am held in high regard by my employer and am being groomed for further promotion; have played a key role in increasing sales at every facility where I have worked.
- In Indiana, was specially selected to act as Equal Employment Counselor because of my tact and diplomacy in resolving management-employee issues.
- Received the highest marks on all annual performance evaluations.

Prior to being recruited into Landry Seafood's management training program, excelled in this track record of promotion with a training organization serving the elderly; enjoyed helping others. The Claremont Home, Harrisburg. IL.
1993-2001: REHABILITATION AIDE. Cross trained into a teaching role and then functioned as a Case Load Manager/Teacher while nursing and caring for moderately impaired handicapped clients; assisted in motor skill training courses for physically impaired clients.

1990-92: FOOD OPERATION ASSISTANT. Learned a great deal about food service in an institutional environment while assisting in food preparation for elderly and physically impaired clients. Performed daily monitoring of clients' food intake. Performed data collection of stock inventory. Assisted in proper food and equipment sanitation.

PERSONAL

Can provide outstanding personal and professional references. Am a take-charge individual with superior skills in organizing and managing projects, people, and events.

Exact Name of Person
Exact Title
Exact Name of Company
Address
City, State, Zip

ASSISTANT MANAGER
for a restaurant
organization

Dear Exact Name of Person (or Dear Sir or Madam if answering a blind ad):

I would appreciate an opportunity to talk with you soon about how I could contribute to your organization through my varied skills including management, media buying, and communications.

As my enclosed resume indicates, in my current situation I was hired at an entry-level position and within two weeks I bypassed the normal progression and moved up to Assistant Manager. I am now in charge of many aspects of the business varying from creative promotional ideas to handling accounting matters.

Although I have excelled and am held in high esteem, I am interested in learning about your organization and how I could rise to the challenge of meeting and exceeding your current goals. I believe I could prove to be an invaluable asset and encourage you to contact me at your convenience in order to schedule a time when we might meet in person to discuss your particular needs and direction.

Sincerely,

Sara Guilford

SARA GUILFORD

1110½ Hay Street, Fayetteville, NC 28305   •   preppub@aol.com   •   (910) 483-6611

OBJECTIVE

To offer a background in the supervision of personnel and administrative activities to an employer that can use a creative professional with a reputation as a skilled communicator who can relate to others and provide good listening skills.

EXPERIENCE

ASSISTANT MANAGER. Hodges Restaurant Systems, Richmond, KY (2003-present). Earned rapid promotions ahead of my peers and now schedule and manage from 15 to 18 employees in a restaurant which takes in approximately $28,000 a month.
- After only two weeks, was singled out for my potential and bypassed the normal career progression to Crew Leader while moving up to Assistant Manager.
- Within six months had achieved a managerial level usually taking five years!
- Use my creative abilities to suggest promotional ideas such as Bingo for senior citizens and other activities resulting in increased customer satisfaction and repeat business.
- Screen and interview prospective employees; train new hires.
- Control food and supply inventories from the ordering stage to stocking.
- Handle accounts payable and receivable.

MEDIA BUYER. Creative Edge Advertising, Lexington, KY (2000-2002). Worked closely with media representatives from TV, radio, magazines, and newspapers while planning, researching, negotiating, and purchasing space and time.
- Made decisions on which avenues to use in order to give each client the maximum media exposure for their advertising dollar.
- Refined computer operating skills by using Lotus and WordPerfect software when maintaining records and filing information.
- Developed a close relationship with the accounting department so that invoices were adjusted and figured accurately to reflect customer expenses.
- Cultivated media representatives so that they kept me in mind when special advertising opportunities were going to be available that would be beneficial to my clients.

SUPERVISORY ADMINISTRATIVE ASSISTANT. Department of Veteran's Affairs, Washington, DC (1997-1999). For the office of the Chief of Veteran's Affairs, earned the respect and high praise of senior officials for my professionalism, dedication to high quality, and talent for ensuring that detailed documentation and records were maintained accurately.
- Supervised new employees and trained them in office operations including the use of Windows and database software as well as operating guidelines and procedures.
- Received, reviewed, and processed correspondence, classified material, performance evaluations, and organizational lists.
- Received and handled phone calls from international and local media representatives as well as the general public.
- Consistently described in official evaluations as exceptionally dedicated and self motivated, was cited as "a valuable asset" who set the example for others.

TRAINING

Completed an advanced training program for clerical/administrative/secretarial specialists at J. Sargeant Reynolds Community College, Richmond, VA (June 1996).

OFFICE SKILLS

Through training and experience, am familiar with standard office equipment including multiline phones, copiers, fax machines, typewriters, and computers.

PERSONAL

Held a volunteer office as treasurer of a 30-member family support group. Quickly earn the respect and trust of those around me. Work well as a team member or in supervisory roles.

Exact Name of Person
Title or Position
Name of Company
Address (no., street)
Address (city, state, zip)

ASSOCIATE MANAGER
for Ponderosa Restaurant

Dear Exact Name of Person: (or Dear Sir or Madam if answering a blind ad.)

I would appreciate an opportunity to meet with you confidentially to discuss the possibility of my joining your organization. As you will see from my resume, I have excelled in a variety of roles within Ponderosa Restaurants, and I have the highest regard for Ponderosa's management team and for my associates. Although I am essentially happy in my current organizational home, I am interested in learning more about your company's strategic direction, because I feel I could contribute to your goals and add value to your company.

While working with Ponderosa for several years, I have had an opportunity to acquire skills in every functional area of restaurant operations. Most recently I played a key role in opening a restaurant which has become the highest-volume unit in the chain's history. While overseeing every aspect of operation in this 235-person restaurant, I have instilled in employees an attitude of "attention to detail" which has produced an exceptionally strong commitment to quality standards.

With a reputation as a dynamic motivator and trainer, I have been commended for my ability to hire, train, develop, and motivate some of the industry's finest human resources. I believe strongly that it is the quality of your people and the way you train them that is the key to success in our highly competitive industry. You will see from my resume that I have won numerous awards and honors, including awards for closing down strong competitors.

You would find me in person to be a gregarious and outgoing fellow who offers a proven ability to relate well to customers and to employees at all levels. I have won numerous awards for my exceptional results in the areas of training, profit, sales, and operations.

I hope you will welcome my call soon to arrange a brief meeting at your convenience to discuss your current and future needs and how I might serve them. Thank you in advance for your time.

Sincerely yours,

Harry Aaron Eames

Alternate last paragraph:
I hope you will call or write me soon to suggest a time convenient for us to meet and discuss your current and future needs and how I might best serve them. Thank you in advance for your time.

HARRY AARON EAMES

1110½ Hay Street, Fayetteville, NC 28305   •   preppub@aol.com   •   (910) 483-6611

OBJECTIVE   To benefit an organization that can use a dynamic and resourceful general manager who offers expertise in restaurant operations including experience in starting up new units, overseeing multiple locations, and troubleshooting problems in existing establishments.

ACHIEVEMENTS
- 2003; Started up a restaurant that is the highest-volume restaurant in the chain's history.
- **Top Training Manager** award, 2002; have been recognized for my expertise in training employees and developing human resources considered the best in the industry.
- **Top Ten Award**, 2002; through my management skills, transformed an average operation into a restaurant in the "top 10%" of the company's units in sales/profits.
- Two **Notch in the Gun** awards, 2002 and 1999; for closing down two competitors.
- **ServSafe**, 2003; received this award from the National Restaurant Association for my impeccable sanitation and health practices.

SUMMARY OF EXPERIENCE   *For the past eight years, worked at Ponderosa Restaurant,* **the largest independently held restaurant chain in Montana;** *have earned a reputation as a dynamic motivator, skilled trainer, creative organizer, and innovative manager.*

ASSOCIATE MANAGER. Ponderosa Restaurants, Bozeman, MT (2002-present). Relocated to Bozeman after completing an extensive executive development training session in the operation of metropolitan units; then opened a restaurant which has become the chain's highest-volume unit.
- *Employee management:* Oversee hiring, training, and scheduling of the restaurant's 235 employees; reduced labor costs 6% within three months after opening.
- *Inventory control*: Cost-effectively manage the purchasing, receipt, and utilization of an inventory of perishable and nonperishable items.
- *Finances*: Prepare profit-and-loss statements; monitor invoicing; oversee payroll.
- *Quality control*: Have instilled in employees an attitude of "attention to detail" that has produced a strong commitment to quality standards.
- *Sales and profitability*: Have exceeded every monthly record established for sales.

PARTNER/MANAGER. Ponderosa Restaurants, Billings, MT (1996-2002). Excelled in a variety of roles because of my versatile management skills.
- *Operations management*: Increased sales in off-season by 35% over a six-year period; learned that persistence and hard work are the keys to achieving sales goals.
- *Competitive spirit*: Despite the disadvantage of having to compete with limited seating space, closed down two competitors and increased sales by 26%.
- *Training and development*: Trained district managers, partner managers, franchise service consultants, and assistant managers.
- *Area supervision*: Functioned as a Temporary Area Supervisor and helped selling units with a variety of problems when the district supervisor was overloaded.

ASSISTANT MANAGER. Ponderosa, Missoula, MT (1995-96). Was commended for my creative approach to community involvement and acquired expertise in guest services while training employees and controlling food/labor costs.

EDUCATION   **B. A. in Business Administration,** The University of Montana-Missoula, MT, 1994. Completed extensive executive/management training, Ponderosa Restaurants, 1995-2003.

PERSONAL   Offer extensive expertise in setting up menu matrices, completing sanitation paperwork, handling purchasing, and performing every job and task in restaurant operations.

CAREER CHANGE

Date

Exact Name of Person
Exact Title
Exact Name of Company
Address
City, State, Zip

Dear Exact Name of Person (or Dear Sir or Madam if answering a blind ad):

With the enclosed resume, I would like to express my strong desire to become a Flight Attendant with Delta Airlines and make you aware of my background which is ideally suited to your needs.

Throughout my working career, I have excelled in the hospitality industry. In an entry-level position at Applebee's Restaurant, I was rapidly promoted to Hostess and given the responsibility for training other employees. While living in Syracuse for two years, I worked as an Airport Rental Agent, and I became skilled at serving both busy business and family travelers.

An expert in mixology, I have excelled as a Bartender, and I am very proud of the fact that I have trained two bartenders who went on to establish successful businesses in the hospitality industry. As an expert bartender, I once founded "from scratch" and managed a respected bar called Dee's Spot which attracted a crowd of regulars who enjoyed the atmosphere. I have become an expert at planning and organizing special events for customers including birthday parties, dinners, celebrations of all types, and surprise parties. I have become skilled at making excellent decisions in special situations and crises. In one job I was awarded a special Letter of Commendation from the Alcohol Law Enforcement (ALE) Agency because of my professional handling of an out-of-control customer.

Because of my excellent reputation as a respected manager and business person in the community, I was recruited for my current job with a local pub. The owner relies on me to manage the bar and train both bartenders and hostesses while he concentrates on other business areas.

I am certain that my professional background and gracious personal style of handling people would be well suited to the needs of Delta Airlines, and I hope you will make the decision to offer me employment as a Flight Attendant. I can provide excellent personal and professional references.

Yours sincerely,

Denise Elizabeth Graves

DENISE ELIZABETH GRAVES

1110½ Hay Street, Fayetteville, NC 28305 • preppub@aol.com • (910) 483-6611

OBJECTIVE

I want to contribute to Delta Airlines as a flight attendant through my extensive background in the hospitality industry which involves dealing with people, serving the public, and handling all types of emergencies and unexpected events in a calm and poised manner.

EXPERIENCE

BAR MANAGER & MANAGEMENT CONSULTANT. Lynagh's Sports Bar, Poughkeepsie, NY (2003-present). Because of my outstanding personal and professional reputation, was recruited for this position which involves acting as a supervisor of this popular meeting place frequented primarily by young professionals.
- Through my extensive experience in business management and in restaurant and bar management in particular, have produced spectacular increases in sales.
- Because the owner/manager knows that I am totally reliable and trustworthy, he is able to concentrate on business while I hire, train, and supervise personnel.

BARTENDER & TRAINING MANAGER. Metro, Poughkeepsie, NY (2002). Trained hostesses and junior bartenders while applying my expert knowledge of mixology. On numerous occasions, provided leadership when customers needed help in getting home.

BUSINESS MANAGER & OWNER. Dee's Spot, Poughkeepsie, NY (1998-2001). Started "from scratch" a business in the hospitality industry which became very successful and which cemented my reputation as a respected business manager in the Poughkeepsie community.
- Worked with an accountant for yearly taxes, but handled all weekly, monthly, and quarterly financial reporting; handled bookkeeping, payroll taxes, and accounting.
- Became skilled in ordering inventory so that inventory carrying costs were as low as possible while maintaining sufficient quantities so that we did not stock out.
- Hired and trained many excellent employees; am proud that I trained (in mixology and management) two bartenders who went on to establish their own successful businesses.

BARTENDER & TRAINING MANAGER. Silver Dollar Saloon, Poughkeepsie, NY (1994-98). Became a valued confidante of the owner of this business, who relied on me to hire and train his employees.
- Received a special Letter of Commendation from the Alcohol Law Enforcement (ALE) agency because of my skill in handling an out-of-control customer.

AIRPORT RENTAL AGENT. Budget Rent-a-Car, Syracuse, NY (1992-94). At the airport in Syracuse, handled car rentals for busy travelers; completed contracts, explained the details and fine points of rental agreements, and provided directions to travelers along with information about fine restaurants and scenic attractions.
- Became skilled in dealing with business travelers and their particular needs.

HOSTESS & TRAINER. Applebee's, Poughkeepsie, NY (1990-92). At the popular restaurant which is a favorite meeting place for professionals of all ages, began in an entry-level position and was promoted to train and develop other employees.
- Was named Employee of the Month and was frequently praised by customers.

EDUCATION

Numerous courses at Dutchess Community College, Poughkeepsie, NY.
Completed management training courses through employers such as Applebee's.

PERSONAL

Excellent personal and professional references are available upon request.

Date

Exact Name of Person
Title or Position
Name of Company
Address (no., street)
Address (city, state, zip)

BARTENDER/WAITER
for a privately owned bar
and grill

Dear Exact Name of Person: (or Dear Sir or Madam if answering a blind ad.)

I would appreciate an opportunity to talk with you soon about how I could contribute to your organization through my vast knowledge of the food and beverage business.

As you will see from my resume, I have contributed to the success of businesses serving the entertainment/recreational needs of people. Most recently as a bartender I have played a key role in building the clientele of a popular bar and grill. I am considered an expert on mixology and have even created my own "signature" drinks.

In other jobs I have supervised lifeguards, instructed fishing and water skiing activities, and controlled inventories of recreational equipment.

I hope we will have the opportunity to talk in person about how I could be of value to your business. I can provide outstanding personal and professional references. You would find me to be someone of the highest character who is known for my willingness to "pitch in" and work as needed when other workers encounter unexpected problems.

I hope you will welcome my call soon when I attempt to determine if your schedule will permit us to meet in the near future. Thank you in advance for your time.

Sincerely yours,

Luis Gonzalez

LUIS GONZALEZ

1110½ Hay Street, Fayetteville, NC 28305　　•　　preppub@aol.com　　•　　(910) 483-6611

OBJECTIVE　　To benefit an organization that can use a hardworking and reliable individual who offers a background in the hospitality industry along with other valuable experiences.

EXPERIENCE　　**BARTENDER/FOOD SERVER**. JD's Bar & Grill, Abilene, TX (2003-present). Am involved in all aspects of operating and managing this popular bar and grill serving a loyal clientele; assure that the bar is perfectly cleaned and well stocked at all times.

- *Mixology*: Considered an expert on mixology, have become knowledgeable of more than 80 different import beers and demonstrated my comprehensive knowledge of mixed drinks; created my own "signature" drinks which became favorites.
- *Management*: Act as assistant manager in his absence; became known for my professionalism and willingness to work "on call, no questions asked."
- *Food preparation*: Responsible for food orders and food preparation.
- *Purchasing/inventory control*: Accountable for beer and liquor inventory; determine product line and order beverages and some foodstuffs.
- *Finances*: Assure proper pricing and handling of in excess of $2,000 daily.
- *Customer relations*: Play a key role in building the clientele.
- *Technical knowledge*: Implement all state laws on alcohol consumption.

SKI MACHINE OPERATOR/MAINTENANCE COORDINATOR. Jenny Lake, Abilene, TX (1999-2003). Was in charge of lifeguards and ski machine on a busy lake used by swimmers, boaters, and water skiers; monitored skiers' safety and assured proper maintenance of equipment.

- As a water skiing instructor, taught thousands of people to water ski.
- Contributed to the image and profitability of this business by making sure it maintained a reputation as a safe and reliable operation.

INVENTORY CONTROLLER and **CUSTOMER SALES REPRESENTATIVE**. KEC Electric, Wichita, KS (1996-99). Began as a truck driver and became very knowledgeable of Central Kansas' road system while loading and driving trucks filled with electrical equipment; was promoted to an inside warehouse job and then to a sales position.

- Controlled and accounted for $16 million in inventory while overseeing warehouse sanitation and internal organization.
- Also excelled in a sales position; handled sales of $200,000 monthly and helped increase sales by my ability to communicate with customers by telephone and in person.

LIFEGUARD/SKI INSTRUCTOR/FISHING GUIDE. Wet 'N Wild Waterpark, Texarkana, TX (1996). Supervised large groups of people and was responsible for the safety of hundreds of people daily while maintaining a 100-person pool and overseeing swimming and water activities.

- Instructed water skiing and drove a boat; instructed fishing.

EDUCATION　　Completed more than two years of college-level courses related to computer programming, networking, small business financing, and supervision/management, Wichita Community College.

PERSONAL　　Am considered a friendly, gregarious team member with leadership strengths. Vast knowledge of food/beverage business. Excellent references on request.

Exact Name of Person
Title or Position
Name of Company
Address (no., street)
Address (city, state, zip)

BARTENDER/WAITRESS

for a popular college "hangout." As you can see from this presentation, not every cover letter has to be long!

Dear Exact Name of Person: (or Dear Sir or Madam if answering a blind ad.)

It is with much enthusiasm that I submit the enclosed resume and application for a position with Planet Hollywood, Inc.

You will see from my resume that I have much to offer your organization. I am skilled in performing nearly every job in restaurant operations, and I earnestly desire to embark on a permanent career with your company. I am willing to relocate world wide according to your needs.

I hope you will contact me soon to suggest a time convenient for us to meet and discuss your current and future goals and how I can help achieve them.

Sincerely,

Tasha N. Epps

TASHA N. EPPS

1110½ Hay Street, Fayetteville, NC 28305 • preppub@aol.com • (910) 483-6611

OBJECTIVE

To benefit an organization that can use a dedicated young professional with extensive experience in the food service/restaurant industry along with proven management potential, customer relations skills, and strong personal initiative.

EDUCATION

Portland Community College, Portland, OR: completed a Bartending Course in the Adult Continuing Education Program.
Completed numerous other courses at Portland Community College and Portland State University in mathematics and other areas.
Graduated from Tate's Creek Senior High School, Portland, OR, 1998.
- Was active in the National Honor Society, S.A.D.D., Tate's Creek Marching Band, Foreign Language Club, Spanish Club, and F.B.L.A; during annual F.B.L.A. competitions, placed at both the district and state levels and then placed in the top 20 at the national convention.
- Was extremely active in band as a junior high school student at Parton's Wood Junior High School, was active in Orchestra, Marching Band, All-County Band, All-State Band.

EXPERIENCE

BARTENDER/WAITRESS. Superstar's, Portland, OR (2002-present). Have been involved in a wide variety of activities for this restaurant which is one of Portland's most popular college spots.
- *Waitressing*: Excelled as a waitress until I was old enough to bartend.
- *Bartending*: Have become skilled in mixology, and am knowledgeable of a wide variety of import and domestic beers.
- *Technical knowledge*: Implement all state laws on alcohol consumption, and apply my expert knowledge of food sanitation and other regulations.
- *Inventory control*: Have become experienced in stocking beer, liquor, and utensils used in bartending.
- *Ordering/purchasing*: Have assumed responsibility for ordering food and beer from distributors; handle grocery shopping as needed and pick up liquor from stores.
- *Facility renovating/modernizing*: Played a key role in renovating this facility; helped create new concepts and themes and then, when it closed down for five weeks for modernization, was totally involved in the physical "facelift" by helping to install carpet and also sanding, painting, and staining fixtures.
- *Opening/closing*: Have been entrusted with opening/closing the facility and with calculating receipts.

BARTENDER/WAITRESS/COOK. The Melodeon, Eugene, OR (1999-2001). Before moving to Portland, worked this job full time; while living and working in Portland, frequently traveled to Eugene and filled in for waitstaff, cooks, and bartenders at this popular night spot.

Other experience: Gained valuable management and public relations skills while working as a youngster and teenager in two family businesses.
- In a contracting company, went out on jobs with my dad and learned a variety of homebuilding and carpentry skills.

PERSONAL

Am single and will relocate worldwide and travel extensively as needed. Am musically inclined and am learning the mandolin and saxophone. Enjoy reading, amateur photography, website design, horseback riding, and baking. Am a curious and intelligent person who continually seeks new ways to improve my mathematics and computer science knowledge.

CAREER CHANGE

Exact Name of Person
Exact Title
Exact Name of Company
Address
City, State, Zip

BREWER

This individual seeks to
return to a previous field.

Dear Exact Name of Person (or Dear Sir or Madam if answering a blind ad):

I am writing to express my strong interest in the position of District Manager. With the enclosed resume, I would like to make you aware of my background as an articulate young professional whose exceptional communication, organizational, and technical abilities have been proven in challenging situations in management, sales, and beverage production environments.

While I have recently excelled as an Art Sales Representative for the Sandlin Gallery in Seattle, most of my work experience has been in brewing or in the management of bars and brewpubs. At Cornerstone Brewing Company, I advanced from a production job on the bottling line to the highest position at the company, that of Brewer. I supervised as many as 10 employees, ran a $500,000 kegging operation and a $1 million bottling machine, and trained my replacements as I moved up to positions of increased responsibility.

In earlier positions, I managed several establishments in the Spokane area, including two locations in which I was involved in the operation from the ground up. At The Hideaway, I assisted with the construction of the building; interviewed, hired, and trained all staff members; and managed all operational aspects from the day the business opened. Through my efforts, the bar became so successful that it attracted the interest of several buyers, and the owners eventually sold the operation for more than five times its initial value.

As you will see, I have earned a Bachelor of Science in Biology from the Gonzaga University in Spokane, where I also received an Exxon grant for marine invertebrate biology research. In addition, I completed the Short Course in Brewing Technology at the Largess Technical Institute and obtained a brewer's license through this program.

If you can use an assertive and motivated young professional with exceptional communication skills as well as a track record of accomplishment in management and sales, I hope you will contact me to suggest a time when we might meet. I can provide outstanding references at the appropriate time.

Sincerely,

John C. Booth

JOHN CLARENCE BOOTH

1110½ Hay Street, Fayetteville, NC 28305　　•　　preppub@aol.com　　•　　(910) 483-6611

OBJECTIVE　　To benefit an organization that can use an educated, articulate young professional with exceptional communication, organizational and technical skills who offers a track record of success in operations management of restaurant and clubs, brewing, and sales.

EDUCATION　　**Bachelor of Science** in **Biology**, with a concentration in Microbiology and Biotechnology, Gonzaga University, Spokane, WA, 1999.
- Named to the Dean's List.
- Received an Exxon grant for marine invertebrate biology research.
- Completed the Short Course in Brewing Technology, Largess Technical Institute, Seattle, WA, 2000.

CERTIFICATIONS　　Earned a Brewer's License through the Largess Technical Institute, one of only ten Brewing Technology programs in the world.

EXPERIENCE　　**SALES REPRESENTATIVE.** Sandlin Gallery, Seattle, WA (2003-present). Performed customer service, cash handling, and display tasks; co-responsible for all aspects of the operation of the gallery in the absence of the Director.
- Performed merchandising and display, presenting each piece of art effectively to maximize its unique appeal and entice the patron.
- Assisted gallery patrons in selecting and purchasing fine art paintings and sculptures.

BREWER and **MACHINE OPERATOR.** Cornerstone Brewing Company, Seattle, WA (2001-03). Started on the bottling line and quickly advanced to positions of increasing responsibility with this nationally-distributed specialty brewery.
- Selected for promotion to Brewer, the highest position at the company; utilized my knowledge of brewing techniques to ensure the quality of the company's products.
- Supervised eight employees in the bottling department; operated a $1 million bottling machine.
- Promoted to sole responsibility for the operation of a $500,000 kegging operation; trained new personnel to perform this job when I was selected for further advancement.

MANAGER and **BARTENDER.** The Hideaway, Spokane, WA (1997-2000). Was involved from the ground up in all stages of this successful establishment, from assisting with construction to interviewing and hiring, to managing the operation.
- Supervised ten employees, including the bar and wait staff.
- Interviewed, hired, and trained all employees, maintaining open lines of communication with staff and sharing their suggestions and concerns with the owners.
- Through my initiative and strong bottom-line orientation, weekly revenues increased from $1,000 per week to more than $9,000 per week; this attracted several interested buyers, and the owners sold the business for more than five times its initial value.

MANAGER and **LEAD BARTENDER.** Southhill Station, Spokane, WA (1994-96). Oversaw the operation of the bar, supervising bar and wait staff, controlling storeroom and bar inventory, and ensuring financial accountability, guest satisfaction, and security.

MANAGER and **BARTENDER.** Carrot Patch Bar & Grill, Spokane, WA (1992-94). Started with this company as a bartender and quickly advanced to weekend shift manager.

PERSONAL　　Excellent personal and professional references are available upon request.

Date

Exact Name of Person
Exact Title
Exact Name of Company
Address
City, State, Zip

BREWPUB MANAGER

This individual seeks a change from operations management to sales representative within his industry.

Dear Exact Name of Person (or Dear Sir or Madam if answering a blind ad):

With the enclosed resume, I would like to make you aware of my interest in exploring employment opportunities with your organization and introduce you to my background and credentials related to the food industry.

As you will see from my resume, I have worked in the restaurant industry for the past 11 years. While earning my B.S. degree in Business Administration, I worked full-time as a Cook and was involved in cooking steaks, seafood, soups, sandwiches, and other items from scratch. After graduating from college, I accepted a job as a Kitchen Manager and Assistant Manager with a home-style restaurant, and I greatly expanded the customer base through innovative menuing as well as private party functions. I saved the restaurant more than $12,000 in one quarter in food and beverage purchases by instituting a program of multiple vendors.

Most recently, I have been involved in starting a successful brewpub which grossed $1.5 million in its first year of operation. While managing Back of House operations, I am in charge of all decisions which involve buying equipment and materials, and I negotiate all terms with vendors.

My wife and I have decided to relocate permanently to Charleston, WV, and I am in the process of resigning from my position as Managing Partner. I have decided that I would like to work as a Sales Representative for a company which provides quality materials to restaurants. I offer a thorough understanding of how the buying process works within organizations ranging from "mom and pop" establishments to chains, and I am certain I could be successful in representing your product line.

With an excellent personal and professional reputation, I can provide outstanding references at the appropriate time. If you can use an outgoing and knowledgeable sales professional to join your team in the Charleston area, I would enjoy an opportunity to talk with you about your needs.

Yours sincerely,

Steven Todd Edgerton, Jr.

STEVEN TODD EDGERTON, JR.

1110½ Hay Street, Fayetteville, NC 28305 • preppub@aol.com • (910) 483-6611

OBJECTIVE

To contribute to an organization that can use a knowledgeable food industry professional who offers outstanding sales and consulting skills along with hands-on experience in restaurant management, kitchen operations, equipment utilization, and vendor relations.

EDUCATION

Bachelor of Science in Business Administration (B.S.B.A.) with extensive coursework in Computer Science, Shepherd College, Shepherdstown, WV, 1997.
- Elected President, Club Sports Council, 1995-96.
- With a college friend, started the university's lacrosse club team; negotiated for funding, lobbied for money for equipment, organized the playing schedule with other schools, and played the sport.
- Graduated from Sayre School, Huntington, WV, 1992.

EXPERIENCE

BREWPUB MANAGER & MANAGING PARTNER. Mountain High Brewing Company, Huntington, WV (2003-present). With a partner, raised $1.5 million in private capital by selling shares at $35,000 a share to finance the creation of a new brewpub which opened in December, 2003, and which grossed $1.5 million in its first year of operation.
- Was instrumental in designing and overseeing the construction of a 250-seat, 10,000-square feet brewpub which caters to an upscale target market aged 25-45.
- Played a key role in developing the day-to-day policies and procedures for the brewpub's 50-plus employees.
- Have skillfully managed Back of House operations, including budgeting expenditures, creating menus and weekly specials, hiring and training employees, directing advertising strategies, as well as planning and coordinating special events.
- Am in charge of all decisions which involve buying equipment and materials from vendors; negotiate contract terms.
- Applied my resourcefulness and in-depth food industry experience with the result that I have achieved food costs of consistently 2% under budget while maintaining quality.

KITCHEN MANAGER & ASSISTANT MANAGER. The Bunnery, Huntington, WV (1997-2003). Made numerous contributions to the bottom line of a restaurant which specializes in home cooking for the working person.
- Began in a management trainee position and took over the kitchen operations after the existing manager quit with no notice; maintained a quality food service operation which cooked everything "from scratch" and then expanded the customer base through innovative menuing as well as private party functions.
- Saved the café more than $12,000 in one quarter in food and beverage purchases by instituting a program of multiple vendors used for comparison shopping purposes.
- Was responsible for all food ordering, the development of inventory systems, as well as the bookings and food preparation for all private functions.
- Became skilled in dealing with different vendors including PYA, Sysco, IFH, EG Forrest, Coca-Cola, and others.

Other experience: COOK. Shades Café, Shepherdstown, WV (1994-97). While earning my degree at Shepherd College, worked 40 hours a week cooking steaks, seafood, soups, sandwiches, and other items.

PERSONAL

Highly motivated and industrious individual. Excellent references on request. Offer a proven ability to "think on my feet" and solve problems resourcefully under tight deadlines.

Date

Exact Name of Person
Exact Title
Exact Name of Company
Address
City, State, Zip

CHAIN RESTAURANT MANAGER

for Chili's Restaurant

Dear Exact Name of Person (or Dear Sir or Madam if answering a blind ad):

With the enclosed resume, I would like to make you aware of my background as an experienced single and multiunit restaurant manager with excellent communication and problem-solving skills and proven expertise in staff development.

Most recently, I have been excelling as a Restaurant Manager for Chili's Restaurant in the Birmingham location. This busy branch of the nationwide chain has annual food sales of $2.75 million and retail sales of $900,000. I supervise a staff of 110 employees, scheduling as many as 3000 labor hours per week in order to fully cover the kitchen and wait staff. Under my management, the Birmingham store has achieved a 10% increase in operating income. This was accomplished through a reduction in turnover, development of sales building programs, and careful monitoring of labor and food expenditures.

At International House of Pancakes, I was hired as an Assistant Manager and quickly advanced to Store Manager and then to Area Manager, overseeing the operation of six locations and supervising as many as 25 managers. During my time there, income in my district increased by 10%, sales by 7.5%, and I was named District Manager of the Year after only 2 years with the company. Several of the managers that I trained went on to become District Managers, and others won Manager of the Year and Store of the Year honors.

Though I am highly regarded by my present employer, and can provide outstanding personal and professional references at the appropriate time, I feel that I would be more fully challenged, and my skills and experience better utilized, in a larger volume or multiunit environment.

If you can use a highly experienced restaurant manager with excellent motivational and staff development skills and a strong background in both single restaurant and multiunit management, I hope you will contact me soon to suggest a time when we might meet to discuss your needs. I assure you in advance that I would rapidly become a valuable addition to your organization.

Sincerely,

Troy J. Converse

TROY J. CONVERSE

1110½ Hay Street, Fayetteville, NC 28305 • preppub@aol.com • (910) 483-6611

OBJECTIVE

To benefit an organization that can use an experienced restaurant manager with exceptional communication and organizational skills who offers a background in managing multiunit operations and proven expertise in staff development.

EXPERIENCE

RESTAURANT MANAGER. Chili's, Birmingham, AL (2003-present). Manage all operational aspects of this local branch of a nationwide chain with annual food sales of $2.75 million and retail sales of $900,000.

- Supervise a staff of 110 employees, with as many as 35 people working a given shift; direct and coordinate wait staff and kitchen crew station assignments and ensure that all tasks are completed in a prompt, courteous, and accurate manner.
- Responsible for all aspects of personnel development; interview, hire, and train new employees; reward excellence and counsel marginal workers to improve performance; conduct periodic employee evaluations.
- Train senior associates and associate managers that are being groomed for advancement.
- Schedule 110 employees utilizing 2400-3000 labor hours per week.
- Prepare and maintain all operational paperwork, including opening and closing reports, daily and weekly sales tracking summaries, and shortage/overage reports.
- Verify accuracy of all invoices and receipts for merchandise, perishable goods, and supplies; negotiate contracts with outside vendors.
- Achieved a 10% increase in operating income through reductions in turnover, development of sales building programs, and careful monitoring of labor and food costs.

At International House of Pancakes I was hired as an Assistant Manager, and was rapidly promoted in the following "track record" of increasing responsibilities:

AREA SUPERVISOR. Birmingham, AL (1994-2003). Monitored the operational, administrative, and financial performance of the stores in my district, in order to maximize sales and controllable profits from each unit.

- Oversaw the operation of six stores, supervising 25 managers and 300-400 employees.
- Improved sales in my district by more than 7.5% and income by more than 10%.
- Trained managers who advanced into district manager positions, as well as several managers who won Store of the Year and Manager of the Year honors.

STORE MANAGER. Birmingham, AL (1993-94). Promoted to this position from Assistant Manager, after only eight months with the company; managed all aspects of the operation of the restaurant, supervising 50-60 employees and three assistant managers.

- Directed the activities of the employees and other managers to ensure smooth operation of the kitchen and wait staff, maximizing customer satisfaction.
- Interviewed, hired, trained, and supervised all new staff members.
- In 1993, my store had the highest percentage of Guest Approval reports.

ASSISTANT MANAGER. Birmingham, AL (1992-93). Assisted the manager in supervising and directing the operation of this busy location.

- Supervised all employees in my area; served in the capacity of manager when the Store Manager was off duty.

Other experience: RESTAURANT MANAGER. Burger King, Huntsville, AL (1986-91). Started with Burger King as a cook and worked my way up to Manager.

PERSONAL

Excellent personal and professional references are available upon request.

CAREER CHANGE

Date

Exact Name of Person
Title or Position
Name of Company
Address (no., street)
Address (city, state, zip)

CHAIN RESTAURANT MANAGER

Notice that this cover letter has been worded so that employers in multiple industries might take notice.

Dear Exact Name of Person: (or Dear Sir or Madam if answering a blind ad.)

Can you use a hardworking young professional who offers outstanding abilities in training and supervising employees, controlling inventory, handling customer relations, and restoring and increasing operational efficiency?

My experience, as you will see from my resume, has given me opportunities to excel in training and motivating employees to work together. On multiple occasions I have been brought into troubled operations and have restored profitability and efficiency. I have consistently built productive teams, reduced employee turnover, and found ways to improve procedures.

I have directly supervised as many as 97 employees while also being involved in areas including conducting inventories, reorganizing storage facilities, preparing daily/weekly/monthly reports, and troubleshooting production and customer service difficulties.

With my experience, I offer a variety of skills which would benefit any organization and I am confident, with my proven adaptability record, that I would be a great asset.

I hope you will welcome my call soon to arrange a brief meeting at your convenience to discuss your current and future needs and how I might serve them. Thank you in advance for your time.

Sincerely yours,

Larry J. Williamson

Alternate last paragraph:
I hope you will call or write soon to suggest a time convenient for us to meet and discuss your current and future needs and how I might serve them. Thank you in advance for your time.

LARRY J. WILLIAMSON

1110½ Hay Street, Fayetteville, NC 28305 • preppub@aol.com • (910) 483-6611

OBJECTIVE

To benefit an organization that can use an experienced manager with a strong bottom-line orientation and excellent staff development skills who offers a track record of accomplishment in restoring profitability and efficiency to troubled operations in the restaurant and retail industries.

EDUCATION & TRAINING

Bachelor of Science degree in **Business Administration** with an emphasis in Management. California State University, Bakersfield, CA, 1990; received the Chancellor's Award for academic excellence, 1989 and 1990.
- Computer skills include: Access, Excel, Lotus 1-2-3, WordPerfect, Microsoft, Windows.
- Have completed rigorous advanced training in retail management and leadership.

EXPERIENCE

ASSISTANT MANAGER. Bob Evans Big Boy, Sacramento, CA (2003-present). Quickly mastered the different operating systems of this large national restaurant chain, honing my management skills while scheduling and supervising the restaurant operations.
- Supervised as many as 50 restaurant personnel; assisted with interviewing, hiring, and training of new employees.
- Conducted daily inspections of the kitchen, service area, and physical location of the restaurant to ensure the highest standards of cleanliness and appearance.

PROJECT MANAGER. Denny's, various locations in Northern & Southern California (2000-03). Was handpicked by the District Manager to troubleshoot problems and transform troubled operations into efficient, profitable restaurants, oversaw all operational aspects at numerous locations.
- Supervised as many as 97 personnel, including General Managers, Front of the House Managers, Kitchen Managers, and kitchen, host, and wait staff.
- Observed and participated in the daily activities of the restaurant, recommending changes to existing training and operations methods to improve performance in all measured proficiencies.
- Trained new personnel and provided refresher training to existing staff, addressing shortcomings in employee performance and raising the skill level of all employees.

ASSISTANT MANAGER. Golden Cafeteria, various locations throughout Southern California (1996-2000). Started with this busy national cafeteria chain as a Manager Trainee and quickly advanced to Assistant Manager; supervised up to 83 people while improving customer and employee relations.
- By carefully scheduling employee hours according to sales forecasts, was able to reduce labor costs to below the company average without adversely effecting customer service.
- Implemented more stringent loss prevention procedures that resulted in decreased theft.
- Increased bottom-line profit by more than $1,000 in a single month.

ASSISTANT MANAGER. True Value Hardware, San Jose, CA (1991-96). Supervised and trained up to 20 employees, providing hands-on management, ensuring fast and accurate customer service, and effectively controlling costs while filling in for absent managers.
- Oversaw the operation of the paint, hardware, floor coverings, housewares, and lumber departments; performed budgeting and forecasting of labor and inventory costs.
- Reduced operation cost through monitoring using cost analysis techniques.
- Was instrumental in the turnaround of a unprofitable store in San Luis Obispo area.

PERSONAL

Excellent personal and professional references are available upon request.

CAREER CHANGE

Date

Exact Name of Person
Title or Position
Name of Company
Address (no., street)
Address (city, state, zip)

CHEF

If you are looking for more
resumes and cover letters
of chefs, you might want to
look at the Executive Sous
Chef on page 80-81.

Dear Exact Name of Person: (or Dear Sir or Madam if answering a blind ad.)

With the enclosed resume, I would like to make you aware of my interest in pursuing employment opportunities with your organization.

As you will see from my resume, I have held a variety of positions in the past ranging from sales to a culinary position; most recently I have owned and operated my own service business. Under my operation, the store has become known as the best business of its kind in the area.

If your organization is currently seeking an energetic and enthusiastic professional with a proven track record of success, I encourage you to consider me for your team. Although I have most recently worked outside the restaurant field, I am eager to return to the hospitality industry. I could become an asset to an organization through my culinary knowledge as well as my extensive service industry knowledge.

I hope you will welcome my call soon to arrange a brief meeting at your convenience to discuss your current and future needs and how I might serve them. Thank you in advance for your time.

Sincerely yours,

Kristy F. Swanson

Alternate last paragraph:
I hope you will call or write soon to suggest a time convenient for us to meet and discuss your current and future needs and how I might serve them. Thank you in advance for your time.

KRISTY F. SWANSON

1110½ Hay Street, Fayetteville, NC 28305 • preppub@aol.com • (910) 483-6611

OBJECTIVE   To offer my enthusiastic and energetic personality, reputation as a talented and effective sales professional, and positive attitude to an organization in need of a versatile, honest, and trustworthy individual who can quickly earn the trust and respect of all.

EXPERIENCE   **NAIL TECHNICIAN.** Swan Nails, Shreveport, LA (2001-present). Built a respected service business from the ground up and within three years was seeing an average of 25 customers a week while handling all aspects of finances, marketing, sales, and services.
- Developed an excellent repeat customer base while earning a reputation as the best nail artist in the city for my skills with sculptured and acrylic nails as well as with more standard manicures and pedicures.
- Recommended to actress Melanie Griffith who was filming a movie in the area, I did her nails and those of her assistants while she was in Shreveport.

CHEF. The Rosebud, Shreveport, LA (1999-2001). Became known as a talented and hardworking young professional who could easily learn and perform a variety of functions in a popular restaurant including preparing foods, controlling inventory, saute cooking, and assisting the head chef.

Excelled in the following track record of promotion with Sonitrol:
1997-99: SALES REPRESENTATIVE. Sonitrol of Baton Rouge, LA. Quickly became a record-producing sales professional and was highly effective in selling my positive attitude, confidence in my sales abilities, and persistent manner to exceed my monthly quotas of sales for these high-ticket home alarm systems.
- Made cold calls on home owners to set up three sales presentations each day.
- Became the top female sales rep for the area six consecutive months!
- Reached the level of sales where trips to Jamaica and Thailand as well as Lake Tahoe, NV, were awarded in recognition of achievements.
- Was promoted to this productive territory after impressive achievements in training with another Sonitrol location.

1995-97: TRAINING SPECIALIST. Sonitrol of Shreveport, LA. Contributed my product knowledge and infectious, positive manner while training new employees in the company's philosophy and motivating them to understand human nature and to find the right approach for different potential buyers.
- Stepped in to troubleshoot problems and help new representatives find the way to close difficult sales and convince reluctant home owners to make a decision on buying the $2,000 alarm systems.
- Was presented with a $1,300 system as a sales incentive and offered a choice of locations and job opportunities for advancement.

Other experience: RECEPTIONIST. Professional Driving Schools of Shreveport, LA (1993-95). Gained my first exposure to telemarketing, sales, and merchandising while taking care of a wide range of day-to-day activities in the training department.

EDUCATION & TRAINING   Studied Advertising at Louisiana State University-Shreveport (1991-93).
Completed a 150-hour course in Nail Technology at Susanne's in Shreveport, LA.

PERSONAL   Attended several workshops from "Step Up," a Baton Rouge-based program emphasizing self awareness, confidence building, and assertiveness.

CAREER CHANGE

Date

Exact Name of Person
Title or Position
Name of Company
Address (number and street)
Address (city, state, and zip)

CLINICAL DIETITIAN

in a medical food service
environment

Dear Exact Name of Person: (or Sir or Madam if answering a blind ad.)

Can you use a bright and articulate young professional who offers the creativity and vision to be effective in marketing concepts and products as well as an education and practical experience as a clinical dietitian? I am interested in transitioning into the hospitality industry and feel I have much to offer.

As you will see from my enclosed resume, I am a versatile and adaptable individual who can manage time for maximum productivity and handle multiple simultaneous projects and responsibilities with ease. The recipient of eight different scholarships my freshman year in college, I earned my B.A. with a concentration in Food/Nutrition and Dietetics with a minor in Psychology. While attending college I was very active in campus organizations, volunteer work in the community, and also completed internships.

Presently a Clinical Dietitian with Delta Healthcare working at Sun Valley Medical Center, Sun Valley, ID, I am actively involved in administrative and clinical responsibilities which include marketing activities. As a member of a multidisciplinary medical team, I am heavily involved in educating, instructing, and informing medical professionals as well as patients on the value of nutritional care and in understanding that attention to diet can reduce the length of a patient's hospitalization. As the Instructor for a "LifeSteps" program with more than 25 participants, I encourage a healthy diet and the need to use group support and behavior modification techniques to reinforce the benefits of a healthy lifestyle.

In this job, as in nearly every other position and activity I have been involved in, I am called on to prepare information used in written and verbal forms, to speak before large groups, and to communicate persuasively with medical professionals as well as members of the public. I am confident that through my education, experience, and background of public service and volunteerism I offer the drive, skills, and personality that would allow me to be successful in marketing services, concepts, or products to any type of audience.

I hope you will welcome my call soon to arrange a brief meeting to discuss your current and future needs and how I might serve them. Thank you in advance for your time.

Sincerely,

Susanne K. Fitzpatrick

SUSANNE KATHERINE FITZPATRICK

1110½ Hay Street, Fayetteville, NC 28305   •   preppub@aol.com   •   (910) 483-6611

OBJECTIVE
To offer my creative abilities, familiarity with marketing concepts and techniques, and experience in training and instructing others to an organization that can benefit from my written and verbal communication skills as well as my education and experience in nutrition.

EDUCATION
B.A. in Liberal Arts with an emphasis on Food/Nutrition and Dietetics, University of Missouri, Saint Louis, MO, 2000; minor concentration in Psychology.
- Completed an internship at the University of Tennessee Hospital and Veterans Administration Medical Center, Knoxville, TN, 2001-02 with clinical, administrative, and community rotations.

EXPERIENCE
Am gaining advancement in health care settings while applying my versatile skills and ability to adapt to new procedures and ideas with ease, Delta Healthcare:
CLINICAL DIETITIAN. Sun Valley Medical Center, Sun Valley, Idaho (2002-present). In a multidisciplinary medical setting with an emphasis on the specialities of pediatrics, surgery, and nephrology, am successfully adding to the knowledge base of medical professionals and emphasizing the importance of teaching patients good nutritional habits in order to reduce patient stays and ensure their awareness of proper diet.
- Develop video presentations and newspaper articles which I combine with my public speaking abilities to educate medical professionals of the advantages of various nutritional supplements.
- Serve as the leader of the Continuous Quality Improvement committee and serve on a hospital nutrition subcommittee.
- Design educational material which promote the importance of nutritional care.
- Selected as **INSTRUCTOR** for a "Passport to Health" program with more than 25 participants, provide counseling in areas which encourage a healthy lifestyle: a combination of group support, nutrition, physical activity, and behavior modification which resulted in weight losses from six to 26 pounds during four months on the program.
- Balance the corporate goals of Delta Healthcare with the hospital's policies and procedures so that both organizations can work together to provide highest quality care.

CLINICAL/ADMINISTRATIVE DIETITIAN. Idaho Falls Hospital, Idaho Falls, ID; and Tennessee Regional Hospital, Knoxville, TN (2000-02). Provided assistance to the existing cafeteria and catering staff as a reserve employee while setting up operations according to corporate guidelines and expectations: created a catering "specials" notebook.
- Represented the corporation in a professional and effective manner in a delicate situation where a new contract brought about changes in procedures and goals.

Highlights of other experience: refined time management, communication, and planning skills in numerous internships, volunteer jobs, and part-time jobs while attending college:
As a **Clinical Dietetic Student,** worked in nursing home and addiction treatment unit of a Veteran's Administration Medical Center: organized and taught a Diet for Sobriety class and instructed patients in basic nutrition and appropriate diets, Knoxville, TN (1998-99).
As a **Nutrition Assistant,** was involved with testing and modification of existing recipes for a college dining service, University of Missouri, St. Louis, MO (1997-98).

PERSONAL
Am an articulate and poised young professional. Offer excellent time management skills and the ability to handle multiple simultaneous projects and tasks effectively. Through 13 years in 4-H, acquired communication, leadership, and organizational skills along with a strong sense of responsibility, work ethic, and dedication.

CAREER CHANGE

Date

Exact Name of Person
Title or Position
Name of Company
Address (number and street)
Address (city, state, and zip)

CONVENTION MANAGER

This experienced hotel convention manager seeks a change into a new field in which she can utilize her strong problem-solving, project management, and customer service skills.

Dear Exact Name of Person: (or Sir or Madam if answering a blind ad.)

Can you use a bright and articulate professional with a broad base of public relations and hospitality experience?

As you will see from my enclosed resume, I am a versatile individual who can organize for maximum productivity and handle multiple simultaneous projects and responsibilities with ease. I have gained much experience dealing with the public and especially in setting up conventions and personal visits so as to ensure the guests' ultimate comfort and enjoyability. While in college, I earned my B.S. with a concentration in Marketing and graduated on the Dean's List. I am highly computer literate with a good knowledge of a variety of programs.

Presently a Corporate Sales Manager with Sheraton Suites, I offer highly refined communication and public relations skills. I am confident that through my education, experience, and background of success that I offer the drive, skills, and personality that would allow me to be successful in your organization.

I hope you will welcome my call soon to arrange a brief meeting to discuss your current and future needs and how I might serve them. Thank you in advance for your time.

Sincerely,

Mary J. Hubbard

Alternate last paragraph:
I hope you will call or write me soon to suggest a time convenient for us to meet and discuss your current and future needs and how I might serve them. Thank you in advance for your time.

MARY J. HUBBARD

1110½ Hay Street, Fayetteville, NC 28305   •   preppub@aol.com   •   (910) 483-6611

OBJECTIVE

To apply my experience in public relations and the hospitality industry to an organization that can use a mature professional skilled in increasing sales, improving merchandising, and strengthening the quality of customer service through outstanding communication abilities.

EXPERIENCE

CORPORATE SALES MANAGER. Sheraton Suites, Lexington, KY (2003-present). For this popular hotel and convention center, use the full range of my communication skills and knowledge of public relations techniques to increase regular and group room sales through personal visits, phone calls, and correspondence.
- Welcome large corporate groups and key meeting planners personally and establish myself as their point of contact for any questions or problems that might arise.
- Plan and carry out an annual theme party for up to 150 regular corporate clients.
- Deal on a regular basis with representatives of area businesses and government entities including the Fayette County Civic Center and the Bluegrass Regional Airport.
- Represent the hotel/convention center to colleges, universities, and schools as well as tour and travel offices to make them aware of the range of available facilities.
- Create informative, attractive brochures to provide potential customers with the total range of facilities and activities available to them.
- Prepare expense accounts, lost business and variance reports, occupancy figures, and monthly itineraries as well as keeping complete and up-to-date lists of all contacts.

CONVENTION SALES ASSISTANT. Greater Cincinnati Convention and Visitor Bureau, Cincinnati, OH (2002-03). Handled a variety of support activities for the convention sales department while gaining a great deal of exposure in dealing with people ranging from the general public, to hotel and motel representatives, to sales professionals.
- Became skilled in using a specialized database for the preparation and maintenance of sales leads, updates, bookings, and lost business reports.
- Worked closely with the sales managers and project coordinator in the preparation of trade shows, special projects, familiarization tours, and sales blitzes.
- Prepared monthly reports detailing leads and sales as well as summaries of year-to-date progress and the status for each sales manager.

SALES ASSISTANT. River City Hilton, Cincinnati, OH (2001-02). Provided the hotel's director of sales with support in areas ranging from dealing with hospitality staff personnel, to preparing reports and correspondence, to scheduling. Was part of a team which coordinated and scheduled civic, professional, and other types of organizations holding conventions.

Highlights of earlier experience: Polished my public relations and communication skills.
As an **Audience Surveyor**, developed a system for cold calling television viewers to persuade them to watch pilot programs on the FOX network and processed the survey forms.
As a **Telemarketer,** implemented a cold calling system, confirmed appointments, and made follow-up calls to people who visited a timeshare condominium complex.

EDUCATION

B.S., Business Administration with concentration in Marketing, Middlebury College, Middlebury, VT, 2000. Held membership in the Marketing Club and made the Dean's List.
A.A., Business Administration with concentration in Marketing, Community College of Vermont, Waterbury, VT, 1995.

PERSONAL

Am creative and have a flair for dealing with people of all types and backgrounds. Am very articulate and also offer the ability to communicate effectively in writing.

Exact Name of Person
Title or Position
Name of Company
Address (no., street)
Address (city, state, zip)

COOK
specializing in pastry
cooking

Dear Exact Name of Person: (or Dear Sir or Madam if answering a blind ad.)

I would appreciate an opportunity to talk with you soon about how I could contribute to your organization through my experience in the food service industry, including my knowledge of the administrative aspects of this industry.

You will see from my resume that I earned a reputation as a knowledgeable, dependable, and respected professional while employed with the University of Georgia. I have overseen operations of dining facilities serving three meals a day to as many as 800 people. I have become skilled at managing the details of inventory control, quality control, sanitation, and production operations while also training employees, maintaining excellent customer relations, and solving difficult and unexpected supply problems.

Especially effective at training others, I am skilled at motivating personnel and developing them into productive teams of workers who are known for providing attractive and nourishing meals. My experience also includes ensuring sanitation and health standards are met and controlling inventories of perishable and nonperishable foods.

I hope you will welcome my call soon to arrange a brief meeting at your convenience to discuss your current and future needs and how I might serve them. Thank you in advance for your time.

Sincerely yours,

Stella L. Preen

Alternate last paragraph:
I hope you will call or write me soon to suggest a time convenient for us to meet and discuss your current and future needs and how I might serve them. Thank you in advance for your time.

STELLA L. PREEN

1110½ Hay Street, Fayetteville, NC 28305   •   preppub@aol.com   •   (910) 483-6611

OBJECTIVE

To offer my management experience, motivational skills, and organizational abilities to a company that can use a hardworking professional with extensive knowledge related to quality control, inventory control, production operations, and service operations.

COMPUTERS

Knowledgeable of software/operating systems including Excel, Word, and Windows.

EXPERIENCE

PASTRY COOK. Outback Steakhouse, Macon, GA (2003-present). Am contributing to the high quality of food served in this full-service restaurant by producing fine baked goods while also preparing/cooking a wide range of items for the brunch buffet; prepare salads, sandwiches, and desserts according to customers' orders.

- Simultaneously apply my skills in a church-sponsored program: use progressive cooking techniques while preparing breakfast for as many as 90 people a day.

COOK. Friendly's Restaurant, Macon, GA (2001-03). Prepared and cooked all varieties of meals and desserts; acted as supervisor in the absence of the manager.

Refined my supervisory and managerial skills in food service operations while working with the University of Georgia in Athens, GA:
SUPERVISORY BAKER. (2000). As a night-shift baker, prepared pastries, pies, cakes, and cookies for a dining facility which fed approximately 1,500 meals a day.

- Taught personnel proper procedures for preparing meals using all kitchen equipment as well as the recommended methods for handling cash and ordering supplies.

FACILITY SUPERVISOR. (1998-2000). Advanced to higher supervisory levels in a cafeteria serving two meals a day to around 500 people; handled responsibilities including ordering supplies, planning meals, training personnel, and preparing reports.

- Reduced the facility's account status to within 3% of allocations; maintained this level.

FOOD SERVICE OPERATIONS MANAGER. (1997-98). Singled out for my demonstrated knowledge and leadership abilities, oversaw ordering supplies and planning menus as well as controlling record keeping and supervising 32 employees.

ASSISTANT MANAGER. (1994-97). Planned menus, prepared reports, and maintained accounts for a campus cafeteria.

Highlights of earlier experience: Learned scheduling, accounting for food items, and health and safety guidelines in previous jobs as a Shift Supervisor and Cook.

- Played an instrumental role in helping a dining facility win a local award as "best overall lunch establishment."

EDUCATION & TRAINING

Completing associate's degree in Business Administration, Macon State College, Macon, GA. Completed training related to inventory management, accounting, supervision, and supply.

PERSONAL

Work well under pressure. Excel at motivating and training other employees. Feel my management skills are transferable to any industry. Familiar with food service equipment such as steam kettles, convection ovens, food slicers, and food processors.

CAREER CHANGE

Date

Exact Name of Person
Title or Position
Name of Company
Address (no., street)
Address (city, state, zip)

COOK FOREMAN
in a hospital environment

Dear Exact Name of Person: (or Dear Sir or Madam if answering a blind ad.)

I would appreciate an opportunity to talk with you soon about how I could contribute to your organization through my extensive experience in food service.

As you will see from my enclosed resume, I offer a proven ability to do outstanding work and achieve superior results. In every job I have ever had, I have been promoted ahead of my peers in record time because of my initiative, supervisory ability, problem-solving skills, and absolute commitment to produce quality results in every area.

You will see from my resume that I am considered an expert in all aspects of food service operations management, from cooking to dietary planning and budget preparation. I am knowledgeable of food service operations in medical/hospital environments, and I am confident my skills would transfer effectively into any environment which requires the preparation of tasty food served to hundreds of people three times a day. I have gained expertise in preparing foods for all types of special diets.

I hope you will call or write me soon to suggest a time convenient for us to meet and discuss your current and future needs and how I might serve them. Thank you in advance for your time.

Sincerely yours,

Sean M. McIntyre

SEAN MICHAEL MCINTYRE

1110½ Hay Street, Fayetteville, NC 28305 • preppub@aol.com • (910) 483-6611

OBJECTIVE To contribute to an organization that can use a skilled food service professional who offers a proven ability to manage people along with extensive knowledge related to food purchasing, dietetic services and menu planning, inventory management, and cost control.

EDUCATION Completed extensive college-level course work at the University of Georgia and at other locations sponsored by the Veterans Administration related to dietary management, supervision, food service operations, and union/management relations.

EXPERIENCE **Have excelled in a track record of promotion with St. Joseph Hospital, Bangor, ME:**

2002-present: COOK FOREMAN and **ASSISTANT CHIEF, FOOD PRODUCTION.** Received the highest evaluations possible on every performance appraisal; was praised for my insistence on top-quality safety and sanitation standards, was commended for my exceptional development of fellow employees and strong support of E.E.O. programs, and was thanked for my outstanding "crisis management" skills displayed during emergencies caused by severe weather.

- At this 800-bed hospital, assigned jobs to a 21-person food preparation staff that included cooks, assistant cooks, and vegetable preparers; continuously trained personnel in portion control and ingredient usage.
- Prepared weekly and daily orders for staple food items, produce, milk, bread, frozen vegetables, dessert, unique items used in supplemental feedings, and other foodstuffs.
- Maintained constant vigilance over stock levels; kept an eye on costs while assuring the availability of all needed products.
- On my own initiative, improved communication and cooperation among hospital personnel by holding conferences with production personnel, ICU professionals, and food service supervisors.
- In the belief that motivating people is the key to quality results, am constantly working with food service personnel to refine their skills and train/motivate them.
- During a severe blizzard in March 2003, took full charge of dietetic operations to ensure the proper feeding and nutrition of patients and staff, despite severe supply problems caused by catastrophic weather.

1999-2001: FOOD SERVICE SUPERVISOR. Because of my excellent performance in this job, was promoted to **Cook Foreman** (the job above), in less time than anyone else in the organization's history.

- Earned a reputation as a tactful communicator and fair manager through my success in establishing procedures to be used in matters related to E.E.O. and the union.
- Instituted computer classes for food service workers WG-3 and above; improved the skills of employees related to using the computer to forecast needs and control costs.
- Scheduled and assigned work daily to 40 employees.
- Became respected for my ability to manage every aspect of the food production process, from ordering food, to controlling ingredients in food preparation, to avoiding problems that could cause work stoppage and productivity loss.

1993-98: COOK. Received numerous awards for my cooking skill and was rapidly promoted to **Food Service Supervisor.** Cooked hospital food and modified food items according to menu.

PERSONAL Am known for my ability to train, motivate, develop, and inspire employees. Have had much experience in working with union officials. Excel in working well with people at all levels.

Date

Exact Name of Person
Title or Position
Name of Company
Address (no., street)
Address (city, state, zip)

**CORRECTIONAL FOOD
SERVICES OFFICER**

for an inmate population

Dear Exact Name of Person: (or Dear Sir or Madam if answering a blind ad.)

I would appreciate an opportunity to talk with you soon about how I could contribute to your organization through my experience and background in the supervision of kitchen and wait staff in both a correctional institution and a restaurant environment.

You will see from my resume that I am currently working at Loudon Correctional Hospital in Jackson, MS where I manage up to 20 personnel while performing other duties including training, monitoring safety and sanitation, and conducting periodic inventories. Working in the correctional environment has ensured me the opportunity to use my natural leadership and organizational skills in a situation quite diverse from my previous occupation. As I have documented on my resume, before becoming involved with the Mississippi Department of Corrections, I managed a "mom-and-pop" type restaurant for many years.

If you can use an experienced food service professional with excellent staff training and organizational skills, I hope you will call or write me soon to suggest a time convenient for us to meet and discuss your current and future needs and how I might serve them. Thank you in advance for your time.

Sincerely yours,

Anthony J. Tombs

Alternate last paragraph:
I hope you will welcome my call soon to arrange a brief meeting at your convenience to discuss your current and future needs and how I might serve them. Thank you in advance for your time.

ANTHONY J. TOMBS

1110½ Hay Street, Fayetteville, NC 28305   •   preppub@aol.com   •   (910) 483-6611

OBJECTIVE   To benefit an organization that can use an experienced food service professional with strong staff training and organizational skills who offers a background in the supervision of kitchen and wait staff in correctional institution and restaurant environments.

EDUCATION   Completed nearly three years of college level course work towards degree programs in Mathematics and Mechanical Drafting.
Completed numerous courses related to food service, supply and support, purchasing, and food preparation, State of Mississippi.

EXPERIENCE   *With the Mississippi Department of Corrections, have advanced in the following "track record" of accomplishment:*
2002-present: **FOOD SERVICES OFFICER.** Loudon Correctional Hospital, Jackson, MS. Promoted to this position from Food Service Assistant; direct the work of inmates and perform a wide variety of food preparation, sanitation, and service tasks.
- Manage up to 20 food service personnel, directing and participating in the training of adult inmates in proper procedures of food service, preparation, and sanitation.
- Conducted periodic inventories, monitoring stock levels in order to control inventory; prepare orders and oversee the purchasing of produce for the facility.
- Ensure that all cooking surfaces and food preparation areas are properly sanitized.
- Oversee preparation of meals, directing the work of all food service personnel to ensure that meals were served on time.
- Monitored safety and sanitation procedures to ensure compliance with local, state, and federal regulations and guidelines.

2000-02: **FOOD SERVICES ASSISTANT.** Jackson Youth Center, Jackson, MS. Performed a variety of supervisory, training, food preparation, and inventory control tasks for the food service department of this busy juvenile correctional facility.
- Oversaw the preparation of breakfast and lunch, directing the work of food service personnel to ensure that these meals were served on time.
- Supervised as many as 14 juvenile inmates and other personnel. Directed and participated in the training of personnel, teaching all aspects of the food service industry.
- Assisted in the planning and development of events and functions, such as special menus and arrangements for Christmas, Thanksgiving, Independence Day, etc.
- Verified that all inmates and other personnel maintained compliance with safety and sanitation rules and regulations.
- Department of Corrections certified; completed Department of Corrections OPUS training.

GENERAL MANAGER. Calico Corner, Hattiesburg, MS (1985-2000). Provided a wide range of food preparation, supervisory, and operational support to the manager of this local full service restaurant.
- Provided supervisory oversight to as many as five employees.
- Oversaw the preparation of meals as well as the sanitation of the kitchen, food preparation and storage areas, and cooking surfaces.
- Assisted the manager with interviewing, hiring, and training of new employees.
- Monitored the performance of all employees, ensuring exceptional customer service and food quality was provided at all times.

PERSONAL   Excellent personal and professional references on request.

CAREER CHANGE

Date

Exact Name of Person
Title or Position
Name of Company
Address (no., street)
Address (city, state, zip)

CUSTOMER SERVICE REPRESENTATIVE

An all-purpose resume such as this one emphasizes skills and experience which are transferable to numerous industries.

Dear Exact Name of Person: (or Dear Sir or Madam if answering a blind ad.)

I would appreciate an opportunity to talk with you soon about how I could contribute to your organization through my versatile experience in serving customers, managing projects, and coordinating a wide range of activities.

As you will see from my resume, I have received rapid promotions and performance-based awards in every job I have ever held. I can provide outstanding personal and professional references which will attest to my strong problem-solving and customer service skills as well as my friendly disposition, professional style, and high personal standards.

In my most recent job with the Hilton Hotel, I was commended for exemplifying the hotel's "Yes I Can" motto through my strong customer service abilities. In a previous job I won a prestigious award and was rapidly promoted to manage four of my peers involved in property management and leasing activities. Although I am known for my outgoing personality and ability to work well with people at all levels, I am a very detail-oriented person and believe that "attention to detail" is an essential ingredient in providing exceptional customer service. You will see from my resume that I have excelled in a job as a Budget/Investment Analyst. In one job for the City of New Orleans, I made investment decisions for the city while also coordinating the research and decision making as well as the compilation and publication of the city's Budget Book.

You would find me in person to be someone who is comfortable walking into new situations and who enjoys a new challenge. I am positive that I could quickly become an asset to your organization.

I hope you will call or write me soon to suggest a time convenient for us to meet and discuss your current and future needs and how I might serve them. Thank you in advance for you time.

Sincerely yours,

Jesse R. Slone, III

Alternate last paragraph:
I hope you will welcome my call soon to arrange a brief meeting at your convenience to discuss your current and future needs and how I might serve them. Thank you in advance for your time.

JESSE R. SLONE, III

1110½ Hay Street, Fayetteville, NC 28305 • preppub@aol.com • (910) 483-6611

OBJECTIVE

To benefit an organization that can use a versatile and dynamic young professional with exceptional organizational, management, customer service, and public relations skills along with a reputation as a creative opportunity finder and problem solver.

EDUCATION

Bachelor of Arts (B.A.) degree, Tulane University, New Orleans, LA, 1998.
- Was elected *Tulane University School Ambassador,* 1997-98.
- Was Faculty Editor, Tulane University Yearbook.

Excelled in graduate courses in Human Relations, University of Central Florida, FL, 2002.

PUBLICATIONS & AWARDS

Researched, compiled, and directed the publication of a financial publication for the City of New Orleans which contained the 1999 city budget.

Have received awards and honors in every job I have ever held including two "Working Friendly" awards, a Spirit of America award, Hospitality Association medals, and a Certificate of Appreciation from the Mayor of New Orleans' office.

COMPUTERS

Proficient with Excel, Access, Lotus 1-2-3, Word, PowerPoint and Windows applications. Have taught myself several software packages.

EXPERIENCE

CUSTOMER SERVICE REPRESENTATIVE. Boardwalk Hilton, Savannah, GA (2003-present). Function as Reservationist while planning, scheduling, and managing a variety of customer service activities which I always perform with a "Yes I Can" attitude.
- Was commended for my poise working in an environment in which last-minute changes and capacity/staffing problems are constant challenges. Coordinate business packages and VIP arrangements; work on a daily basis with travel agents and other hospitality industry professionals.
- On a daily basis, compile an occupancy report as well as a ten-day forecast.

HOUSING MANAGEMENT ASSISTANT. Sunshine Realty and Relocation Specialists, Orlando, FL (2001-03). Received a prestigious award recognizing my exceptional performance in handling a difficult relocation management project, and was quickly promoted to Lead Housing Counselor, which put me in the position of training and managing four people.
- Conducted group and individual counseling with families relocating to/from the area.
- Negotiated with local property owners, worked with managers of temporary lodgings.

BUDGET ASSISTANT. Jenkins Contractors, Orlando, FL (2001). Was responsible for requesting and consolidating budget input data for supplies, equipment, and other contractual services for 15 regional contracting offices throughout Florida, Georgia, and Alabama.

BUDGET/INVESTMENT ANALYST II. City of New Orleans, New Orleans, LA (1998-2001). Supervised the work of a Budget/Investment Analyst I while personally formulating, analyzing, and controlling numerous departmental annual budgets, including operating and revenue-sharing budgets; prepared budgets after analyzing historical expenditures and projecting future needs.
- Negotiated interest rates with savings and loan institutions in order to invest idle city funds in interest-bearing securities.
- Prepared and filed tax returns for all city funds; prepared detailed reports and data tables for use in budget hearings; prepared the 1999 City Budget Book for publication.

PERSONAL

Can provide exceptionally strong personal and professional references. Will travel.

CAREER CHANGE

Date

Exact Name of Person
Title or Position
Name of Company
Address (no., street)
Address (city, state, zip)

**CUSTOMER SERVICE
SPECIALIST**

in a hotel environment

Dear Exact Name of Person: (or Dear Sir or Madam if answering a blind ad.)

I would appreciate an opportunity to talk with you soon about how I could contribute to your organization through my proven skills in the areas of sales, quality control, customer service, and accounting.

As you will see from my enclosed resume, I excel in working with people and have a record of providing outstanding customer service. I have worked in both motel and restaurant environments where I earned a reputation for contributing to increased sales and customer satisfaction.

Earlier experience in quality control jobs helped me acquire an eye for detail and the ability to work with specialists in other departments to develop cost-effective methods and procedures.

I feel certain that I could contribute to your organization through my skills and abilities as well as through maturity and dedication to quality. I hope you will welcome my call soon to arrange a brief meeting at your convenience to discuss your current and future needs and how I might serve them. Thank you in advance for your time.

Sincerely yours,

Alicia E. Watson

(Alternate last paragraph:
I hope you will call or write soon to suggest a time convenient for us to meet and discuss your current and future needs and how I might serve them. Thank you in advance for your time.)

ALICIA E. WATSON

1110½ Hay Street, Fayetteville, NC 28305 • preppub@aol.com • (910) 483-6611

OBJECTIVE To apply my communication and sales abilities to an organization in need of a hard worker who also offers experience related to quality control and a talent for working with figures.

EXPERIENCE **CUSTOMER SERVICE SPECIALIST.** Day's Inn Hotel, Somerset, KY (2002-present). Earned a reputation as a dedicated worker with a true desire to provide quality customer service while handling operations including:

    Serving customers; making reservations
    Answering phones and providing information
    Ensuring guests enjoyed pleasant meals and good service
    Taking customers' payments and operating a cash register

- Gained experience related to accounting and handling money and am skilled in working with figures. Became known for my ability to satisfy customers of fine dining.

BOOKKEEPER. The Richmond Pub and Eatery, Richmond, KY (1998-2001). Assisted in keeping books for a family-owned restaurant with four employees.

- Apply my mathematical abilities to ensure "error-free" record keeping.

QUALITY CONTROL SPECIALIST. Delilah's, Somerset, KY (1995-97). Performed quality checks on measurements, colors, lines, and styles for a company manufacturing high-quality men's and women's clothing.

- Was recognized for my attention to detail in inspecting products to ensure they met quality standards.
- Supervised 12 employees involved in pulling samples, inspecting new items before they went into mass production, and preparing production reports.

CUSTOMER SERVICE SPECIALIST. Fanny's Fabrics, Richmond, KY (1991-94). Assisted customers in selecting fabrics and coordinating colors and styles to be used in home decorating.

- Applied my mathematical skills to estimate fabric costs and to measure materials.
- Contributed to increased sales through my ability to help customers "see" how their decorating projects would look when completed.

Other experience: Gained experience in quality control and bookkeeping in a manufacturing environment.

- Checked procedures and made calculations in order to ensure that corrections were made.
- Coordinated with laboratory employees to ensure the quality of new designs and colors.
- Trained employees in several different positions within the department.
- Learned to work with people of varied capacities and skills and gained the understanding that every employee has knowledge and skills to contribute.
- Worked with the chief engineer to set up the most cost effective procedures whenever new product lines were introduced.
- Maintained records and prepared taxes for a leather goods business.

TRAINING & Completed the Notary Public course on legal procedures, Somerset Community College,
CERTIFICATION Somerset, KY. Certified as a Notary Public.
Studied accounting and business, Elizabethtown Community College, Elizabethtown, KY, 1990-91.

PERSONAL Enjoy contributing to my community by doing volunteer work with handicapped children and senior citizens. Possess very strong communication and sales skills.

Exact Name of Person
Title or Position
Name of Company
Address (no., street)
Address (city, state, zip)

DIETARY AIDE
in a nursing home
environment. This
individual is making a
career in the food service
field in institutional
settings.

Dear Exact Name of Person: (or Dear Sir or Madam if answering a blind ad.)

With the enclosed resume, I would like to make you aware of my interest in exploring employment opportunities with your organization and introduce you to my experience.

As you will see from my resume, I recently resigned from my position at the Pine Forest Home in Ohio and have relocated to Iowa in order to be closer to family. In my spare time, I completed numerous courses at the local community college.

In my previous position, I was cross trained in multiple areas including the dietary services area. As a Dietary Aide, I gained an excellent understanding of special diets including diabetic and low cholesterol diets, and I set up food trays and prepared beverages for meals. I also gained experience in the housekeeping and laundry services area, and I previously worked as a Certified Nursing Assistant.

I am confident that I could make a valuable contribution to an organization that can use a hard worker who is well organized, honest, and dependable. If my background and skills interest you, I hope you will contact me to suggest a time when we could meet in person to discuss your needs. Thank you.

Yours sincerely,

Daria Joanne Dawson

DARIA JOANNE DAWSON

1110½ Hay Street, Fayetteville, NC 28305   •   preppub@aol.com   •   (910) 483-6611

OBJECTIVE
To contribute to an organization that can use an experienced support services provider who offers a versatile background in dietary services and housekeeping operations in institutional and nursing home environments.

EXPERIENCE
DIETARY AIDE, HOUSEKEEPING AIDE, & CNA. Pine Forest Home, Parma, OH (2001-present). Became experienced in setting up food trays and preparing beverages for meals while gaining a comprehensive understanding of various diets including diabetic and low-cholesterol diets.
- Delivered and collected trays.
- Assisted in food preparation and substituted food as appropriate for specific dietary needs.
- Operated dishwasher according to established procedures.
- Previously worked as a Certified Nursing Assistant (CNA).
- Recently resigned my position at the Pine Forest Home in order to relocate to Iowa to live near family.

DIETARY AIDE. Cuyahoga County Hospital, Parma, OH (1999-01). Set up food trays and prepared beverages for meals.
- Developed an excellent understanding of basic diets and substituted food as necessary.
- Delivered and collected trays; operated dishwasher.

NURSING ASSISTANT. Chrysalis House, Akron, OH (1998-99). Assisted residents with necessary daily hygiene and general housekeeping.
- Distributed meals and assisted with intake; charted residents' daily routine.

Other experience:
PREP PERSON. Mary's Kitchen, Marion, IN. Became known for my strong work ethic and industrious attitude in this restaurant environment.
DIETARY AIDE. Riverside Nursing Home, Marion, IN. Became knowledgeable of special diets and acceptable food substitutions while working with elderly people.
CAFE HOSTESS. Natasha's Cafe, Medina, OH. Prepared food daily, served customers, operated cash register, handled large amounts of money, and closed shop daily.

EDUCATION
Completed coursework in English and math, Cuyahoga County Community College, Parma, OH, 2002.
Previously graduated from Medina Senior High School, Medina, OH.

SPECIAL SKILLS
Dietary aide services: Extensive experience in dietary food service.
Housekeeping: Knowledgeable of institutional housekeeping procedures, including laundry.

PERSONAL
Highly motivated individual who desires to work as part of a dedicated team. In my spare time, enjoy swimming, dancing, outdoor activities, and reading. Able to follow strict guidelines; can handle hard, physical labor. Well organized, dependable, honest.

Exact Name of Person
Title or Position
Name of Company
Address (no., street)
Address (city, state, zip)

**DIETARY MANAGER
APPRENTICE**

in a hospital setting

Dear Exact Name of Person: (or Dear Sir or Madam if answering a blind ad.)

    I would appreciate an opportunity to talk with you soon about how I could contribute to your organization through my education related to nutrition, dietary management, and meal planning as well as through my hardworking nature and positive, outgoing disposition.

    As you will see from my resume, I offer a proven commitment to the field of dietetics and nutrition. In a recent apprenticeship while earning my B.S. degree in home economics, nutrition, and meal management from the University of New Mexico, I worked in a hospital environment where I became involved in food preparation, menu planning, and inventory control. I became acquainted with every aspect of the job of the hospital dietary manager.

    You will also see from my resume that I began working at the age of 15 and demonstrated at a young age my ability to handle responsibility and deal with people. I have excelled at several jobs while working part-time, summer, and holiday jobs to finance my college degree. In one work-study job at the university, I used a computer software program called "The Food Processor" to analyze and plan menus, and I played a key role in planning and serving at major receptions and university events. I also worked part-time as a waitress/hostess at a restaurant, where I was involved in every aspect of operations.

    I have also worked in nonfood environments. In fact, while working as a sales representative for McAlpin's Department Store, I received the company's second-highest award for sales achievements. This was an unusual honor for a person as young as I was and with no previous sales experience.

    You would find me to be a congenial young person who tries hard to excel in all that I do. I can provide outstanding personal and professional references upon your request.

    I hope you will welcome my call soon to try to arrange a time when we might meet to discuss your needs and how I might serve them. Thank you in advance for your time.

Sincerely yours,

Amy L. Bowers

AMY LYNN BOWERS

1110½ Hay Street, Fayetteville, NC 28305　　•　　preppub@aol.com　　•　　(910) 483-6611

OBJECTIVE

To contribute to an organization that can use a hardworking young professional who offers expert knowledge of nutrition, diet, institutional cooking, and meal management along with exceptionally strong skills related to customer service and public relations.

EDUCATION

Earned a **Bachelor of Science (B.S.)** degree in Home Economics, Nutrition, and Meal Management, University of New Mexico, Albuquerque, NM, 2003.
- Received the Kathleen E. Dmitruk Scholarship, 2001-03.
- Excelled academically and was named to the Dean's List.
- Was elected Secretary of the university's Home Economics Club.

EXPERIENCE

APPRENTICE TO DIETARY MANAGER. Albuquerque Hospital, Albuquerque, NM (2003). In a formal apprenticeship while completing my college degree, functioned as the "shadow" of the hospital's Dietary Manager; gained an overview of what is involved in managing nutrition and planning meals in a hospital environment.
- Assisted the kitchen staff by constructing diet cards for meals, by labeling special diets, and by sanitizing trays and utensils; learned the importance of monitoring sanitation and observing hygiene practices of food service workers.
- Participated as an observer in patient/family consultations conducted by the dietary manager.
- Prepared patient menus; was trained in the fundamentals of purchasing and inventory control.
- Became aware of the many different kinds of diets provided to patients including pureed food, low-calorie diets, and low-sodium meals.

CATERER/HOME ECONOMICS DEPARTMENT ASSISTANT. University of New Mexico, Albuquerque, NM (2002-03). Became skilled in using a computer program called "The Food Processor" as an aid in analyzing menus while also assisting the Home Economics Chairperson in planning menus for a local prison as well as in planning and managing the food served at major events and receptions.
- Learned how important it is to be well organized when managing numerous projects.

WAITRESS/HOSTESS. Emmet's, Albuquerque, NM (2002-present). Constantly operate according to the philosophy that "the customer is always right" while participating in every area of this restaurant; help the cooks in the kitchen, book parties, seat customers, make beverages, help serve at catered functions, work on the serving line, run the cash register, account for cash, and take orders by telephone.

SALES REPRESENTATIVE. McAlpin's Department Store, Abilene, TX (2000-02). After being with McAlpin's for only a year, won the second-highest award given by the company for sales achievements—the "Bronze" Award; this is considered a great honor and it was unusual for a young college student with no previous sales experience to win this award.
- Was commended for my positive attitude and "peppy" disposition.
- Worked part-time selling jewelry, shoes, handbags, and accessories to finance college.

COMPUTERS

Have worked with Word and other software; have an ability to rapidly master new software.

PERSONAL

Take pride in my neat and professional appearance. Am a very self-confident person who has an ability to work easily with others. Am patient and determined and enjoy challenges.

Date

Exact Name of Person
Title or Position
Name of Company
Address (no., street)
Address (city, state, zip)

DINING FACILITY
MANAGER
for a cruiseship

Dear Exact Name of Person: (or Dear Sir or Madam if answering a blind ad.)

I would appreciate an opportunity to talk with you soon about how I could contribute to your organization through my thorough knowledge of food service operations and extensive management experience.

While beginning my working career as a cashier in a fast food restaurant, I rapidly advanced to Assistant Manager and have progressively advanced in all subsequent positions.

Currently I supervise the preparation, cooking, and serving of meals in a cruiseship's main dining facility, serving as many as 700 people per meal. Working on the cruiseship has proven especially challenging in that the kitchen must be adequately stocked to serve the travelers at all times. With fresh produce and other supplies arriving on board in only specific port locations, excellent organizational skills and attention to detail is imperative.

As you will see from my resume, in a previous job I was chosen to provide instruction to an average of 400 students a month while conducting classes in large quantity food preparation and cooking. Area institutions sent their food service employees to these classes as part of their training programs.

If you can use a dynamic professional with expertise in managing and operating large scale food service operations, I hope you will call or write soon to suggest a time convenient for us to meet and discuss your current and future needs and how I might serve them. Thank you in advance for your time.

Sincerely yours,

Antonio M. Sandoval

Alternate last paragraph:
I hope you will welcome my call soon to arrange a brief meeting at your convenience to discuss your current and future needs and how I might serve them. Thank you in advance for your time.

ANTONIO MIGUEL SANDOVAL

1110½ Hay Street, Fayetteville, NC 28305 • preppub@aol.com • (910) 483-6611

OBJECTIVE To benefit an organization through my expertise in food service operations as well as my management experience and skills in supervising employees.

EXPERIENCE **DINING FACILITY MANAGER.** Carnival Cruiselines, Miami, FL (2003-present). Supervised twenty-six food service specialists preparing three full meals a day for 700 people.
- Recognized for my personnel and budgetary management knowledge, controlled $1.5 million worth of equipment.
- Was selected to attend a prestigious two-week special menu-planning school sponsored by Carnival Cruiselines and held in Kingston, Jamaica.

ASSISTANT FOOD SERVICE MANAGER. Carnival Cruiselines, Miami, FL (2001-03). Worked closely with the senior manager in the ship's kitchen which prepared three hot meals a day for 600 vacationing tourists.
- Learned to supervise personnel, take careful inventory, and place orders.
- Earned rapid advancement to above position and an award for my excellent efforts.

SUPERVISORY DINING FACILITY MANAGER. Foothills Hospital, Sevierville, TN (1999-2001). Directed the performance of food service specialists while cooking, preparing, and serving three meals a day to 500 people in the hospital's cafeteria.
- Maintained $300,000 worth of equipment. Learned to take the responsibility for seeing that even the smallest details were taken care of to guarantee good service.

INSTRUCTOR. Foothills Hospital, Sevierville, TN (1999-2000). In a simultaneous job with the one described above, chosen to conduct classes in food preparation and cooking procedures including how to weigh and measure foods for cooking in large quantities.
- Earned praise for my skills and knowledge while working with an average of 400 students from various regional institutions every month.

ASSISTANT MANAGER. Shoney's Restaurant, Evansville, IN (1997-99). Supervised 15 food service specialists in cooking, preparing, and serving in this national chain restaurant.
- Was credited as a key factor in the restaurant's consistently high levels of cleanliness and quality service as noted in inspections.

ASSISTANT MANAGER. Burger King, Evansville, IN (1995-97). Started as a cashier and within six months was promoted to Assistant Manager, providing leadership for up to 20 employees preparing and serving in the busy fast food restaurant.
- Refined my leadership skills learning to deal with employees effectively.

EDUCATION & TRAINING Studied Food Service Management at Evansville Community College, Evansville, IN, and Volunteer State Community College, Gallatin, TN; completed course work including:

purchasing/receiving/issuing	culinary art/buffet
personnel and human relations	nutrition/menu planning
business math	cafeteria management

Completed approximately 500 hours of training in advanced and basic culinary skills, dining facility management, and human relations/counseling.

PERSONAL Am known for sticking to a job until it's done. Have a reputation as a good listener.

CAREER CHANGE

Date

Exact Name of Person
Title or Position
Name of Company
Address (no., street)
Address (city, state, zip)

DINING FACILITY MANAGER

for a hospital. This individual seeks a career path that will allow him to utilize his strong counseling skills.

Dear Exact Name of Person: (or Dear Sir or Madam if answering a blind ad.)

Can you use an energetic and enthusiastic professional who offers a background of service in supervisory, managerial, and leadership roles which have required outstanding counseling and motivational abilities?

While working at my current job at Central Baptist Hospital, I was formally evaluated as "a leader who sets the standards," and "one who can be counted on to go the extra mile." I excel in finding ways to improve morale, increase productivity, and ensure extremely high standards of service. My experience as a dining facility manager placed me in supervisory roles where I often had many very young employees working in their first jobs. This situation required me to remain patient while transforming them into hardworking personnel who cared about providing quality service.

Although I have excelled in the food service field, I have felt a powerful motivation to move toward a position which utilizes my counseling abilities. I have recently earned my B.A. in Counseling while attending college at night over a six-year period.

I feel that through my training and work history I have gained insights into how to "reach" people through counseling. I have a true concern for people along with the physical conditioning, ability to handle pressure and deadlines, and administrative skills required to excel in difficult conditions.

I hope you will welcome my call soon to arrange a brief meeting at your convenience to discuss your current and future needs and how I might serve them. Thank you in advance for your time.

Sincerely yours,

Christopher David Graves

Alternate last paragraph:
I hope you will call or write soon to suggest a time convenient for us to meet and discuss your current and future needs and how I might serve them. Thank you in advance for your time.

CHRISTOPHER DAVID GRAVES

1110½ Hay Street, Fayetteville, NC 28305   •   preppub@aol.com   •   (910) 483-6611

OBJECTIVE

To benefit an organization in need of a mature professional who offers outstanding communication and counseling abilities along with a reputation as a dedicated and concerned leader, hard worker, and "good listener" with boundless enthusiasm and energy.

EDUCATION

Bachelor of Arts (B.A.) degree in Counseling, University of Chicago, Chicago, IL, 2003. Completed extensive training related to drug and alcohol abuse counseling, leadership and management development, counseling skills for the supervisor, and food service supervision.

EXPERIENCE

SENIOR DINING FACILITY MANAGER and **PERSONNEL SUPERVISOR.** Central Baptist Hospital, Chicago, IL (2001-present). Supervised as many as 187 employees and controlled up to $1.7 million worth of property, equipment, and raw materials as the senior person in several different cafeteria and dining facilities in this large hospital system.
- Provided leadership and guidance to many young employees in their first job.
- Advised executives on training and personnel assignments as well as on the actual preparation, storage, and serving of food.
- Managed one facility which served more than 3,500 people.
- Transformed this troubled facility into an operation with a reputation for excellent service.
- Officially commended for my ability to motivate employees to work together to produce outstanding results as a team, was described as "constantly teaching and showing concern for employees."
- Managed a complex renovation project ahead of schedule and under budget.

DINING FACILITY MANAGER. Good Samaritan Hospital, Chicago, IL (1996-00). Was evaluated as "a consistently outstanding performer" while involved in scheduling, training, and supervising 39 employees; managed a dining facility which served 600 people.
- Handled paperwork and record keeping to include such areas as controlling food accounts and planning menus.
- Developed innovations which improved the quality of service for customers and the work environment for employees.
- Earned the respect of senior executives for my ability to overcome the restraints of personnel shortages and a high employee turnover rate.
- Transformed a "mediocre" facility into one widely recognized as a "model."

FOOD SERVICE SUPERVISOR. Northwestern University, Evanston, IL (1994-96). Advanced from assisting the manager of a dining facility to supervise employees and manage a 48-employee food service center named "the best" of its kind for three consecutive quarters.
- Was named as a key player and leader through my attention to detail, exceptional efforts in administrative areas, and ability to maximize employee contributions.

Highlights of other experience: Gained skills in supervising employees and earned a reputation as a hardworking and dedicated leader.

HONORS

Was honored with numerous commendation and achievement awards for meritorious performance as a leader, manager, and supervisor.

PERSONAL

Enjoy working with young people while counseling them and helping them make important personal and professional decisions. Specialize in "leadership by example."

Exact Name of Person
Title or Position
Name of Company
Address (no., street)
Address (city, state, zip)

**DINING FACILITY
SUPERVISOR**

for youth camp dining
facilities.

Dear Exact Name of Person: (or Dear Sir or Madam if answering a blind ad.)

Can you use a professional with extensive management and operations experience in the food service industry?

As you will see from my resume, I have built a respectable career in the food service industry. Most recently, I have worked in management positions at various youth camp dining facilities. My responsibilities range from overseeing actual facility construction to planning well-balanced meals for an average of 500 campers and staff three times daily. I have been commended for my flawless planning and have a reputation for consistently reducing employee turnover and product loss rates.

I hope you will welcome my call soon to arrange a brief meeting at your convenience to discuss your current and future needs and how I might serve them. Thank you in advance for your time.

Sincerely yours,

Dennis C. Lauderbeck

Alternate last paragraph:
If you can use a dynamic professional with expertise in managing and operating large scale food service operations, I hope you will call or write soon to suggest a time convenient for us to meet and discuss your current and future needs and how I might serve them. Thank you in advance for your time.

DENNIS C. LAUDERBECK

1110½ Hay Street, Fayetteville, NC 28305 • preppub@aol.com • (910) 483-6611

OBJECTIVE
To offer my outstanding knowledge of food service operations to an organization that can benefit from my well-rounded background in management, personnel supervision, preparation, and sanitation activities.

EXPERIENCE
DINING HALL SUPERVISOR. Camp Chief Hector, Redding, CA (2003-present). In recognition of my proven abilities, was handpicked to manage a renovated $1.5 million dining facility which fed approximately 500 people daily, including weekends.
- Was commended for my flawless planning which allowed the facility to open a week ahead of schedule and provided excellent service despite being only 68% staffed.
- Played an important role in negotiating, and then supervising, a $1 million contract.
- Led employees to reach high team work and morale levels while opening the facility during a health inspection and ensuring that operations continued to run smoothly.
- Plan highly nutritional menus for young campers, and account for any special diets.

FOOD SERVICE SUPPORT MANAGER. Camp Chief Joseph, Napa, CA (1998-2002). Procured, stored, issued, and inventoried $4,300 in monthly purchases with an average daily stock of $2,200.
- Provided technical guidance to food preparation specialists; was credited as a major reason for the camp's dining facility receiving favorable responses for quality of service.
- Resulting from success with this job, was promoted to the above job with a sister camp.

DINING FACILITY MANAGER. Waccamaw Nature Camp, Dubois, OR (1997-98). Designed, oversaw construction, and managed a camp dining facility which served 1,500 meals daily to campers and staff in a position usually reserved for a higher ranking manager.
- Monitored a $2 million monthly food inventory budget.
- Became widely recognized for innovative menus, unusual for a high volume operation.

ACTING MANAGER and **QUALITY ASSURANCE INSPECTOR.** Jasper Jarvis High School, Portland, OR (1992-97). Held dual roles in a high school cafeteria which served approximately 30,000 meals a month while also ensuring the quality of services provided by contractors in the cafeteria.
- Received praise for my commitment to training and guiding younger personnel in modern food preparation techniques. Demonstrated talents for problem-solving and finding ways to improve productivity, work methods, and operations.

SUPERVISORY FOOD SERVICE SPECIALIST and **QUALITY CONTROL ADVISOR.** Friendly's Restaurant, Portland, OR (1986-91). Oversaw hiring, training, and scheduling of the restaurant's 85 employees; reduced labor costs 6% within three months.
- Prepared profit-and-loss statements; monitor invoicing; oversee payroll administration.
- Instilled in employees an attitude of "attention to detail" that produced a strong commitment to quality standards.
- Developed inexperienced personnel into well-coordinated and highly functioning teams.
- Achieved noteworthy and extremely high ratings in no-notice sanitation inspections.

EDUCATION & TRAINING
Completed approximately 46 semester hours, Portland Community College.
Attended training programs emphasizing leadership as well as methods for instructing and evaluating in quality assurance programs.

PERSONAL
Am known as a tireless worker. Excel in training and molding effective and productive teams.

Exact Name of Person
Exact Title
Exact Name of Company
Address
City, State, Zip

DIRECTOR OF CATERING
for a major hotel.

Dear Exact Name of Person (or Dear Sir or Madam if answering a blind ad):

With the enclosed resume, I would like to make you aware of my background as a detail-oriented sales and hospitality industry professional with exceptional communication, time management, and customer service skills and experience in account management, direct sales, and public relations.

In my current position as a Director of Catering for Marriot Hospitality at the Sunnydale Marriot in Phoenix, I oversee all aspects of the catering department, including direct sales, planning, and execution of all meetings and conferences for the 6,000 square foot meeting space. I am responsible for generating projected annual sales of $660,000 for the hotel. In addition to supervising one assistant and a Banquet Manager, I prepare catering forecasts, predicting future sales based on current bookings.

In previous positions with The Radisson Bougainvillea in Tallahassee, Florida, I started as a sales assistant and was quickly promoted due to my exemplary job performance and dedication. As Sales and Catering Coordinator, I provided administrative support to two departments. My organizational expertise and detail-oriented approach to problem-solving allowed me to assist the Director of Sales, the Corporate Sales Manager, and the Director of Catering, ensuring that functions were carried out smoothly and to the customer's complete satisfaction. After my promotion to Catering Manager, I assisted the Director of Catering in planning weddings, small meetings, and conferences for this 12,000 square-foot meeting space.

Prior to entering the hospitality industry, I excelled as Legislative Assistant to a member of the California House of Representatives, providing a wide range of clerical and office management services while handling all correspondence from the Representative's constituents.

If you can use a self-motivated, articulate sales and hospitality industry professional with outstanding communication, organizational, and customer service abilities, I look forward to hearing from you soon to arrange a time when we might meet to discuss your needs, and how I might meet them. I can assure you in advance that I have an excellent reputation, and would quickly become a valuable asset to your organization.

Sincerely,

Marissa P. Newsome

MARISSA P. NEWSOME

1110½ Hay Street, Fayetteville, NC 28305   •   preppub@aol.com   •   (910) 483-6611

OBJECTIVE   To benefit an organization that can use a detail-oriented sales and hospitality industry professional with exceptional communication, time management, and customer service skills as well as a background in account management, direct sales, public relations, and catering.

EXPERIENCE   **DIRECTOR OF CATERING.** Marriot Hospitality, Inc., Sunnydale Marriot, Phoenix, AZ (2002-present). Oversee all operational aspects of the catering department in this busy hotel; responsible for direct sales, planning, and execution of all meetings and conferences for this 6,000 square foot meeting space.
- Supervise one assistant and a Banquet Manager; plan food and beverage/catering needs for all small meetings and conferences.
- Service existing accounts and develop new business, selling meeting space and catering services to associations, corporations, and military accounts.
- Prepare catering forecasts, determining future business based on current bookings.
- Work closely with the sales department to coordinate event planning and ensure that all details are handled smoothly and carried out to the satisfaction of the customer.

CATERING MANAGER. The Radisson Bougainvillea, Tallahassee, FL (2000-01). Promoted to Catering Manager; planned all small meetings, weddings, and small conferences for the catering department; earned respect for my attention to detail in catering all types of functions for a meeting space over 12,000 square feet.
- Led the hotel to earn a reputation as "the best meeting place in town."
- Worked closely with the Director of Catering as Catering Manager.

SALES AND CATERING COORDINATOR. The Radisson Bougainvillea, Tallahassee, FL (1998-2000). Became thoroughly knowledgeable of the hospitality industry in this job requiring a versatile and adaptable professional; provided administrative support to two departments — sales and catering — which work closely and share some of the same personnel and areas of operation.
- Provided the Director of Sales, the Corporate Sales Manager, and the Director of Catering with my expertise in coordinating details so that functions were carried out smoothly and to the customer's satisfaction.
- Worked closely with clients to plan small meetings and a variety of events for the hotel's banquet and conference facilities.
- Excelled in handling multiple simultaneous responsibilities under tight deadlines.
- Assisted the General Manager when his regular assistant was unavailable.
- Was promoted to this position after six months as a Sales Assistant.

LEGISLATIVE ASSISTANT. The California House of Representatives, Sacramento, CA (1984-97). Provided a wide range of secretarial and office management activities for an elected representative including handling problems and concerns from constituents in a three-county area which was the largest geographical district in the state.
- Worked closely with the representative to ensure that all direct, written, or telephone inquiries were responded to promptly and to the constituent's satisfaction.

TRAINING   Proficient in using Breeze Systems and software including Microsoft Word.
Completed business coursework, California State University extension.

PERSONAL   Have a real knack for putting people at ease, defusing difficult situations, and getting along with others. Enjoy fast-paced environments and meeting challenges. Excellent references.

Date

Exact Name of Person
Exact Title
Exact Name of Company
Address
City, State, Zip

Dear Exact Name of Person (or Dear Sir or Madam if answering a blind ad):

With the enclosed resume, I would like to make you aware of an experienced food service professional with exceptional motivational, communication, and organizational skills as well as a background as a restaurant General Manager and Director of Operations who has demonstrated the ability to produce extraordinary "bottom-line" results.

With Dudley's restaurant, I was aggressively recruited and hired to design, coordinate the construction of, and manage the kitchen for the opening of this location. My exemplary management skills were quickly recognized, and I was promoted to Director of Operations, with final accountability for all aspects of the operation of a busy restaurant with annual sales of $1.5 million. I train and supervise the Kitchen Manager, Bar Manager, and Front End manager as well as the kitchen, wait and bar staff, totaling 65 employees. I prepare and manage the monthly operations budget, evaluating all expenses to maximize profits and ensure budget compliance.

In previous positions with The White Buffalo, I first coordinated the construction and development of this family restaurant, and then was actively sought out by the owners to "turn around" the operation, taking over at a time when it was on the verge of bankruptcy. Using the same innovative, cost-cutting inventory control procedures I had implemented when I first worked for the company, I quickly transformed the restaurant into a popular and profitable organization with a $200,000 increase in sales.

If you can use an experienced General Manager and Director of Operations whose supervisory and leadership skills have been tested in a variety of restaurant environments, I hope you will contact me soon to suggest a time when we might meet to discuss your needs. I can provide excellent references at the appropriate time.

Sincerely,

Roger S. Chin

ROGER S. CHIN

1110½ Hay Street, Fayetteville, NC 28305 • preppub@aol.com • (910) 483-6611

OBJECTIVE

To contribute to an organization that can use an experienced food service professional who can produce extraordinary "bottom-line" results through applying sales and management skills gained in a variety of restaurant General Manager and Operations Manager positions.

EXPERIENCE

DIRECTOR OF OPERATIONS. Dudley's, Lawrence, KS (2003-present). Aggressively recruited to design and manage the kitchen for this newly opened restaurant; quickly advanced to Director of Operations, responsible for all aspects of the operation of this busy local eatery with annual sales of $1.5 million.

- Train and direct the activities of three managers, including the Bar Manager, Kitchen Manager, and Front End Manager. Supervise the bar, kitchen, and wait staff, totaling more than 60 employees.
- Prepare and manage monthly operations budget, evaluating all expenses to ensure budget compliance and maximize profits. Oversee the creation and development of innovative marketing plans and promotions to increase catering and banquet sales.
- As Kitchen Manager, directed the construction, maintenance, and purchasing of all equipment for the initial setup of the cooking stations and preparation areas.

OWNER-OPERATOR. Roger's Grille and Pub, Lawrence, KS (2001-03). Opened, managed, and oversaw the operation of a busy local restaurant and tavern.

GENERAL MANAGER. The White Buffalo, Emporia, KS (1999-2001). Actively recruited by my former employer, I took over at a time when this restaurant was on the brink of bankruptcy. Quickly transformed it into a popular and profitable organization with a $200,000 increase in sales; supervised a staff of 25 employees.

- Applied my exceptional motivational skills and my expert purchasing and cost-control knowhow to produce dramatic results, quickly "turning around" this ailing operation.
- Trained and motivated employees who became known for exceptional customer service.

MANAGER. Friday's, Lawrence, Emporia, and Topeka, KS (1995-99). Excelled in a variety of management roles in this large restaurant chain.

- **Kitchen Manager**: (Lawrence). Prepared and managed a budget of $200,000; by increasing efficiency and controlling waste, made this restaurant one of the most profitable in 11 states.
- **Service Manager**: (Emporia). Trained and motivated 70 bar and wait staff personnel; carefully budgeted labor hours; controlled liquor costs.

GENERAL MANAGER. The White Buffalo, Emporia, KS (1993-95). After coordinating the construction and development of this family restaurant and creating its menu, excelled in making it one of the area's most popular.

- Decreased food and labor costs with no loss of quality in food or service.
- Implemented innovative, cost-cutting inventory control procedures.

Other Experience:
RESTAURANT MANAGER. Victor Steak Pub, Victor, KS (1990-92). Increased this company's sales to the $1 million level by starting a new department which catered to parties of up to 800 people. Motivated a 75-person staff and molded them into an efficient team.

EDUCATION

Completed the National Restaurant Association Seminar on Catering, Lawrence, KS, and training related to Health and Sanitation in Food Handling, Emporia College, Emporia, KS.

Date

Exact Name of Person
Title or Position
Name of Company
Address (no., street)
Address (city, state, zip)

DIRECTOR OF OPERATIONS

for a major hotel

Dear Exact Name of Person: (or Dear Sir or Madam if answering a blind ad.)

I would appreciate an opportunity to talk with you soon about how I could contribute to your organization through my expertise in operations, project management, and inventory control, as well as my exceptional analytical and decision-making abilities refined throughout years in the hospitality industry.

You will see from my resume that I have been involved in all aspects of designing, coordinating, and implementing housing, recreation, and building renovation programs. I also have recently received a B.S. degree in Hotel Administration from the University of Nevada-Las Vegas. Throughout my career I have attended courses and seminars and studied on my own to remain knowledgeable of my main areas of skills.

In my most recent job as Assistant Director of Operations at Best Western, I utilize my excellent time-management and coordinating skills to manage a popular hotel, including supervising all inventory control and personnel. I significantly improved production while directing catering services at the Days Inn Hotel in Coeur D'Alene, ID.

I feel that I offer a unique combination of creativity and vision, practical technical knowledge, and extensive experience which are transferable to many situations where I could make important contributions.

I hope you will call or write me soon to suggest a time convenient for us to meet and discuss your current and future needs and how I might serve them. Thank you in advance for your time.

Sincerely yours,

Keith Lawrence Hayes

KEITH LAWRENCE HAYES

1110½ Hay Street, Fayetteville, NC 28305   •   preppub@aol.com   •   (910) 483-6611

OBJECTIVE

To benefit an organization seeking a hardworking professional experienced in areas related to operations, project management, and inventory control who possesses excellent planning, communication, and motivational abilities.

EDUCATION

Bachelor of Science (B.S.) in Hotel Administration, University of Nevada-Las Vegas, Las Vegas, NV, 2003.

Received a certificate in the Human Communications program, North Idaho College, Coeur D'Alene, ID, 1992.

Attended a wide range of continuing education courses, including classes in First-Aid, CPR, time-management, leadership, and verbal and written communication skills.

EXPERIENCE

ASSISTANT DIRECTOR OF OPERATIONS. Best Western Hotels, Las Vegas, NV (2002-present). Have refined my communication and accounting skills while overseeing all front desk activities in this popular hotel right off "The Strip" in a very busy tourist atmosphere.
- Coordinate training and work schedules for full-time, part-time, and temporary employees.
- Praised for professionally processing a wide range of accounting functions, including consistently maintaining 100% register reconciliation.
- Have learned to quickly and courteously resolve the thorniest customer-service problems.

DIRECTOR OF OPERATIONS. YMCA of Las Vegas, Las Vegas, NV (2000-02). Excelled at developing, organizing, and promoting all sports-related programs and activities for a 400-person organization while also supervising a staff of 35.
- Designed and interpreted departmental policies and procedures.
- Assisted in creating "how to" workshops and in the renovation of the recreation center.
- Coordinated all children's plays, concerts, and dances.
- Earned a reputation for easily establishing a rapport with people from diverse cultural and socioeconomic backgrounds.
- Ensured the safety and operation of all recreation center equipment and facilities.

ASSISTANT OPERATIONS MANAGER. Days Inn West, Coeur D'Alene, ID (1998-00). Utilized excellent inventory management and organizational abilities planning the catering needs for the hotel banquet facility; trained, supervised, and evaluated food service staff.
- Controlled all inventory ordering and disbursement in addition to performing general ledger accounting procedures.
- Oversaw departmental sanitation; commended by top-level management for significantly raising sanitation inspection ratings. Cited by supervisor as a professional who "demonstrates dedication, enthusiasm, and initiative towards learning new tasks."

DORMITORY MANAGER. North Idaho College, Coeur D'Alene, ID (1993-97). Directed the operations of a 250-room college dormitory while also ordering and maintaining all furnishings.
- Scheduled and tracked maintenance orders. Commended for running the college's best dormitory. Saved a significant amount of renovation costs by coordinating and implementing several projects.

PERSONAL

Am a self-starter who enjoys challenges, problem-solving, and decision-making. Have a knack for motivating personnel. Have consistently received outstanding work evaluations, awards, and letters of commendation. Excellent references.

Date

Exact Name of Person
Title or Position
Name of Company
Address (no., street)
Address (city, state, zip)

Dear Exact Name of Person:

With the enclosed resume, I would like to indicate my interest in the position of Director of Regional Sales for Marriot Hotels International in the Western KY Region. Joan Hendrick, Marriot Hotels International's Director of Regional Services for North and South Carolina, telephoned me to let me know about your search for a Director of Regional Sales and, as she suspected, I am very interested in discussing the position with you.

Currently excelling as Director of Sales for the Sheraton Hotel in Owensboro, I am managing a $1.638 million yearly budget while coordinating the efforts of four sales professionals. In my prior position I was Director of Sales — and routinely functioned as General Manager — for the Day's Inn River's Edge hotel, where I helped manage a $2.5 million budget. In that job I was credited as being the driving force behind the hotel's receiving the Gold Award. In both of those jobs, and in an earlier job as Corporate Sales Manager, I made impressive contributions to yield management while optimizing the effectiveness of the reservation system and building revenue per available room. For example, the Day's Inn River's Edge, we increased the Average Daily Rate from $43.00 to $52.00 and occupancy increased 6%.

My career in the hospitality industry actually began when I was a college student earning a degree in Psychology (which I have put to excellent use in our industry!). To finance my education, I worked as a Hostess/Waitress in fine dining restaurants and became knowledgeable of various wines, tableside service, and food preparation. I am proud of the fact that I learned to take an order for a six-course meal for up to eight people from memory and eye contact! That job gave me a nuts-and-bolts understanding of the "behind-the-scenes" activities of our hospitality industry.

Although I am well regarded by the Sheraton Corporation and am being groomed for rapid promotion into higher management, I have a preference for many of the systems and procedures of Marriot Hotels International. I am quite confident that I would be able to build a close rapport among Marriot Directors of Sales within the region.

I can provide excellent references at the appropriate time, but please treat this resume and letter of inquiry as confidential at this point. I hope you will call or write me soon to suggest a time convenient for us to meet and discuss your current and future needs and how I might serve them. Thank you in advance for your time.

Sincerely yours,

Claudia M. Perez

CLAUDIA M. PEREZ

1110½ Hay Street, Fayetteville, NC 28305   •   preppub@aol.com   •   (910) 483-6611

OBJECTIVE

To benefit Marriot Hotels International as its Director of Regional Sales for the Western KY Region; I offer a proven ability to become a valuable part of a hotel management team while using my sales, marketing, management, and customer service skills to optimize yield, build revenue per available room, build rapport among hotel staff, and maximize the effectiveness of the reservation system.

EXPERIENCE

DIRECTOR OF SALES. Sheraton Hotel, Owensboro, KY (2003-present). Manage a $1.638 million yearly budget for group rooms and catering for a 200-room hotel with 15,000 square feet of banquet space.
- On my own initiative, developed "from scratch" a Trace File System which has dramatically improved the sales efforts of the staff.
- Coordinate the efforts of four people including the Sales Manager, Director of Catering, Catering and Sales Coordinator, and Sales Secretary.
- Am active in the Manager-on-Duty Program in the absence of the General Manager to resolve all customer complaints and employee problems.
- Have received the highest evaluations of my performance, and am being groomed for rapid promotion to higher management levels.
- Make outside sales calls, perform telemarketing, and aggressively book business including sleeping rooms, meeting space, and banquets in the corporate, association, tour and travel, and SMERF markets.

DIRECTOR OF SALES/ASSISTANT GENERAL MANAGER. Day's Inn River's Edge, Owensboro, KY (2000-03). Was credited as being the driving force behind this hotel receiving the Gold Award in 2003; increased the Average Daily Rate (ADR) from $43.00 to $52.00 and increased occupancy by 6%.
- Exceeded every goal for profitability and cost control while helping to manage a $2.5 million budget for this 176-room hotel with 3,000 square feet of meeting space.
- Booked business in all market segments: transient, group, and rack rated.
- Frequently acted as General Manager when the GM was out of town or on vacation; managed the 55-person staff in his absence and became a respected problem solver.
- While filling the shoes of the GM, became extremely knowledgeable of profit-and-loss statements and operating budgets.

CORPORATE SALES MANAGER. Comfort Inn Owensboro, Owensboro, KY (1993-99). Was promoted to Corporate Sales Manager after excelling as Assistant Guest Services Manager. Acquired and maintained local corporate accounts as well as feeder city corporate business from Somerset, Louisville, and Lexington; met or exceeded all sales and budget revenue goals set by the Director of Sales for this 300-room hotel with 40,000 square feet of banquet space, two restaurants, and two bars.

EDUCATION

Received Bachelor of Science (B.S.) degree in Psychology, University of Louisville, Louisville, KY, 1993.
Completed Sheraton Hotels' "Sales Management" course in effectively operating a hotel sales department. At Day's Inn University, studied Guest Service Management, Customer Service, and Employment Management. Completed Comfort Inn International's "Gold Award Program" which taught the steps necessary to become a Gold Award property.

PERSONAL

Believe effective teamwork is the key to success in the hotel industry, and pride myself on my ability to mold and manage teams of loyal employees. Exceptional references.

Date

Exact Name of Person
Title or Position
Name of Company
Address (no., street)
Address (city, state, zip)

DISTRICT MANAGER

of a multiunit restaurant
operation.

Dear Exact Name of Person: (or Dear Sir or Madam if answering a blind ad.)

Can you use an experienced restaurant manager who excels in ensuring profitability, hiring and training productive teams of employees, and increasing profits while reducing costs?

Within a year of joining Denny's Inc. as a single-unit Operations Manager, I had been recognized as the Best Rookie Unit Manager out of 75 units in the region and was promoted to District Manager with three locations. In this capacity I have opened one completely new restaurant with full responsibility for advertising, staffing and training, and administration. I also completely reorganized two neglected and substandard sites and transformed them into profitability and productivity.

In both single-unit and multiunit operations I have accomplished above-average percentages in food costs, operating costs, and payroll and offer the highest hourly employee stability rate of 87 restaurants in the area.

Prior to my experience with Denny's I excelled in new car sales and as an Administrative Manager at a top notch ski resort. In both fields I earned recognition for surpassing my peers in performance and job knowledge and was selected for numerous leadership positions.

I offer a reputation as a person of boundless energy, unquestioned integrity, and superb analytical and problem-solving skills.

I hope you will welcome my call soon to arrange a brief meeting at your convenience to discuss your current and future needs and how I might serve them. Thank you in advance for your time.

Sincerely yours,

Jerome E. Taylor

Alternate last paragraph:
I hope you will call or write soon to suggest a time convenient for us to meet and discuss your current and future needs and how I might serve them. Thank you in advance for your time.

JEROME E. TAYLOR

1110½ Hay Street, Fayetteville, NC 28305 • preppub@aol.com • (910) 483-6611

OBJECTIVE

To contribute my talents for team building, problem-solving, and planning for the smallest details to an organization that can use my proven managerial abilities, "bottom line" orientation, and ability to find and correct inefficient procedures.

EXPERIENCE

Earned Rapid Advancement with Denny's, Inc.:

DISTRICT MANAGER. Gros Ventre, Lander, and Jackson, WY (2002-present). Am successful in ensuring the profitability of a three-unit district in a food service business operating 24-hour days every day of the year; currently run at 105% of guideline profits.
- Restored two neglected restaurants to profitability after personally cleaning, staffing, and reorganizing both locations.
- Handled all aspects of advertising, staffing, ordering supplies, and training employees in order to open a new location.
- Established outstanding year-to-date figures including: maintaining food costs at 28.9% and average payroll at 18.5% while holding operating supplies to 2.5%.
- Set up sales contests for employees which led to a 4.2% increase in year-to-date "real sales" on top of last year's impressive 15% increase.
- Excel in selecting employees who perform as a team.

OPERATIONS MANAGER. Jackson, WY (2001). Learned the management techniques unique to Denny's and led the location to a 35% rate of payroll/food costs in relation to total sales — first place out of 75 units in the region.
- Was recognized as the "Number One Rookie Unit Manager."
- Managed a 29-person staff in a 24-hour-a-day, 365-day-a-year operation.
- Earned advancement to multiunit management within a year.
- Achieved the following rates: food costs 28.5%, payroll 18.5%, and operating costs 2%.

SENIOR NEW CAR SALES ASSOCIATE. Hopkins Lincoln-Mercury, Lander, WY (1998-2000). Refined my communication and "sales" abilities as the leader of a five-person sales team.
- Won a national-level sales contest.

SALES MANAGER. Lander Subaru, Lander, WY (1997-98). Learned sales techniques from "the ground up" and advanced to a management position within five months of joining the company.
- Increased the average monthly new-car delivery rate to 82 from the previous rate of 50.

ADMINISTRATIVE MANAGER. Snow King Ski Corporation, Jackson, WY (1995-97). Provided quality administrative, clerical, and logistic support for a busy ski resort and also acted as the liaison between company executives and a headquarters operation.
- Was credited with transforming "the worst" department into "the best."
- Consistently received "perfect" evaluations and was handpicked for the position on the basis of my "boundless enthusiasm" and "attention to detail."

TRAINING

Excelled in corporate management and sales training programs.

PERSONAL

Offer boundless energy and enthusiasm. Am skilled in organizing my time for maximum effectiveness and can "juggle" numerous tasks simultaneously. Will relocate.

Exact Name of Person
Title or Position
Name of Company
Address (no., street)
Address (city, state, zip)

EXECUTIVE CHEF
You can find other resumes and cover letters of cooks and chefs in this book. Consult the table of contents.

Dear Exact Name of Person: (or Dear Sir or Madam if answering a blind ad.)

With the enclosed resume describing my experience and skills, I would like to formally initiate the process of being considered for a culinary position within your organization.

As you will see from my resume, I have excelled as an Executive Chef and Executive Sous Chef and have been a Certified Executive Chef for many years. I am a member of numerous professional organizations including the American Culinary Federation of Chefs, the Academy of Chefs, the American Culinary Federation, the Canadian Chef Federation, as well as other clubs for the world's top culinary experts.

In my current job I am an Executive Chef associated with Yankee Stadium. For the Platinum Club Membership comprised of 7,000 members, I handle meal preparation and variety of catered events for VIPs. I also personally cater to the needs of 116 skyboxes which belong to the owners of Yankees as well as private individuals and corporations. While managing 22 seasonal and part-time chefs, cooks, and others, I have managed a payroll budget with outstanding results. Although payroll costs were projected to be at 26% of our food and beverage sales of $33.8 million (the largest-ever annual sales) for this year, we brought payroll costs in at only 22% of food and beverage sales. This was in a year when we hosted the World Series. I offer a reputation as an outstanding manager of human, financial, and material resources.

In a previous job I was Executive Chef with the Gratz Park Inn in Providence, RI, where I managed an 18-person staff and was extensively involved in the production of banquets and special events ranging from weddings to corporate functions. In previous positions I have excelled as Chef for an athletic club, as Executive Chef for a yacht club, and as Executive Chef for both hotels and businesses.

You would find me in person to be a congenial individual who prides myself on doing every job to the best of my ability. I have managed budgets, people, and special projects with flair as well as with a bottom-line orientation.

If you can use a culinary professional with my expert technical skills and extensive professional experience, I hope you will call or write me to suggest a time when we could meet in person to discuss your needs and how I might serve them. I can provide excellent references at the appropriate time.

Yours sincerely,

Kelly F. Staehr, CEC

KELLY F. STAEHR, CEC

1110½ Hay Street, Fayetteville, NC 28305 • preppub@aol.com • (910) 483-6611

OBJECTIVE

I want to contribute to an organization that can use an imaginative, highly motivated chef with extensive experience in budgeting and financial control, personnel training and management, marketing and promotion, as well as club and hotel administration.

EXPERIENCE

EXECUTIVE CHEF. Yankee Food Services, Yankee Stadium, New York, NY (2002-present). For the Platinum Club Membership comprised of 7,000 members, handle meal preparation and a variety of catered functions and events for VIPs.
- Personally cater to the needs of 116 skyboxes, which belong to the team's owners, as well as private individuals and corporations. Manage 22 people including chefs.
- Manage a payroll budget which was projected to be 26% of the total $33.8 million in food and beverage sales – the largest-ever sales achieved in a single year; I actually have brought payroll in at 22% of sales when Yankee Stadium hosted the World Series.

EXECUTIVE CHEF. Gratz Park Inn, Providence, RI (2001-02). Added an international touch to the cuisine of this fine hotel through my extensive culinary background; trained and retrained key staff people with the result that the kitchen is now operating more harmoniously and efficiently.
- Managed an 18-person staff; was involved in banquets and special events.

RESTAURANT MANAGER/TEMPORARY EXECUTIVE CHEF. Vermont Inn, Rutland, VT (1996-01). Excelled in a temporary six-month assignment in which I had an option to purchase the restaurant from the owner of the inn; I decided not to exercise my option.
- Managed all kitchen and restaurant operations including purchasing all food and beverages, food preparation, sales and marketing, and all bookkeeping functions.

CHEF. Worcester Racquet Club, Worcester, MA (1994-96). Planned and directed all food services related to both restaurant operations as well as special banquets for a club with a membership of 1200 along with a full athletic staff. Served luncheons daily to 500 people.
- Dramatically cut food costs as a percentage of total budget while increasing food quality and customer satisfaction; maintained 28% food cost and 17% labor cost.

EXECUTIVE CHEF. Steigler Enterprises, Inc., Salem, MA (1992-93). Served 2500 employee meals each day. Produced outstanding meals considered excellent quality for the money.
- Based on average purchase of $4.75, maintained a 38% food cost and 45% labor cost.

EXECUTIVE CHEF. Glocksbury Yacht Club, Boston, MA (1990-91). At a private yacht club with 2600 members around the world, managed food preparation and food service provided six days a week at two restaurants each with its own menu and in a different geographical location. Oversaw food sales totaling $2.3 annually.

AFFILIATIONS

Certified Executive Chef   American Culinary Federation of Chefs
Member of the Academy of Chefs   Member of American Culinary Federation
Member of Canadian Chef Federation   Member of Atlantic Coast Chefs in Boston

EDUCATION

Completed Trade School for Cooking and Pastry Apprenticeship
Have completed numerous professional development courses through the years.

PERSONAL

Offer a culinary background with kitchen proficiency in German, English, and Spanish. Excellent references. Extensive P & L responsibility. Expert in cost control.

CAREER CHANGE

Date

Exact Name of Person
Title or Position
Name of Company
Address (no., street)
Address (city, state, zip)

EXTERMINATOR

transitioning from pest
control to restaurant
control.
At first glance, you might
ask, "What's an
exterminator doing in a
book about restaurants and
the food industry?" This
successful entrepreneur
sold a business and has a
non-compete restriction
which bars him from
working in the industry
where he gained most of
his experience. He feels he
has experience relevant to
the food industry, however,
and his resume stresses his
skills and experience
relevant to the food
industry.

Dear Exact Name of Person: (or Dear Sir or Madam if answering a blind ad.)

I would appreciate an opportunity to talk with you soon about how I could contribute to your organization through my demonstrated ability to pinpoint new business opportunities and to develop business activities that address those opportunities.

As you will see from my resume, I have most recently been a successful entrepreneur and recently sold a pest control business which I founded to one of the largest pest elimination service companies in the country. It is not viable for me to remain with the company since its "promotion from within" policy would require me to accept an entry-level position within the corporation, and I feel that my extensive management and sales skills would not be fully utilized at such a level.

Essentially I obtained my pest control license at the age of 21 and then, on my own initiative, transformed myself, through education and hard work, into a highly knowledgeable industry professional.

Throughout my experience in pest control, I have had many working relationships with the food industry. I have performed quality assurance inspections with a large supermarket chain to safeguard against poor handling, storage, and temperature control on multiple occasions. I also have experience evaluating employee adherence to local health codes. At this point, I feel like I would like to move forward with my career and work exclusively with sanitation practices in the food and restaurant industry.

I feel confident I could succeed in your organization because of my proven ability to communicate ideas to others, my exceptionally strong problem-solving skills, and my ability to formulate new ideas based on information obtained from multiple sources. I have an outgoing and self-confident personality that enables me to rapidly earn the trust of others.

I hope you will review my skills and experience in order to determine if they could be of value to you. I am a proven performer and I will add considerable value to any company I am a part of. I am writing to you because I know of your company's fine reputation, and I believe I could contribute significantly to your bottom line. Please give me a call if you feel there is a fit between your needs and what I offer. Thank you in advance for your time, and I shall look forward to the possibility of meeting you.

Yours sincerely,

Travis J. Greer

TRAVIS J. GREER

1110½ Hay Street, Fayetteville, NC 28305 • preppub@aol.com • (910) 483-6611

OBJECTIVE

To contribute to an organization that can use a dynamic professional who offers exceptionally strong sales and management abilities which could be valuable to any industry.

HIGHLIGHTS OF BUSINESS SKILLS

Am an extremely versatile professional with skills/experience in the following areas:

starting up new business operations	purchasing materials
selecting and training employees	controlling inventory
writing reports and proposals	accounting/preparing financial reports
handling sales, marketing, public relations	dealing with regulatory agencies

TECHNICAL EDUCATION

Completed specialized education at the **University of Toledo** in Pest Control Technology.
• Excelled in extensive pest control course work at **West Virginia University**.
Completed advanced courses at **Eastern Washington University** at the Wood Destroying Organisms Institute.
Completed corporate training sponsored by leading industry firms including Orkin Chemicals, Ball Distribution, and Shandow Research Laboratories.

FOOD INDUSTRY KNOWLEDGE

Studied food processing sanitation/hygiene, American Institute of Bakers.
Acquired "hands-on" expertise in treating and inspecting large food processing facilities.
Performed quality assurance inspections of a large supermarket chain.

EXPERIENCE

FOUNDER/PRESIDENT. Begone Services, Inc., Spokane, WA (2002-present). Started "from scratch" a company which was recently bought out by one of the largest pest elimination service companies in the country.
• Have succeeded as an entrepreneur and business manager in a highly competitive industry because of my ability to communicate ideas to others, my problem-solving skills, my ability to formulate new ideas based on information obtained from multiple sources, and my outgoing and self-confident nature.
• Established the company in Spokane and then expanded the service area from Cheney, WA to Coeur D'Alene, ID.
• Handled all financial matters including budgets, profit-and-loss quotas, tax planning, insurance, and purchasing.
• Was involved in a project with a large supermarket chain which involved performing quality assurance inspections throughout each store; evaluated the chain's pest control program, assessed food handling and storage procedures, and monitored temperature control in critical areas such as deli/bakeries, meat and seafood shops, and cooler/freezer; also evaluated employee adherence to local health codes.
• Acquired considerable experience in dealing with government regulatory agencies and in preparing the paperwork necessary to document programs in critical situations.

EXTERMINATOR. Turner Exterminating, Inc., Spokane, WA (1994-2002). Was a major force in the company's growth over eight years of 15% yearly; helped establish formal training and hiring policies; began in sales and in my fourth year was promoted to supervisor overseeing clean-out coordination, termite control coordination, equipment maintenance, and troubleshooting in all areas of service.
• In my fifth year was promoted to **Vice President of Sales and Training**; had responsibility for setting/achieving branch goals and for defining/implementing training.

PERSONAL

Will travel and relocate as needed. Excellent references.

CAREER CHANGE

Date

Exact Name of Person
Title or Position
Name of Company
Address (no., street)
Address (city, state, zip)

FAST FOOD MANAGER

at Burger King seeks new career.

Dear Exact Name of Person: (or Dear Sir or Madam if answering a blind ad.)

Can you use a hardworking young professional who offers a proven "track record" of hard work and dependability along with strong planning, organizational, and management skills?

In order to finance my B.A. degree in Psychology, I commuted every weekend for four years to my managerial position at Burger King. It is this kind of dedication and determination that I offer your organization. While working at Burger King I used my psychology education to help create and implement motivational programs that helped to boost employee productivity and improve morale. Although I am very appreciative of the experience I have earned in the food industry, I would now like to make use of my degree in a different field.

My experience, as you will see from my resume, has given me opportunities to excel in training and motivating employees to work together. I have consistently built productive teams, found ways to improve procedures, and have been known as a diligent worker.

I feel that I offer a mix of experience and skills which could be easily transferred to other organizations because of my adaptability and dedication to any situation.

I hope you will welcome my call soon to arrange a brief meeting at your convenience to discuss your current and future needs and how I might serve them. Thank you in advance for your time.

Sincerely yours,

Sally Ireland

Alternate last paragraph:
I hope you will call or write soon to suggest a time convenient for us to meet and discuss your current and future needs and how I might serve them. Thank you in advance for your time.

SALLY IRELAND

1110½ Hay Street, Fayetteville, NC 28305   •   preppub@aol.com   •   (910) 483-6611

OBJECTIVE

I want to contribute to an organization that can use a hardworking young professional who offers a proven "track record" of hard work and dependability along with strong planning, organizational, and management skills.

EDUCATION

Earned **B.A. degree in Psychology,** University of Rochester, Rochester, NY, 2003.
- Worked every weekend as a manager at Burger King from 1998-03 in order to finance my college education; this required me to travel from Rochester to Elmira every weekend for four years.
- Was handpicked for a prestigious six-month assignment my senior year as **Assistant to Psychologist**; refined my research and writing skills while compiling and organizing statistics and operating a computer.

Completed course work to receive certification in Food Service Management, Elmira Community College, Elmira, NY, 2000.

Graduated from Elmira High School as an **Honor Roll Student**, 1998.
- Was elected Vice President of the Psychology Club.
- Member, Beta Club.

EXPERIENCE

MANAGER. Burger King Restaurant, Elmira, NY (1998-present). Used my psychology education to help create and implement motivational programs that boosted employee productivity and improved morale.
- Trained and supervised up to 10 employees.
- Controlled cash flow of up to $16,000 daily; made bank deposits.
- Ordered and controlled an inventory of perishable and nonperishable goods which experienced a rapid turnover.
- Developed a highly motivated team which became known for providing excellent customer service.

MATH LAB ASSISTANT. University of Rochester Math Department, Rochester, NY (1999-03). Was successful in helping many students eliminate their "math fear" while monitoring students with math deficiencies, administering and grading tests, and tutoring students on levels ranging from basic to advanced mathematics.
- Began as a tutor in the Math Lab and quickly advanced to help plan and manage all tutoring services provided.
- Assisted athletes in "time management": aided in planning their course schedules and establishing specific study sessions to help them acquire good study habits.
- Also worked as an **Aerobics Tutor**.

CASHIER. Burger King Restaurant, Elmira, NY (1995-98). Was commended for my poise in handling the public in my first job; learned to work in a fast-paced environment which required accurate handling of money while rapidly assembling orders and greeting customers.

BUS DRIVER. N.Y. Board of Education, Elmira, NY (1995-98). Became known as a disciplined hard worker and was named "Bus Driver of the Year" in 1997 because of my perfect safety record and courteous behavior.

PERSONAL

Offer a proven ability to motivate others. Am highly motivated to excel.

CAREER CHANGE

Date

Exact Name of Person
Title or Position
Name of Company
Address (no., street)
Address (city, state, zip)

Dear Exact Name of Person: (or Dear Sir or Madam if answering a blind ad.)

Can you use a hardworking young professional who offers outstanding customer service abilities along with communication skills, a knowledge of computer and office operations, and experience in training and management?

My experience in management with Hardee's has given me the chance to become skilled in office operations, training, supervision, inventory control, and general management. I have advanced rapidly and was selected to assist in the set up of a new management team for a franchise where I helped hire and train employees.

I have earned a reputation for my customer service expertise and skill in providing training and guidance to my employees. Several of the people I trained have quickly advanced to management roles.

I offer an open mind, the ability to easily and quickly learn new things, and a natural intelligence which would contribute to my ability to become a productive and valued member of your organization.

I hope you will welcome my call soon to arrange a brief meeting at your convenience to discuss your current and future needs and how I might serve them. Thank you in advance for your time.

Sincerely yours,

Joseph T. Palumbo

Alternate last paragraph:
I hope you will call or write soon to suggest a time convenient for us to meet and discuss your current and future needs and how I might serve them. Thank you in advance for your time.

JOSEPH TAYLOR PALUMBO

1110½ Hay Street, Fayetteville, NC 28305 • preppub@aol.com • (910) 483-6611

OBJECTIVE   To contribute to an organization that can use a mature, intelligent, and dependable young professional who offers proven management experience and a knowledge of office and computer operations.

SPECIAL   Offer knowledge related to these and other special interest areas:
SKILLS
   Personal computers   Windows operating systems
   computer graphics design   drafting and commercial art design

TRAINING   Gained rapid advancement to management positions at a very young age with Hardee's Corporation:

   OPERATIONS MANAGER. Sims Avenue, Spartanburg, SC (2003-present). Supervise 35-40 employees involved in food preparation and service as well as maintenance and clean up while handling up to $5,000.
   • Excelled as an effective trainer: developed high-quality employees and had two students earn management positions in only two months.
   • Succeeded in improving the store's customer service reputation.

   MANAGER. Spencer Street, Spartanburg, SC (2002-03). Supervised and trained employees while managing funds and overseeing receipt and storage of all perishable and nonperishable supplies.
   • Led the location to a 9.5% sales increase while reducing costs 6%.
   • Gained valuable management experience and insight into the advantages of working to build a cohesive team.
   • Was handpicked to assist in setting up a new management team for a Greenville, SC franchise: selected and trained a team of employees, gained experience in working under pressure in a high-volume facility, and contributed to the development of a team which continues to increase sales and profit.

   FOOD SERVICE MANAGER. Sims Avenue, Spartanburg, SC (2001). Supervised employees while also overseeing supply operations and developing more effective waste reduction procedures. Reduced food costs 9% by applying effective cost control guidelines.

   OPERATIONS AND TRAINING MANAGER. Spencer Street, Spartanburg, SC (1998-00). Earned rapid promotion from training manager to overseeing all aspects of store operations from supervising employees, to handling up to $8,000 in daily receipts and inventory control.
   • Learned to "think on my feet" while working in a busy, fast-paced food service atmosphere, solving problems and ensuring smooth operations.
   • Developed numerous employees who are now successful restaurant managers.

   CUSTOMER SERVICE SPECIALIST. Honor Street, Spartanburg, SC (1997). Learned to work with others to provide fast customer service.

EDUCATION   Completed more than 500 hours of public speaking and religious education at the Spartanburg Theological Seminary, Spartanburg, SC.
   Received the Future Business Leader's of America Award for superior knowledge in marketing techniques, Silas Creek High School, Spartanburg, SC.

PERSONAL   Am described as a "kind and friendly" person who can put others at ease. Learn very quickly.

Exact Name of Person
Title or Position
Name of Company
Address (no., street)
Address (city, state, zip)

FINANCE CHIEF
for a large restaurant

Dear Exact Name of Person: (or Dear Sir or Madam if answering a blind ad.)

I would appreciate an opportunity to talk with you soon about how I could contribute to your organization through my expertise related to merchandising, finance, customer service, and employee training/placement.

As you will see from my resume, I have enjoyed a "track record" of promotion to increasing responsibilities because of the contributions I have made to my employers. I am proud of the fact that I have made these contributions to companies which are themselves considered some of the most successful retailers in the world.

Most recently I have excelled in directing operations and managing finances at a large restaurant in a chain of family restaurants. I have used my motivational skills to inspire employees to participate in lowering food costs, and as a team we lowered food costs 4% in the first two years. I recently won the corporation's "Notch in the Gun" award for closing down a competitor in the same price range offering a similar product line.

In previous jobs with Pic 'n' Save, Rose's, and Boyle's, I feel that I earned my "Ph.D" in merchandising and retailing. After developing expertise in Rose's "plan-o-gram" system of retailing and merchandising, I was recruited by Pic 'n' Save to manage a 33-person store where I increased profitability in numerous areas through my creativity, merchandising flair, and "common sense." I also developed teamwork among employees in reducing inventory shrinkage/shortage to less than 3% — well below the company average.

You would find me to be a warm and personable individual who believes that a "hands-on" management style is the key to profitability and excellent customer service. At Perkins I recently made one of the top two scores in the corporation on a test measuring my understanding of a "personality profile" which the company uses to identify the right people to hire and then place them in the "right" jobs.

I hope you will call or write me soon to suggest a time convenient for us to meet and discuss your current and future needs and how I might serve them. Thank you in advance for your time.

Sincerely yours,

Timothy Charles Richards

TIMOTHY CHARLES RICHARDS

1110½ Hay Street, Fayetteville, NC 28305   •   preppub@aol.com   •   (910) 483-6611

OBJECTIVE

To contribute to the profitability of an organization that can use a skilled restaurant/retail manager with the proven ability to excel as a district/operations manager through my financial knowhow, inventory control expertise, motivational skills, and industry knowledge.

EXPERIENCE

OPERATIONS MANAGER/FINANCE CHIEF. Perkins Restaurants, Reading, PA (2003-present). Personally direct all financial activities including the preparation of budgets, ledgers, financial statements, and paperwork turned in to the regional office while also scheduling 50 employees, controlling inventory, and handling customer service/employee relations.

- Used my motivational skills to inspire employees to participate in lowering food costs and controlling inventory; cut food costs 4% within the first six months and have maintained this standard.
- Applied my understanding of the Standard Personality Profile (SRI) to hire the right people and then place them in jobs that best suited their profile and the restaurant's needs; made one of the top two scores in the corporation on a test measuring SRI understanding and its relevance to employee placement.
- Was named to the Perkins Family Club for learning to recognize customer names, faces, and occupations.
- Won the corporation's "Notch in the Gun" award for closing down a competitor (Denny's Restaurant) in the same price range with a very similar product line.

STORE MANAGER. Pic 'n' Save, York, PA (2001-03). Supervised 33 employees and two assistant managers while opening new stores and earning a reputation as a distinguished merchandiser; received a promotion to a higher-volume store because of my managerial and merchandising skills.

- Through employee education/motivation and vigilant management, reduced inventory shrinkage/shortage to less than 3% — well below the company average..
- Increase profitability through my merchandising flair: designed counters so that they generated higher turnover of low-cost items and increased "impulse buys," which in turn boosted overall profitability.

STORE MANAGER. Rose's, York, PA (1999-2000). Became skilled in managing seasonal merchandise while supervising 10 salespeople and directing customer relations, inventory control, and merchandise flow through the traffic and receiving departments.

- Developed expertise in implementing "plan-o-grams" to maximize profitability.
- Color coordinated soft goods to increase sales while also maintaining the lowest possible safe inventory level in the stockroom in order to balance stockout considerations against inventory carrying costs.

GROUP MANAGER. Boyle's, Scranton and York, PA (1996-99). Began with Boyle's as a Shipping Clerk and was rapidly promoted to Stocker, Foreman, and Receiving Manager in charge of all incoming and outgoing shipments; supervised five employees while monitoring ticketing, overages, shortages, damages, invoices, merchandise transfers, and vendor drop shipments.

- Learned how to set realistic goals that could be achieved; led employees to achieve a goal of increasing sales by 3% while shaving 1% off labor costs.

EDUCATION

Completed two years of college in business administration, Reading Area Community College, Reading, PA; named to **Dean's List**.

Excelled in extensive corporate training related to sales, merchandising, and finance.

Date

Exact Name of Person
Title or Position
Name of Company
Address (no., street)
Address (city, state, zip)

FOOD PREPARER

for a restaurant.
Interested in seeing similar
resumes and cover letters?
Look for "cook" and "chef"
in this book's alphabetical
listings.

Dear Exact Name of Person: (or Dear Sir or Madam if answering a blind ad.)

I would appreciate an opportunity to talk with you soon about how I could contribute to your organization through my knowledge of restaurant operations, experience in food preparation and cooking, and skills in customer service and inventory control.

You will see when you look at my resume that I offer experience which ranges from fast food, to dining room only, to restaurant settings. At the present time I am working at two popular local restaurants simultaneously. At Antonio's I prepare and cook all menu items in a family-style Italian restaurant. At Ramsey's, which is known primarily for its rib specialties, I am involved in all phases of food preparation.

I feel that I am a well-rounded professional who can make a difference through my skills and knowledge as well as my personal qualities of drive and determination.

I hope you will welcome my call soon to arrange a brief meeting at your convenience to discuss your current and future needs and how I might serve them. Thank you in advance for your time.

Sincerely yours,

Vlad A. Paraschiv

Alternate last paragraph:
I hope you will call or write me soon to suggest a time convenient for us to meet and discuss your current and future needs and how I might serve them. Thank you in advance for your time.

VLAD A. PARASCHIV

1110½ Hay Street, Fayetteville, NC 28305   •   preppub@aol.com   •   (910) 483-6611

OBJECTIVE

To offer my reputation as a young professional who knows the value of hard work and importance of contributing to team efforts to an organization that can benefit from my broad base of food service experience, inventory control know how, and sales skills.

EXPERIENCE

Have become known as an individual who can be counted on to work until the job is done right and who offers excellent time management skills refined in part- and full-time jobs sometimes held simultaneously:

COOK. Antonio's Restaurant, Madison, WI (2002-present). For a popular family-style restaurant, provide the know how and skills to do the work of two or three people while preparing and cooking meals to order.
- Successfully trained five employees who have become dependable, skilled personnel.
- Became very effective reducing waste during the preparation of all menu items for this popular Italian restaurant.
- Gained familiarity with inventory control and food rotation procedures.
- Closed the kitchen at the end of the day and saw that all equipment and areas of the facility were cleaned and sanitized.

COOK and **FOOD PREPARER.** Ramsey's Restaurant, Madison, WI (2001-2002). Became skilled in preparing various types of food items for assembly and in cooking them at this popular restaurant.
- Contributed to kitchen crew efficiency by preparing the ingredients for salads and batter for onion rings, assembling sandwich and meat sets for other dishes, and portioning chicken tenders and cheese sticks so they were ready to be cooked.
- Have become skilled in preparing and precooking a wide range of meat items including baby back ribs, spare ribs, and beef ribs as well as chicken and pork loins.
- Gained recognition for being faster in all phases of preparation than is usual.
- Reorganized the stock room and kept it cooler and cleaner than before.

KITCHEN ASSISTANT. Tony Roma's Ribs, Milwaukee, WI (2001). Provided assistance in various areas of kitchen operations from pastry, to deep frying, to salads, to pizzas, to soups.

COOK and **CASHIER.** Checker's Hamburgers, Milwaukee, WI (1997-2000). Learned to provide rapid and friendly customer service in a fast food environment.
- Earned a reputation as a hard worker who could be counted on to do anything needed from unloading trucks, to cleaning, to stocking.

CAFETERIA CLEANING TEAM MEMBER. Bellevue Foods, University of Wisconsin-Milwaukee (1995-97). Worked as part of a five-person team charged with cleaning a 500-person dining facility.
- Was selected to help serve meals when formal dinners were held.

EDUCATION

Have completed approximately 2-1/2 years of college course work leading to a bachelor's degree in Business Administration, University of Wisconsin-Madison.

SPECIAL SKILLS

Through my varied experience, offer a unique blend of skills including such things as fork lift operations, typing, and familiarity with restaurant procedures.

PERSONAL

Am a well-rounded individual who as a high school student lettered in wrestling and was a member of the all-county youth orchestra. Excellent references available upon request.

Exact Name of Person
Exact Title
Exact Name of Company
Address
City, State, Zip

**FOOD SERVICE
MANAGER**

for a theme restaurant and
tour groups

Dear Exact Name of Person: (or Dear Sir or Madam if answering a blind ad):

With the enclosed resume, I would like to make you aware of my interest in exploring employment opportunities with your organization.

As you will see from my resume, I offer extensive experience in food service management. Currently, I manage food service personnel responsible for preparing large-scale meals for two daily tourist groups. This organization provides chuckwagon rides followed by nightly dinner theatre. In a prior position, I gained experience working in a large amusement park dining facility where I became acquainted with several specialized menus and introduced a variety of "fun" foods to complement the guests' park experience.

Because I began my career as a Cook, I am skilled at cooking nearly any type of food. After I was promoted into management, I became responsible for quality assurance, sanitation management, portion control, inventory management, receiving and storage, and personnel management. I have been responsible for millions of dollars in equipment and inventory.

My experience with various organizations catering to tourists and recreation have proven invaluable to my guest service and hospitality skills. I understand the importance of the customers' enjoyment and will stop at nothing to ensure them a memorable and pleasurable experience. These positions have also offered exciting challenges which I have continually met and surpassed. It is with confidence that I assure you that my prior experience has prepared me to be an asset to any organization.

I hope you will welcome my call soon to arrange a brief meeting at your convenience to discuss your current and future needs and how I might serve them. Thank you in advance for your time.

Sincerely,

Hugh Nevins Burkhart

Alternate last paragraph:
I hope you will contact me to suggest a time when we might talk about your needs. I can provide outstanding references.

HUGH NEVINS BURKHART

1110½ Hay Street, Fayetteville, NC 28305　　•　　preppub@aol.com　　•　　(910) 483-6611

OBJECTIVE　　To contribute to an organization that can use a skilled food industry professional who offers vast knowledge of all aspects of food preparation along with experience in managing unique food service operations catering to vacationing families while controlling quality, nutritional content, and sanitation.

EDUCATION　　Completed two years of college course work in the food service field at institutions including Tarrant County Junior College and the University of Texas-Dallas.

EXPERIENCE　　**FOOD SERVICE MANAGER.** Bar-J Chuckwagon Tours, Waxahachie, TX (2003-present). Manage up to 40 food service personnel responsible for preparing a meal each for two different daily tourist groups (approximately 500 people) in the "old west" dining area of an operation that includes chuckwagon rides followed by nightly dinner theatre. Supervise the preparation of all types of food and baked goods.

FOOD SERVICE MANAGER. Snake River Rafting Co., Jackson, WY (2002-03). Managed up to 15 food service professionals preparing 4 outdoor meals a day for various tour groups with this rafting company. The tours stopped at a halfway point on the float to enjoy a meal prepared in an outdoor kitchen. The menus usually consisted of some sort of "traditional regional" dish, such as buffalo stew. Supervised the preparation and regulated for sanitary practices.

FOOD SERVICE SUPERVISOR. Six Flags over Texas, Dallas, TX (1998-01). While managing food preparation in a family amusement park environment, became knowledgeable of special diets for diabetes, vegetarians, and "fun" foods.
- *Quality Control:* Gained experience in inspecting personnel, equipment, sanitation facilities, and other matters related to safety, lighting, hygiene, and cleanliness.
- *Inventory Control:* Ordered perishable and nonperishable food stuffs and assured proper storage; monitored stock rotation according to "first in, first out." Maintained vigilance related to the dates on all products.
- *Personnel Management:* Trained, motivated, and evaluated all types of personnel in the park's dining facility.
- *Marketing/Menu Planning:* Created several "fun" food items for the park's dining facility menu that were designed to complement the guests' overall park experience.

FOOD SERVICE MANAGER. Chuck E. Cheese Restaurants, Ft. Worth, TX (1992-97). Managed 14 kitchen and dining room employees and accounted for equipment valued at up to $1 million.
- Credited with playing a key role in winning the statewide "Best Chuck E. Cheese Store."
- On a formal performance evaluation, was praised for "outstanding managerial abilities."
- Provided leadership during multiple special projects which required creative problem solving related to financial and personnel resources. Was praised for overcoming all obstacles and completing the projects with professionalism and expertise.

FOOD SERVICE SUPERVISOR & COOK. Cosmo's, Ft. Worth, TX (1987-92). In entry-level jobs as a Cook, performed a variety of cooking and food service duties to facilitate food preparation, and learned to operate all types of food preparation and cooking equipment.

PERSONAL　　Excellent personal and professional references on request.

Exact Name of Person
Exact Title
Exact Name of Company
Address
City, State, Zip

FOOD SERVICE SPECIALIST

(COOK) in a recovery clinic serving substance abusers

Dear Exact Name of Person (or Dear Sir or Madam if answering a blind ad):

With the enclosed resume, I would like to make you aware of my interest in exploring employment opportunities with your organization and introduce you to my background related to your business.

As you will see from my resume, I am currently a Cook and Food Service Specialist at the world's largest substance abuse and plastic surgery recovery clinic. I have completed extensive technical and supervisory training related to food service, and have received Food Service Specialist Certification from Modesto Junior College. I work with an efficient team which serves up to 1,200 meals daily to 350 clients. In addition to cooking a wide variety of items, I was singled out because of my management ability for special responsibilities related to managing production, controlling inventory, and scheduling employees.

You will also notice from my resume that, prior to this position, I advanced into supervisory positions with a banking facility which operated 11 branches. I managed dozens of employees, held the keys and security clearance to three of the 11 branches, and was entrusted with handling and depositing large amounts of cash. I was placed in charge of other employees because of my strong customer service and problem-solving abilities.

If my background and skills interest you, I hope you will contact me to suggest a time when we could meet in person to discuss your needs. Thank you.

Yours sincerely,

Lizanne M. Dougherty

LIZANNE M. DOUGHERTY

1110½ Hay Street, Fayetteville, NC 28305　　•　　preppub@aol.com　　•　　(910) 483-6611

OBJECTIVE

I want to contribute to an organization that can use a skilled and highly trained young manager who offers experience in food preparation and food service, inventory control and financial accounting, as well as personnel supervision and training.

TRAINING

Completed the **Food Service Specialist Course,** Modesto Junior College, Modesto, CA, 2001. Extensive training related to food preparation, production operations, and customer service,
* Have become skilled at cooking and baking as well as food service operations.

COMPUTERS

Studied Accounting at San Diego State University, 1998-99; excelled in full-time academic studies while also working full-time to finance my college education.
Have utilized automated systems for ordering, purchasing, distribution, and inventory control of food items and food preparation equipment.

EXPERIENCE

COOK & FOOD SERVICE SPECIALIST. Chrysalis Recovery Clinic, Modesto, CA (2001-present). At the world's largest substance abuse and plastic surgery recovery clinic, perform with distinction in food service facilities serving up 1,200 meals daily to 350 clients, which requires working long hours on a regular basis.
* Prepare and schedule or cook menu items on the production schedule.
* Bake, steam, braise, boil, simmer, and sauté gourmet foods as prescribed by client's personal diets.
* Garnish food items heavily.
* Set up serving lines. Receive and store subsistence items.
* Apply food protection and sanitation measures.
* Have learned valuable food service skills including the following:
  How to identify and effectively use spices: garlic powder, poultry seasoning, thyme, oregano, chicken and beef bastes, etc. I have excellent taste buds, and specialize in preparing tasty sauces and gravies.
  How to cook poultry and dressing until internal temperatures reach 165 degrees F.
  How to use proper cooking methods for many different types of ingredients: e.g., both tomato and milk products, because of their acidity, will burn or scorch very quickly.
  How to substitute ingredients: e.g., I have often substituted ketchup for tomato paste, sage for poultry seasoning, etc. As a cook, when dietary restraints or lack of supplies present a problem, my knowledge of substitution of ingredients has helped me.
  How to determine correct ingredient measurements: As a cook, I weighed ingredients using a very accurate scale and can make measurements by sight with many products.
  How to use proper, safe, and sanitary methods to store food: e.g., putting foods in shallow containers (flat pans) and marking the date and time of refrigeration; after initial chilling, refrigerating foods at temperatures at or below 45 degrees F; etc.

SUPERVISOR & TELLER. Central Bank, San Diego, CA (1999-01). At a banking facility, was promoted rapidly to supervise other tellers because of my strong customer service skills and attention to detail in cash control.
* Served up to 250 customers a day performing a variety of banking responsibilities.
* Managed 10-12 employees and trained them in accuracy, attention to detail, and customer service. Scheduled employees. Trained new employees.

PERSONAL

Highly motivated individual known as a hard worker with an excellent attitude.

Date

Exact Name of Person
Title or Position
Name of Company
Address (no., street)
Address (city, state, zip)

Dear Exact Name of Person: (or Dear Sir or Madam if answering a blind ad.)

I would appreciate an opportunity to talk with you soon about how I could contribute to your organization through my education and experience related to the field of restaurant and hotel management.

I have recently received an Associate's degree in Hotel and Restaurant Management from the University of Colorado at Boulder. I have been working since I was in high school as a hostess, waitress, and banquet coordinator. After starting with a family-style restaurant at a young age, I quickly earned a reputation as a mature and responsible young person. I earned the trust of the owner and was soon working all shifts and filling in during the manager's absence.

Very customer service oriented, I am known for my ability to remain calm and in control even when things are very hectic and busy. I am a team player who motivates others to follow my example of professionalism and dedication to quality service.

I hope you will welcome my call soon to arrange a brief meeting at your convenience to discuss your current and future needs and how I might serve them. Thank you in advance for your time.

Sincerely yours,

Christine D. Li

Alternate last paragraph:
I hope you will call or write me soon to suggest a time convenient for us to meet and discuss your current and future needs and how I might serve them. Thank you in advance for your time.

CHRISTINE D. LI

1110½ Hay Street, Fayetteville, NC 28305 • preppub@aol.com • (910) 483-6611

OBJECTIVE

To contribute through my education and experience related to restaurant and hotel management by offering my motivational and communication skills along with my energy, enthusiasm, and reputation as a dependable and knowledgeable young professional.

EDUCATION

Associate's degree in **Hotel and Restaurant Management,** University of Colorado at Boulder, Boulder, CO, 2002.
- Supervised up to seven people while planning, organizing, cooking for, and serving at campus special events, thereby gaining an opportunity to manage details while remaining in control when problems arose (college-sponsored Hotel/Restaurant Society).

Studied **Marketing and Small Business Management,** Arapahoe Community College, Littleton, CO.

TRAINING

Sanitation Certification: learned food diseases, bacteria prevention, proper water temperatures, and insect control, University of Colorado at Boulder, Boulder, CO, 2002.
Cooking Course: emphasis on preparing, measuring, cooking, and serving food, Arapahoe Community College, Littleton, CO, 1999.

SPECIAL KNOWLEDGE

Through training and experience, have gained knowledge of the restaurant business from concept to operation including the following areas:

break-even point analysis	forecasting sales	job descriptions
cleaning/operating supplies	positions and tasks	profit management
preparation and portion control	personnel management	task and job analysis

staffing: recruitment, selection, interviewing, orientation, training
food purchasing: purchasing, storage of different types of food
sanitation: acidity and bacterial growth, food protection, pest control

Use computer software for word processing and spreadsheets.

EXPERIENCE

FOOD SERVICE TEAM LEADER. Howard Johnson Inc., Denver, CO (2003-present). Because of my education and experience in the restaurant business, have been able to quickly become familiar with the variety of positions it takes to make a busy hotel restaurant operate smoothly and provide courteous service in all areas.
- Ensure that customers have a quality dining experience.
- Supervise up to 15 team members per shift, including kitchen and wait staff.
- Responsible for hiring, firing, and training of all personnel. Take inventory, place orders, account for profits and losses. Use my accounting skills to balance books nightly.

HOSTESS and **WAITRESS.** Celia's, Boulder, CO (2001-2002). Expanded my knowledge of food service by handling functions ranging from greeting customers and seating them, to explaining menu choices, to taking orders, to serving food, to stocking servers' stations, to totaling bills and collecting payments.
- Learned to use the Omron computer system for adding bills.

HOSTESS and **WAITRESS.** Ed and Fred's, Littleton, CO (1995-2000). Began working while still in high school and gained a reputation as a mature and responsible young person who learned quickly and could be counted on to work hard to ensure customer satisfaction, especially at peak periods.

PERSONAL

Am a positive and optimistic individual. Offer an energetic, enthusiastic, and outgoing personality. Enjoy contributing to team efforts and seeing customers enjoy services.

Exact Name of Person
Exact Title
Exact Name of Company
Address
City, State, Zip

**FRANCHISE GENERAL
MANAGER**

of a Popeye's restaurant
chain

Dear Exact Name of Person (or Dear Sir or Madam if answering a blind ad):

With the enclosed resume, I would like to make you aware of my background as a seasoned restaurant manager with exceptional motivational, staff development, and organizational skills whose abilities as a leader have been tested in stressful and fast-paced environments.

Most recently, I have been excelling as a General Manager with Popeye's Chicken Inc., where I supervise a staff of 29 employees, including two Assistant Managers and two Shift Managers in the operation of this busy franchise location with annual sales of $900,000. Through my careful management, this has become one of the more profitable locations in the franchise group, with total labor and management costs of only 26% and an average controllable profit of 31.2%. In addition, this store was recognized as a Golden Wing winner, ranking #41 out of 6,000 Popeye's nationwide in all measured proficiencies.

In an earlier position as General Manager of Ritzy's, I learned to control expenditures, carefully manage labor hours and human resources, and maximize profits in an environment where a low volume of sales was the norm. Despite these constraints, I was able to keep all cost, profit, and sales figures within company guidelines. Prior to that, I began my restaurant management career as a General Manager with a different Popeye's location, providing managerial oversight and supervision to a staff of 30 employees at a franchise location with average yearly sales of $1.3 million.

As you will see, I have completed nearly five years of college-level course work in Criminal Justice, Computer Science, and Sociology, which I have supplemented with numerous professional development and food services training courses.

If you can use an enthusiastic and articulate restaurant management professional with proven abilities related to training, human resources management, and increasing profitability, I hope you will contact me to suggest a time when we might meet. I can provide outstanding references.

Sincerely,

Neville H. Radcliffe

NEVILLE H. RADCLIFFE

1110½ Hay Street, Fayetteville, NC 28305 • preppub@aol.com • (910) 483-6611

OBJECTIVE

To benefit an organization that can use an experienced restaurant manager with exceptional communication and organizational skills who offers a track record of accomplishment in the areas of human resources, inventory control, P & L, quality control, and customer service.

EDUCATION

Completed more than four years of college-level course work in Criminal Justice, Computer Science, and Sociology.

Finished several professional development and food services training courses, including:
- Serve Safe, Food Sanitation Certification, 40 hours, Little Rock, AR, 2003.
- Popeye's Manager Training Course, 72 hours, 2000.
- Conflict Mediation Course, 40 hours, Westark Community College, Fort Smith, AR, 1998.

EXPERIENCE

GENERAL MANAGER. Popeye's Chicken, Inc., Little Rock, AR (2002-present). Manage all aspects of the operation of this busy franchise branch of the large national restaurant with an annual volume of $900,000; oversee human resources, inventory control, profit & loss, quality control, and customer service.
- Supervise 29 employees including two Assistant Managers, two Shift Managers, and a 25-person crew.
- Interview, hire, and train all new employees; conduct periodic employee performance appraisals and develop plans of action to increase employee achievement levels.
- Conduct weekly and monthly inventories to track usage and control loss; order paper and food products.
- Prepare weekly employee schedules and daily task assignments to ensure each work station is adequately staffed with the most competent employees.
- Ensure that labor hours are within guidelines based on total volume of sales; total crew and management labor costs are at an extremely low 26%.
- Design and implement the business plan, producing P & L, G & L, and other cost/profit projections; achieved an exceptional level of profitability, averaging 31.2% of all controllable profits.
- Perform daily, weekly, and monthly audits to ensure accuracy of cash handling and facilitate loss prevention.
- Recognized as a winner in the Golden Wing competition; my store was ranked #41 out of 6,000 Popeye's nationwide.

GENERAL MANAGER. Ritzy's, Jonesboro, AR (2001-02). Provided managerial oversight and supervision for this local drive-through-only fast-food operation; kept all labor hours and other cost/profit figures within company guidelines, despite a low volume of only $2,500 per week.
- Supervised 15 employees, including one Assistant Manager, one Shift Manager, and a crew of 13 full and part-time associates. Interviewed, hired, and trained all new employees; conducted employee evaluations and counseled marginal employee.

GENERAL MANAGER. Popeye's Chicken, Inc., Jonesboro, AR (2000-01). Supervised a 30-employee staff, including one Assistant Manager and two Shift Managers while overseeing all operational aspects of this $1.3 million location of the nationwide fast-food chain.
- Prepared the business plan for the store, producing cost/profit analyses and sales projections in order to maximize controllable profits.

PERSONAL

Excellent personal and professional references are available upon request.

Date

Exact Name of Person
Exact Title
Exact Name of Company
Address
City, State, Zip

FRONT DESK SUPERVISOR

in a Hampton Inn hotel

Dear Exact Name of Person (or Dear Sir or Madam if answering a blind ad):

With the enclosed resume, I would like to make you aware of my desire to explore employment opportunities with your hotel.

As you will see from my resume, I have excelled in all aspects of front desk management at hotels in Minnesota and Connecticut. At two Day's Inns in Saint Paul, MN, I was extensively trained in auditing and office operations while learning to handle the full range of responsibilities which go into effective front desk management.

In my current job as Front Desk Supervisor, I handle all front desk responsibilities and am totally committed to the hotel's goals of achieving the highest standards of customer satisfaction. I also perform the audit every Sunday which requires me to balance all hotel accounts.

I am held in high regard by my current employer and can provide outstanding personal and professional references at the appropriate time. If you can use an astute and experienced hospitality industry professional with the proven ability to impact your bottom line in profitable ways, I hope you will contact me to suggest a time when we might meet to discuss your needs. Thank you in advance for whatever time and professional courtesies you can extend.

Sincerely,

Hind J. Haidar

HIND J. HAIDAR

1110½ Hay Street, Fayetteville, NC 28305   •   preppub@aol.com   •   (910) 483-6611

OBJECTIVE

I want to contribute to an organization that can use an experienced hospitality industry professional with a proven ability to solve problems and maximize customer satisfaction as well as occupancy.

EDUCATION

B.S. in Computer Technology, Southern Connecticut State University, New Haven, CT. Excelled academically and graduated cum laude with a 3.8 GPA; was a member of Phi Beta Kappa Sorority.
A.A. in Hotel Hospitality, Three Rivers Community-Technical College, Norwich, CT.
A.A. in Office Technology, St. Paul Technical College, Saint Paul, MN.
A.A. in Business Management, St. Paul Technical College, Saint Paul, MN.

EXPERIENCE

FRONT DESK SUPERVISOR. Hampton Inn, Norwich, CT (2003-present). For this 168-room hotel, am excelling at all aspects of this job which involves extensive responsibilities related to customer service for large accounts and individuals, accounting and auditing, billing, as well as training new front desk clerks.
- Currently begin work at 7 AM and handle the heavy volume of customer complaints and questions which occur between 7 AM and 10 AM.
- Work routinely with large accounts to book blocks of rooms and coordinate special events; provide customer service in the booking process and provide liaison regarding any special banquets and events which are set up.
- Handle a wide range of responsibilities related to billing, accounting, and auditing; for two months acted at the hotel's auditor until the position was filled, and am continuing to perform the audit every Sunday which requires me to balance all hotel accounts.
- Handle the billing, and deal with coupons; prepare the ledger.
- Am totally committed to the hotel's policy of assuring customer satisfaction, no matter what, and routinely solve problems to assure guest satisfaction and repeat business.
- Book up to 150 rooms monthly while providing courteous and friendly customer service.
- Have received numerous letters of appreciation because of my professionalism and dedication to the highest standards of customer support and assistance.

STORE MANAGER. Boston Market, Norwich, CT (2001-02). After relocating from Minnesota back to Connecticut, accepted a job as a store manager and managed a staff of 12.
- Emphasized adherence to the highest standards of cleanliness and sanitation, and led the store to receive an O.S.H.A. award for food service and management.
- Coordinated the store's certification by S.A.F.E. for safety and sanitation.

FRONT DESK REPRESENTATIVE. Day's Inn, St. Paul, MN (1998-01). For this 176-room Day's Inn, played a key role in the hotel's receiving the Gold Star for superior service.
- Received extensive formal and on-the-job training related to auditing, customer service, switchboard operations, reservations and office work, and sales.
- Was frequently commended for my sunny disposition and outgoing personality, and excelled in all aspects of customer service.

TRAVEL & TOURISM PHONE OPERATOR. CT Travel & Tourism, New Haven, CT (1994-97). In this summer job, underwent an intensive training program which made me an expert on the state of Connecticut; became knowledgeable of facts and trivia about the state.

PERSONAL

Am a highly self-motivated individual known for my professional attitude. In my spare time, enjoy jazz music and the study of religions.

Exact Name of Person
Exact Title
Exact Name of Company
Address
City, State, Zip

FRONT OF THE
HOUSE MANAGER

in an upscale restaurant

Dear Exact Name of Person (or Dear Sir or Madam if answering a blind ad):

With the enclosed resume, I would like to make you aware of my desire to explore employment opportunities with your restaurant.

As you will see from my resume, I have excelled in all aspects of Front of the House management in my current job at Hatch's Café in Las Cruces. I have also worked as a bookkeeper, an operations supervisor at a large 24-hour gym, and a bar manager at a popular local restaurant. I've been successful in each of these positions and have learned skills from wine and cigar appreciation to supervising staffs of up to 36 while being responsible for millions of dollars worth of equipment.

I have an outgoing and enthusiastic personality which is conducive to both working in the front of the house in a restaurant and training and supervising the wait staff efficiently. I thoroughly enjoy my work and can conquer any dilemmas I meet quickly and precisely so as to not affect the smooth operation of the restaurant.

I am held in high regard by my current employer and can provide outstanding personal and professional references at the appropriate time. If you can use an enthusiastic team player sure to provide quality service, I hope you will contact me to suggest a time when we might meet to discuss your needs. Thank you in advance for your time.

Sincerely,

Cynthia Louise Masterson

CYNTHIA LOUISE MASTERSON

1110½ Hay Street, Fayetteville, NC 28305 • preppub@aol.com • (910) 483-6611

OBJECTIVE   To offer a strong background as a team player with superior skills in training and supervising employees. Provide an enthusiastic personality to a restaurant in need of a professional with experience in fine dining environments and well-defined "people" skills.

EDUCATION   Currently studying **Food Service Management** at Dona Ana Branch Community College, Las Cruces, NM.

EXPERIENCE   **FRONT OF THE HOUSE (F.O.H.) MANAGER**. Hatch's Café, Las Cruces, NM (2002-present). For this popular dining facility which has become one of "the" places to dine in the city, have learned the fine details of preparation and service in a fine dining atmosphere.
- Train wait staff in all aspects of fine dining restaurant operations and in the nuances of providing quality service and proper presentation of food.
- Structure the restaurant in all facets of fine dining for any amount of business on any given night. Assist in design of limited menus including food and wine selections.
- Have learned extensive knowledge of state-of-the-art POS restaurant systems.
- Have developed an extensive knowledge of all aspects of wine.
- Gained appreciation of cigars and of how to store them properly and what brands are considered the highest quality by those who appreciate the best.
- Gained extensive gourmet food preparation knowledge.
- Have been a member of the Hatch's Cafe wait staff team since the restaurant's opening.
- Contributed to the restaurant's recognition with these 2003 honors during only its second year of existence: People's Choice Award for Best Restaurant and "Best Entree Award" in the American Red Cross Chef's Auction.
- Recruit new employees for all positions to cover F.O.H. operations.

BOOKKEEPER and **SALES ASSOCIATE**. Myer's Fitness Shop, Las Cruces, NM (2001-02). Decreased time needed to keep this company's books while preparing bank deposits, ordering stock, balancing the books daily, and counting register drawers.
- Was entrusted with as much as $100,000 at a time while processing bank deposits.
- Compiled and maintained the accuracy of data related to AP/AR and delinquent accounts.
- Ordered stock and assisted in inventory control.
- Gained a great deal of experience in dealing with the public while assisting customers in the selection of clothing and accessories as well as while finding service prices.

GYM OPERATIONS SUPERVISOR. Gold's Gym, Boca Raton, FL (1996-2001). Trained and then supervised as many as 36 employees while preparing schedules for a 24-hour-a-day operation. Earned instructor qualification.
- Held responsibility for controlling a $10 million equipment inventory.

BAR MANAGER. The Merry Piglets, Boca Raton, FL (1994-96). Increased bar sales by providing excellent service in a full-service bar in this popular local restaurant: established a "Happy Hour" promotion which increased sales as much as $500 on each of the three nights a week it was in effect.
- Trained and then supervised five bartenders; mixed drinks.
- Counted registers and controlled inventory.

PERSONAL   Thoroughly enjoy preparing a restaurant and staff for opening. Ensure a smooth flow throughout the night. Enjoy conquering dilemmas quickly and precisely.

Date

Exact Name of Person
Title or Position
Name of Company
Address (number and street)
Address (city, state, and zip)

**GROCERY CUSTOMER
SERVICE MANAGER**

with the Kroger Food chain

Dear Exact Name of Person: (or Sir or Madam if answering a blind ad)

Can you use a motivated and detail-oriented young professional with a background of excellence in staff development and training, management, and customer service?

As you will see from my enclosed resume, I have been working for the 1,200-store Kroger grocery chain for several years. I started with the organization as a cashier when I was in high school and have progressively moved up the ladder to reach my current position as Customer Service Manager. I supervise as many as 30 employees, interview and hire new staff, provide training, and am known as the top performer in cash handling, speed, and accuracy. I was selected for this position when the store opened at a new location because my high standards were recognized and valued.

I am a versatile individual who can organize for maximum productivity and handle multiple simultaneous projects and responsibilities with ease. I have gained much experience dealing with the public and supervising employees. I am currently working towards my Bachelor of Science degree in Business Administration, which I have found complements my work and assists me in becoming an even more valued asset. I am confident that through my education, experience, and background of success that I offer the drive, skills, and personality that would allow me to be successful in your organization.

I hope you will welcome my call soon to arrange a brief meeting to discuss your current and future needs and how I might serve them. Thank you in advance for your time.

Sincerely,

Tenille D. Jackson

Alternate last paragraph:
I hope you will call or write me soon to suggest a time convenient for us to meet and discuss your current and future needs and how I might serve them. Thank you in advance for your time.

TENILLE D. JACKSON

1110½ Hay Street, Fayetteville, NC 28305 • preppub@aol.com • (910) 483-6611

OBJECTIVE To benefit an organization that can use a motivated and detail-oriented young professional with exceptional communication, planning, and organizational skills who offers a background of excellence in staff development and training, management, and customer service.

COMPUTERS Skilled in utilizing grocery bar scanning technology and mainframe computers on a daily basis – operate specialized systems linked to the home office in OH.

EXPERIENCE *Have built a reputation as a dedicated team player and skilled trainer while excelling in the following "track record" with the 1,200-store Kroger grocery chain:*

2003-present: **CUSTOMER SERVICE MANAGER.** Manchester, NH. Selected to help open the new location on Village Road to ensure that high standards in training, customer service, and cash controls were met or exceeded from day one; assist the other managers in implementing company programs, policies, and standards.
- Supervise as many as 30 cashiers and baggers; interview and hire new employees.
- Known for my patient, effective training style, provide instruction to new store managers on Kroger office procedures.
- Provide training to newly hired cashiers and customer service personnel, effectively presenting new and existing company programs, policies, and procedures.
- Consistently the top performer in cash handling, register speed, accuracy, and efficiency.

2002-03: **CUSTOMER SERVICE MANAGER.** Manchester, NH. Transferred to the Northpark location to resolve existing problems, rapidly improved cash controls, reducing losses and increasing customer satisfaction by providing friendly and efficient service.
- Provided supervision and training to 20-30 cashiers and baggers; oversee employee performance to ensure high standards of customer service and cash handling.
- Trained new store managers in company procedures related to office operations.

1994-2002: **CUSTOMER SERVICE MANAGER.** Manchester, NH. Promoted to this position in recognition of my exceptional performance as Bookkeeper at the Snyder Street location; supervised and trained more than 25 cashiers, baggers, and office personnel.
- Entrusted with additional responsibility as Front End Trainer for the area, instructing new customer service managers, cashiers, and other customer service personnel.
- Conducted interviews and made hiring decisions on new employees.

1993-94: **BOOKKEEPER.** Manchester, NH. After excelling as an Office Assistant, advanced to this position upon graduating from high school; entrusted with handling all office responsibilities, cash controls, and supervision of personnel; interviewed and hired new employees. Supervised as many as 30 cashiers and baggers.

OFFICE ASSISTANT. Started with Kroger as a **CASHIER** when I was 16; was rapidly promoted based on my maturity and ability to effectively meet challenges.

EDUCATION Completed nearly two years of college-level course work towards a Bachelor of Science in Business Administration, New Hampshire College, Manchester, NH.
Finished numerous training courses sponsored by Kroger, including Women in Conference, a Vendor Training class, NGAA Training (new office procedures), and Western Union/Money Order, as well as Kroger Library course.

PERSONAL Have received many outstanding performance awards. Excellent references upon request.

CAREER CHANGE

Exact Name of Person
Exact Title
Exact Name of Company
Address
City, State, Zip

GUEST SERVICES SUPERVISOR

for a hotel. After years of experience in the hospitality industry, this professional has decided to make a change and become a travel agent with an airline. Notice how the resume stresses experience which is relevant to aviation.

Dear Exact Name of Person (or Dear Sir or Madam if answering a blind ad):

With the enclosed resume, I would like to express my strong desire to become a Flight Attendant with Continental Airlines and make you aware of my background which is ideally suited to your needs.

Throughout my working career, I have excelled in the hospitality industry. I am currently working at Winchester Inn (a local hotel chain) as a Guest Services Supervisor. I started with the chain as a Guest Services Agent and have moved up the promotional ladder. I supervise desk clerks, hire and train new employees, book bus tours, and deal with the hotel guest relations on all levels.

Through graciously and effectively resolving all guest complaints, I have gained invaluable experience that I am certain would be well suited to the needs of Continental Airlines. I hope you will be in touch with me soon to set up a time when we might meet and further discuss my qualifications. I can provide excellent personal and professional references. Thank you in advance for your time.

Yours sincerely,

Kathleen M. Olson

KATHLEEN M. OLSON

1110½ Hay Street, Fayetteville, NC 28305 • preppub@aol.com • (910) 483-6611

OBJECTIVE To obtain a position as a flight attendant with Continental Airlines.

EXPERIENCE *With Dalton Hospitality, Inc., a regional holding company that owns a number of chain hotels, advanced in a "track record" of increasing responsibilities:*
2003-present: **GUEST SERVICES SUPERVISOR.** Winchester Inn, Tulsa, OK.
Was promoted to this position from Guest Services Agent; perform a variety of supervisory, administrative, and customer service tasks for this busy branch of a local hotel chain.
- Supervise five front desk clerks, directing their activities to guarantee maximum guest satisfaction.
- Participate in interviewing, hiring, training, development, and evaluation of Guest Services employees.
- Train new Guest Services associates in all front desk procedures as well as in the handling of guests' questions, problems, etc.; continually provide feedback and guidance to staff.
- Prepare weekly work schedules for Guest Services employees, controlling labor hours to minimize overtime and ensure optimum front desk coverage.
- Provide documentation to justify overtime hours to the General Manager; maintain records of staff attendance and tardiness.
- Perform direct sales of hotel services to organizations, such as booking bus tours into the facility.
- Verify accuracy of cash drawer at start of shift and supervise end-of-shift closeout of register and cash receipts; ensure timely and accurate completion of paperwork.
- Listen to, analyze, and resolve all guest complaints in accordance with policies and procedures of the hotel.
- Notify upper-level management if unusual incidents or emergencies arise or if a customer service issue cannot be resolved without higher approval.

2000-03: **GUEST SERVICES AGENT.** Winchester Inn, Benning, OK. Provided a number of customer relations, clerical, and administrative tasks to guests during their stay at this branch of a local hotel chain.
- Checked guests into and out of the hotel; scheduled and canceled guest reservations.
- Answered multiline telephone and operated a switchboard, directing guests' calls to the correct extension and taking messages when guests were not available.
- Performed clerical and secretarial functions, including typing, filing, photocopying, and operating a variety of office equipment.
- Provided assistance to guests, addressing and resolving questions and complaints when possible or directing them to the Guest Services Supervisor when necessary.
- Operated a guest reservation terminal, cash register, credit card terminal, and ten-key calculator.

Other experience:
CASHIER. Friendly's, Tulsa, OK. Provided customer service, unloaded shipments of ice cream and supplies, ran the cash register, and took customer orders for ice cream cakes.
CREW MEMBER. Rally's Hamburgers, Tulsa, OK. Served customers, prepared food, opened and closed the store, and performed cash handling duties.

PERSONAL Excellent personal and professional references are available upon request.

Date

Exact Name of Person
Exact Title
Exact Name of Company
Address
City, State, Zip

HEAD BAR MANAGER

with a popular pub.

Dear Exact Name of Person (or Dear Sir or Madam if answering a blind ad):

Please accept my enclosed resume as indication of my interest in pursuing employment with your organization.

As you will see from my resume, I offer a reputation as a highly honest and reliable professional who is known for a positive attitude as well as strong personal initiative and a dedication to achieving results. With my exceptional background in the hospitality/service industries, I am a skilled manager of time as well as of human, fiscal, and material resources.

In addition to my versatile education in banking and finance as well as in technology with a concentration in engineering, I have excelled in jobs where well-developed customer service skills and knowledge of human nature were of utmost importance. My varied experience in accounting, inventory control, and employee supervision has earned me a reputation for effective problem solving and the ability to make sound decisions.

I am confident that my skills as a tactful, articulate communicator and natural leader could quickly make me a valuable asset to your organization. Thank you again for your consideration.

Sincerely,

Nick Greene

IAN NICHOLAS GREENE ("Nick")

1110½ Hay Street, Fayetteville, NC 28305 • preppub@aol.com • (910) 483-6611

OBJECTIVE

To benefit an organization that can use an articulate professional who offers a genuine enthusiasm for finance and accounting as well as practical experience in supervision, cost management, inventory control, and training in the hospitality industry/service industries.

EDUCATION

Have completed one year of course work in pursuit of a **B.S.** degree in **Banking and Finance**, University of Colorado at Denver.

Earned a **A.A.S.** in **Technology**, Community College of Denver, Denver, CO— was an honor student with a concentration in **Engineering**.

COMPUTERS

Offer the ability to quickly master new software and operating systems; familiar with Windows, Microsoft Word, Excel, and Access as well as Paintshop Pro, and Corel Draw.

EXPERIENCE

Have earned a reputation as a highly honest and reliable professional with a vibrant and enthusiastic personality while excelling in the hospitality/service industries:

HEAD BAR MANAGER. Palamino Pub, Denver, CO (2003-present). Supervise as many as nine bar staff personnel and two members of the wait staff.

- Develop schedules based on business forecasts in order to ensure adequate covering while controlling labor costs.
- Supervise activities in all bar areas including a lounge, a sport area, and a party room – each of which have different serving needs because of different types of functions and activities taking place.
- In a mainly cash business with a portable and easily pilfered inventory, oversee the important close of business activities including securing stock and money.
- Monitor and record daily waste and consumption, resulting in excellent inventory control figures.
- Was described, in writing, by the Managing Partner, as "very conscientious ..displays good flexibility... timekeeping and punctuality are without fault."

BAR MANAGER. Brown Palace Hotel, Denver, CO (2000-02). Supervised a staff of approximately 20 people working in six bars and party rooms while overseeing such support functions as inventory control, booking events, and maintaining ledger accounts.

CASINO CASHIER. Bally's Casinos Inc., Atlantic City, NJ (1999-00). Was described by my employer as a "very honest, reliable person with a vibrant and lively character" in recognition of my skills and knowledge of the casino industry.

- Involved in conducting the "casino count" at the end of each night; accounted for large amounts of money, entering figures into the appropriate ledger categories.

PURSER. Princess Cruiselines, Miami, FL (1998-99). For a cruise ship line, handled basic accounting and financial support duties while also participating as a staff member in activities which kept passengers comfortable and satisfied with ship services.

HEAD BAR MANAGER. Brown Palace Hotel, Denver, CO (1990-98). Originally hired as a Night Porter, earned advancement based on my initiative and confident manner.

- Supervised a staff of 20 working in six bars and party rooms.
- Oversaw inventory control, ordering, and stocking of supplies and beverages.

PERSONAL

Am a tactful and diplomatic individual who works well with others in supervisory roles or while pursuing corporate goals. Excellent references are available upon request.

Exact Name of Person
Exact Title
Exact Name of Company
Address
City, State, Zip

HEAD CHEF   Dear Exact Name of Person (or Dear Sir or Madam if answering a blind ad):

I would appreciate an opportunity to talk with you soon about how I could contribute to your organization through my experience as a chef and restaurant manager as well as through my desire to create environments where individual growth and learning are encouraged.

I am presently the Head Chef and Managing Partner of the Georgetown Café in Washington, D.C. I was involved in building this business from the ground up — from site selection, to hiring and training of the staff, to making decisions on menu choices and design — and have seen it grow into a million-dollar producing business. Georgetown Cafe quickly became one of "the" places to go in the city and earned both the People's Choice Award for Best Restaurant as well as "Best Entree Award" in the March of Dimes Chefs Auction in only its second year in business.

I graduated from the famed Johnson and Wales Culinary Institute in Charleston, SC, and completed a rewarding "externship" in a popular Charleston restaurant where I received exposure to quality control, baking and pastry preparation, private party catering, and the proper fundamentals of cooking.

With a reputation as a creative and talented professional, I am confident that I possess the vision, knowledge, and expertise to allow me to continue to produce productive and effective teams of employees. I excel in motivating those around me to give their best efforts to ensure the highest quality of food, preparation, and service.

I hope you will call or write me soon to suggest a time convenient for us to meet and discuss your current and future needs and how I might serve them. Thank you in advance for your time.

Sincerely,

Herman Armando Suarez

HERMAN ARMANDO SUAREZ

1110½ Hay Street, Fayetteville, NC 28305　•　preppub@aol.com　•　(910) 483-6611

OBJECTIVE　　To offer my experience as a chef and management professional as well as my educational background in culinary arts to an organization that can use an individual who enjoys the challenge of creating a productive and positive environment where continual learning and personal growth are encouraged.

EDUCATION　　Earned an **A.O.S. degree in *Culinary Arts*** from Johnson and Wales Culinary Institute, Charleston, SC, 2000.

HONORS　　During only its second year of existence, led the Georgetown Cafe to recognition with these honors: People's Choice Award for Best Restaurant "Best Entree Award" in the March of Dimes Chef's Auction.

EXPERIENCE　　**HEAD CHEF** and **MANAGING PARTNER.** Georgetown Café and Restaurant, Washington, D.C. (2002-present). For this popular dining facility which has become one of "the" places to dine in the city, have built a prospering business from the ground up and seen it grow to take in $1 million dollars annually.
- Provide the creative spark which has allowed this restaurant to develop and grow.
- Develop new menu items and oversee all aspects of restaurant operations.
- Hire, train, and manage the staff which now numbers about 30 employees.
- Developed the restaurant layout and actual physical design.
- Design menus including layout and making price determinations.
- Oversee all stages of food preparation and daily a la carte service.
- Gained experience in accepting full responsibility for all bottom line profits, expenses, and payroll processing.
- Manage the inventory control process including ordering perishable and nonperishable food items and equipment.
- Monitor all aspects of restaurant operations to ensure the highest quality of customer service and food preparation.

SOUS CHEF. Luigi's Italian Restaurant, Arlington, VA (2000-02). Learned to produce quality products in a high-volume kitchen while contributing my skills in food preparation at all work stations within the kitchen.
- Contributed ideas and suggestions in menu development and design.
- Assisted in inventory control by coordinating ordering for products each day in order to prepare adequately. Scheduled, hired, and fired employees.
- Applied my creativity and knowledge while developing recipes and testing them to ensure consistency and quality. Prepared soups, stocks, sauces, and specials.

STUDENT CHEF. The Rosebud, Charleston, SC (1999). As a Johnson and Wales student, received an excellent introduction and training in the proper basic fundamentals of cooking.
- Gained exposure to the quality control environment in a professional kitchen under the classical brigade system. Handled preparation and production in line stations.
- Learned basic baking and pastry skills needed to build a base for the future.
- Assisted in supporting private parties and special functions.

CERTIFICATION　Environmental Virginia State Food and Management Sanitation Certificate, 2000.

.

CAREER CHANGE

Date

Exact Name of Person
Exact Title
Exact Name of Company
Address
City, State, Zip

HEAD SERVER
in a fine dining
establishment

Dear Exact Name of Person: (or Dear Sir or Madam if answering a blind ad):

With the enclosed resume, I would like to make you aware of my strong background in customer service, public relations, and business development and to acquaint you with the leadership, exceptional training skills, and education in business and computers that I could put to work for your company.

As you will see from my resume, I have completed an Associate's degree in Business Administration from the University of Hawaii-Honolulu Community College, where I maintained a 3.5 GPA while working an average of 30 hours per week. While completing this program, I discovered a strong interest in computers, and I have now earned both an A+ and a Microsoft Certified Systems Engineer certification.

Most recently, I have excelled as Head Server at Theissen's, Honolulu's premiere fine dining establishment. In addition to ensuring an elegant and satisfying experience for patrons, I held additional responsibility for many important aspects of the restaurant's operation. I trained new service staff members, instructing them in all areas of providing the exemplary service expected by our customers. My ability to respond to rapidly shifting priorities was proven time and again, as I handled duties that ranged from ordering and maintaining the wine selection, to assisting patrons in planning and organizing special events, while consistently increasing profits through my exceptional sales ability.

Throughout my career in customer service and retail environments, I have consistently been placed in leadership roles, where my employers have benefited from my ability to train and motivate others to greater levels of efficiency and productivity.

Although I am highly regarded by my employer and have been offered promotion into a management position, I have decided instead to explore other options where I can more fully utilize my growing education and interest in computers and technology. If you can use an articulate, self-motivated young professional with exceptional interpersonal skills and the proven ability to motivate others and increase bottom-line profits, I hope you will welcome my call soon when I try to arrange a brief meeting to discuss your goals and how my background might serve your needs. I can provide outstanding references at the appropriate time.

Sincerely,

Corinne Driewer

CORINNE DRIEWER

1110½ Hay Street, Fayetteville, NC 28305   •   preppub@aol.com   •   (910) 483-6611

OBJECTIVE

To contribute to an organization that could benefit from an articulate and enthusiastic young professional with exceptional motivational, training, and organizational skills who offers a strong customer service background and an education in business and computers.

EDUCATION

Associate's degree in Business Administration, University of Hawaii-Honolulu Community College, Honolulu, HI, 2002; maintained a 3.5 GPA while working an average of 30 hours per week.
A+ and Microsoft Certified Systems Engineer Certifications, 2003.

COMPUTERS

Proficient in operating many of the most popular computer operating systems and software, including Windows; Microsoft Word, Excel, and PowerPoint; and others.

EXPERIENCE

HEAD SERVER. Theissen's, Honolulu, HI (2003-present). Coordinate and direct six servers, ensuring exceptional service to patrons of Honolulu's finest dining establishment; provide instruction to new service staff members, training them in service techniques to ensure an elegant dining experience for customers.

- Maintain the restaurant's wine inventory, monitoring stock levels and ordering to satisfy customer demand while controlling costs.
- Assist in planning events and parties for large groups, increasing sales by building Theissen's reputation for providing the perfect atmosphere for special celebrations.
- Greet patrons and effectively present a number of special items and events, maximizing profit for the restaurant through my exceptional sales ability.
- Quickly built an excellent rapport with customers, generating repeat and referral business through my strong public relations skills and attentive service.
- Excel in this fast-paced customer service environment through my strong problem-solving skills and ability to effectively respond to rapidly shifting priorities.

SHIFT MANAGER, TRAINER, and **HEAD SERVER.** Trader Vic's (Meier Restaurants, Inc.), Honolulu, HI (2000-02). Provided leadership and training to the professional service and host staff at this innovative and successful local restaurant.

- Served as shift supervisor for the service staff, directing the completion of opening, ongoing, and end-of-day side-work and monitoring employee performance.
- Expertly trained a staff of 18 individuals in all aspects of restaurant operations and service; as a result of my efforts, guest service was maximized, food and beverage sales soared to record levels, customer base increased, and financial controls improved.
- Provided valuable input at monthly management meetings to ensure the development of realistic objectives in both sales and customer satisfaction.
- Helped plan and organize special events and parties, including charitable events.

SERVER. Blackbeard's Hideaway, Honolulu, HI (1999-2000). Provided exceptional customer service to restaurant patrons at this busy local seafood restaurant; greeted guests, took customer's orders, and ensured a pleasant dining experience.

- Responsible for performing setup and preparing the restaurant for the upcoming shift; supervised ongoing side-work and ensured guest satisfaction.

LANGUAGES

Bilingual and fully fluent in both written and spoken Dutch.

PERSONAL

Have built a reputation as a self-motivated, hard working professional with the ability to develop effective relationships with customers. Excellent references upon request.

Exact Name of Person
Title or Position
Name of Company
Address (no., street)
Address (city, state, zip)

HOSPITALITY OPERATIONS SUPERVISOR
in a Howard Johnson Hotel

Dear Exact Name of Person: (or Dear Sir or Madam if answering a blind ad)

I would appreciate an opportunity to talk with you soon about how I could contribute to your organization through my versatility in the areas of food service and hospitality industry management.

Known as a quick learner, I have excelled in finding ways to improve the quality of training, customer service, and operational efficiency while reducing waste and unnecessary costs. I enjoy training employees and motivating them to reach my performance standards while raising their own.

At this time I am working for the major international hotel chain Howard Johnson as an Auditor and Operations Supervisor. As you will see from my resume, I have also worked for the widely known Carl's Jr., Arby's, and Kentucky Fried Chicken chains and have been very effective in supervising as many as 50 employees. In one case I brought a restaurant from a loss to half-a-million in profits.

I feel that I offer a proven "track record" of management expertise and could apply my skills for the benefit of your organization.

I hope you will welcome my call soon to arrange a brief meeting at your convenience to discuss your current and future needs and how I might serve them. Thank you in advance for your time.

Sincerely yours,

Penny M. Powers

Alternate last paragraph:
I hope you will call or write soon to suggest a time convenient for us to meet and discuss your current and future needs and how I might serve them. Thank you in advance for your time.

PENNY M. POWERS

1110½ Hay Street, Fayetteville, NC 28305　　•　　preppub@aol.com　　•　　(910) 483-6611

OBJECTIVE

To apply my experience in hospitality management to an organization that can benefit from my outstanding motivational and interpersonal communications abilities as well as my inventory management "knowhow."

EXPERIENCE

HOSPITALITY OPERATIONS SUPERVISOR & AUDITOR. Howard Johnson Hotels, Ogden, UT (2002-present). Coordinate accounting and balance daily income received in all areas of the hospitality complex including the restaurant, bar, and hotel.

- Keep accurate records of hundreds of thousands of dollars monthly.
- Have developed a reputation for my skills handling the complex records and paperwork involved.
- Demonstrate tact and patience working with all types of people.

HOSPITALITY SPECIALIST. Howard Johnson Hotels, Ogden, UT (2001-02). Checked guests registering into this major international hotel chain and checked them out on departure; answered phone and in-person inquiries.

- Received paperwork from five employees on my shift, checked for accuracy, and balanced daily records. Accepted cash and credit card payments and completed required paperwork.

SALES REPRESENTATIVE. Northwestern Foods Co., Ogden, UT (2000-01). Applied my communication and sales abilities calling on potential customers for a business selling wholesale and bulk groceries in a "shop-at-home" program.

SENIOR ASSISTANT MANAGER. Carl's Jr., Provo, UT (1999-2000). Coordinated all operational aspects of overseeing a busy fast-food restaurant with average daily sales ranging from $1,200 to $5,000.

- Scheduled, supervised, and trained a staff of 50.
- "Turned around" a disorganized and inefficiently run operation.
- Implemented an effective new method of training.

RESTAURANT MANAGER. Arby's, Provo, UT (1998). Supervised 20 employees in a fast-food restaurant averaging $700 to $2,000 a day while overseeing daily functions including cash control, maintenance and cleanup, and hiring, training, and scheduling employees.

- Took over a restaurant with a poor reputation and turned it around into a store that set cleanliness and fast service standards.

ASSISTANT MANAGER. Kentucky Fried Chicken, Provo, UT (1996-98). Transformed a store suffering from major losses and led it to a $500,000 profit during my first year in its management. Hired, motivated, and trained 50 employees.

SPECIAL SKILLS

- Familiar with software including Word, Access, and the HoJo 3000 system used by Howard Johnson Hotels of America.
- Offer additional experience operating 40-line telephone systems, fax machines, copiers, 10-key adding machines, and type 65 wpm.

EDUCATION & TRAINING

Received nearly 200 hours of Carl's Jr. management training.
Completed community college-level work in Business Administration.

PERSONAL

Enjoy developing creative ways to improve training and motivate employees. Am an adaptable quick learner. Will relocate.

Date

Exact Name of Person
Exact Title
Exact Name of Company
Address
City, State, Zip

**HOTEL FRONT
OFFICE SUPERVISOR**
for The Sheraton

Dear Exact Name of Person (or Dear Sir or Madam if answering a blind ad):

With the enclosed resume, I would like to make you aware of my desire to explore employment opportunities with Marriot International.

As you will see from my resume, I have excelled in all aspects of Hotel Front Office management as well as in other positions in the hospitality industry. I am bilingual and have done extensive traveling throughout my life which I have found useful in relating to guests in this line of work. I am extremely articulate as well as highly motivated and will go the extra mile to ensure guest satisfaction.

I was employed with the Peachtree Inn in Atlanta when the hotel was bought by Marriot International. It was during this time that I first became familiar with Marriot's standard operating procedures. I have since worked for other companies in the hospitality industry and have found that I prefer the way that your organization operates. I would like to resume employment with Marriot International in any of your worldwide hotels, and offer my talents as an articulate manager, skilled motivator, and creative problem solver.

I hope you will welcome my call soon to arrange a brief meeting at your convenience to discuss your current and future needs and how I might serve them. Thank you in advance for your time.

Sincerely,

Demetrius W. Kerns

DEMETRIUS W. KERNS

1110½ Hay Street, Fayetteville, NC 28305   •   preppub@aol.com   •   (910) 483-6611

OBJECTIVE

To contribute to the success and prosperity of Marriot International while offering my talents as an articulate manager, skilled motivator, and creative problem solver.

EDUCATION

B.S., Political Science, Georgia State University, Atlanta, GA, 1999.

EXPERIENCE

FRONT OFFICE SUPERVISOR. The Sheraton Westmont, Grand Rapids, MI (2003-present). Juggle multiple responsibilities within this busy front office serving corporate-level customers from around the world.

- Compute and monitor average daily rate (ADR). Have refined computer knowledge while working on a variety of systems including Linux, MSI, Tesa Lock System, Word, and Windows.
- Gained valuable knowledge of Sheraton's Standards of Operations. Offer a track record of success using Signature Marketing Program after three months of extensive implementation.
- Have developed excellent communication, organization, and customer relations skills while making reservations and scheduling group conventions, forecasting, and reconciling rate discrepancies.
- Honed general accounting skills while performing accounts payable/receivable functions.
- Demonstrated a comprehensive knowledge of night auditing procedures conducted manually and through MSI.

FRONT OFFICE MANAGER. Hampton Inn, Grand Rapids, MI (2000-03). Supervised 15 desk clerks and the housekeeping staff while ensuring that the administrative operations of the organization are precisely followed.

- Performed payroll functions including managing time cards; handled promotions and raises. Ensured that employees were scheduled according to booking ratios.
- Acquired skills in night auditing using manual procedures and MSI.

PERSONAL AIDE. Department of Foreign Affairs, U.S. Consulate Internship, Athens, Greece (1998-99). Handled administrative functions as the personal aide to a foreign dignitary including assisting U.S. citizens in obtaining extensions on VISAs.

- Interpreted English to Greek and vice versa for business and personal contacts.
- Gained extensive travel experience.

At the Peachtree Inn in Atlanta, GA, the hotel was bought by Marriot International. I continued to work with the hotel during and after the transformation:
FRONT DESK SUPERVISOR. Marriot Peachtree, Atlanta, GA (1997-98). Refined management and organizational skills while administratively supervising this 425-room hotel with 10 three-bedroom suites, catering to foreign dignitaries and VIPs.

- Used my bilingual skills to help register international guests and dignitaries.

FRONT DESK SUPERVISOR. Peachtree Inn, Atlanta, GA (1995-97). Quickly advanced from restaurant supervisor to desk clerk and then to Front Desk Supervisor when the inn was bought by Marriott.

- Performed opening and closing operations of restaurant.
- Conducted staffing/hiring/training, inventory control, and cost accountability functions.

PERSONAL

Am an extremely articulate and highly motivated team player with a "do whatever it takes" attitude; always willing to go the extra mile for the satisfaction in a job well done.

Date

Exact Name of Person
Exact Title
Exact Name of Company
Address
City, State, Zip

HOTEL GENERAL MANAGER

Dear Exact Name of Person (or Dear Sir or Madam if answering a blind ad):

With the enclosed resume, I would like to make you aware of my desire to explore employment opportunities at the senior management or multiunit operations management level with your corporation.

Since gaining my B.S. degree in Hospitality Management at the University of New England, I have led several establishments to success by increasing profits, boosting guest satisfaction, increasing A.D.R.'s while maintaining high occupancy levels and reducing turnover. I offer experience in supervising and training personnel in all hotel departments. I have experience managing property through major renovation projects as well as turning around troubled operations.

Among other accomplishments, I've recently increased the food and beverage profit levels by 35% while supervising a staff of 120 associates at the Black Hills Radisson. I offer a reputation as an exceptional leader with highly refined communication and staff development skills. While working with the Hyatt Regency in Augusta, Maine, I corrected an ongoing problem by reducing the turnover in the housekeeping department by 45% through effective hiring and incentive programs.

I thoroughly enjoy my role in the hospitality industry and never tire of introducing and implementing innovative training programs and ways to strengthen my organization's distinctive image in the community.

If you can use a highly motivated and experienced senior manager with the proven ability to increase profitability and guest satisfaction, I hope you will contact me to suggest a time when we might meet to discuss your needs. Thank you in advance for your time.

Sincerely,

Raymond L. Morris

RAYMOND L. MORRIS

1110½ Hay Street, Fayetteville, NC 28305   •   preppub@aol.com   •   (910) 483-6611

OBJECTIVE   To benefit an organization that can use an experienced hotel general manager with exceptional leadership and communication skills who offers a strong background in staff development and the proven ability to increase property profitability and guest satisfaction.

EXPERIENCE   **GENERAL MANAGER.** Black Hills Radisson, Bismarck, ND (2003-present). Supervise and develop a staff of 120 hotel associates while formulating and implementing capital and operational budgets.
- Increased food and beverage profit levels by 35% through staff reductions and containment of other expenses. Maintain hotel rev/par index of 110%.
- Provide strong leadership to the sales and marketing team.
- Imaginatively communicated the direction and vision of the hotel and strengthened its distinctive image in the community.

Joined Hyatt Hotels, Inc. in 1994, and was promoted in the following "track record" of increasing responsibilities:
GENERAL MANAGER. Hyatt Inn, Oshkosh, WI (2001-03). Increased hotel rev/par index by 12% over a two-year period while reducing payroll 8% through job consolidation and departmental reorganization.
- Boosted overall guest satisfaction levels by eight percentage points, according to service scores provided by Bueller and Associates.
- Prepared and oversaw the implementation of operational and capital budgets.
- Effectively managed the property through a major renovation project.

ROOMS DIVISION MANAGER. Hyatt Regency, Augusta, ME (1998-2001). Increased the hotel's A.D.R. 13% over a two-year period while maintaining high occupancy levels.
- Supervised the operation of the front office and the housekeeping department; reduced turnover in housekeeping department by 45% through effective hiring and incentive programs. Prepared the operating budgets for the Rooms Division.
- Developed transient rate and yield strategies for the property.
- Responsible for all aspects of training and staff retention.

HUMAN RESOURCES DIRECTOR. Southfork Hyatt, Bangor, ME (1994-98). Reduced hotel medical benefits program by 20% while implementing the hotel Guest Services training program and the Hyatt Shining Star training program.
- Directed the recruitment, interviewing, and hiring of hotel staff.
- Responsible for overseeing the employee review process, disciplinary compliance, and hotel recognition programs, and maintaining all personnel files.
- Administered the hotel benefits program.

Other experience: **MANAGEMENT TRAINEE.** Atlantic Star Companies, Hilton Forest Edge Inn, Bangor, ME (1993-94). Interim position as Human Resource Director for the hotel.
- Implemented the Hilton "Yes I Can" training program.

EDUCATION   **Bachelor of Science degree in Hospitality Management,** University of New England, Biddeford, ME, 1993.
C.H.A. Certification, Hospitality Educational Institute.
Hyatt Reservation Training (32-hour course); Hyatt Priority One Training.

PERSONAL   Excellent personal and professional references on request.

Date

Exact Name of Person
Exact Title
Exact Name of Company
Address
City, State, Zip

HOTEL GENERAL
MANAGER

with a large property
management company

Dear Exact Name of Person (or Dear Sir or Madam if answering a blind ad):

With the enclosed resume, I would like to make you aware of my desire to explore employment opportunities at the senior management or multiunit operations management level.

As you will see from my resume, since graduating with a B.S. degree in Hotel and Restaurant Management, I have established a reputation as a proven performer and highly skilled General Manager. Since shortly after college graduation, I have worked for only two employers—Star Hotel Management Company and Pacific Hospitality— and I have succeeded in managing and "turning around" a variety of properties. With a reputation as a strong leader with an optimistic attitude and effective interpersonal skills, I have especially enjoyed troubleshooting problems. In one assignment with Pacific Hospitality, I took over a Sleep Inn with a troubled front office and rapidly instilled discipline and focus in the work force. On another occasion while I was a General Manager of a Motel 6, I led a team which took over three new Pacific properties and converted them to the policies and procedures of their new owner.

In another position with Pacific as General Manager of a Sleep Inn in Oregon, I played a key role in the property's being named "Region 3's Hotel of the Year." Prior to that, I took over a Motel 6 in Redding, CA, where I modified an outdated pricing structure and made other changes which transformed a property in foreclosure into an attractive motel which was sold.

Although I am held in high regard by my current employer and can provide outstanding personal and professional references at the appropriate time, I would appreciate your holding my expression of interest in your company in confidence at this time. If you can use an astute and experienced senior manager with the proven ability to impact your bottom line in profitable ways, I hope you will contact me to suggest a time when we might meet to discuss your needs. Thank you in advance for whatever time and professional courtesies you can extend.

Sincerely,

Anthony V. Sabotino

ANTHONY V. SABOTINO

1110½ Hay Street, Fayetteville, NC 28305   •   preppub@aol.com   •   (910) 483-6611

OBJECTIVE   I want to contribute to an organization that can use an experienced hospitality industry professional with a proven ability to solve problems and maximize the profitability of properties while managing operations for maximum efficiency and customer satisfaction.

EDUCATION   **B.S. in Hotel and Restaurant Management,** University of Michigan, Ann Arbor, MI. Trained at the Educational Institute of the American Hotel and Motel Association.

EXPERIENCE   *Pacific Hospitality, Los Angeles, CA (2000-present). Have excelled in the following positions at properties managed by Pacific:*
11/03-present: GENERAL MANAGER. Sleep Inn, Bakersfield, CA. Am improving revenue, increasing guest satisfaction, and boosting occupancy rates. At this 122-room hotel, am responsible for sales and revenue management, rooms division operations, accounting and payroll, and all expenses.

8/03-11/03: TASK FORCE GENERAL MANAGER. Sleep Inn, Fresno, CA. Took over an operation with a troubled front office and rapidly instilled discipline and focus in the work force; retrained the Assistant General Manager. Directed operations of a 122-room hotel and played a key role in developing market analysis and pricing structure; negotiated numerous contractual details.

2/02-8/03: GENERAL MANAGER. Sleep Inn, Eugene, OR. Improved guest satisfaction scores 10 percent at this 60-room hotel, and played a key role in the property's being named "2002's Pacific Hospitality's Hotel of the Year, Region 3."

4/01-2/02: GENERAL MANAGER. Motel 6, Bellingham, WA. Functioned in the role of multiunit troubleshooter while managing this 63-room motel. At three different properties acquired by Pacific Hospitality, I led the team which took over the properties and converted them to the policies and procedures of the new owner.

6/00-3/01: GENERAL MANAGER. Motel 6, Redding, CA. At this 98-room hotel, altered an outdated pricing structure and made numerous changes that transformed a property in foreclosure into an attractive hotel which the bank sold.

Star Hotel Management Company, Austin, TX (1990-2000). Worked in the following positions with Star:
1/00-6/00: ASSISTANT GENERAL MANAGER. Hamburg Hotel, Odessa, TX. Managed operations of an 89-room hotel with restaurant.
4/97-1/00: GENERAL MANAGER. Highway Inn, Manhattan, KS. Managed operations of a 98-room hotel and prepared advertising in various media for lounge, hotel, and restaurant.
10/94-4/97: GENERAL MANAGER. Rosehill Inn, Stillwater, OK. At this 114-room hotel, increased occupancy and revenue through special promotions targeting motor coach, family reunions, and transient travelers.
5/90-9/94: Various positions, Sherwood Inn, Abilene, TX. At this 168-room hotel, worked in the food and beverage department. Was in charge in the absence of the General Manager.

AFFILIATIONS   Member, California and Texas Lodging Boards of Directors.

PERSONAL   Offer strong leadership skills as well as an optimistic attitude which have been the keys to my successful years in property management. Proven ability to manage multiple priorities.

Date

Exact Name of Person
Exact Title
Exact Name of Company
Address
City, State, Zip

HOTEL MANAGER

with Family Inn.
This individual seeks to
transfer skills gained in a
family-run hotel to a new
field.

Dear Exact Name of Person (or Dear Sir or Madam if answering a blind ad):

I would appreciate an opportunity to talk with you soon about how I could contribute to your organization through my versatility, education in the area of biology, and experience in small business management.

As you will see from my enclosed resume, I have received my bachelor's degree in Biology from Kent State University-Stark Campus. I have completed more than 300 hours as a Lab Technician in biology, chemistry, and organic chemistry labs while in college at Kent State and earlier while studying Organic Chemistry at Eastern Tennessee State University (Johnson City, TN).

Through my experience in helping build a family-owned business to increased profitability, I have gained valuable exposure to bookkeeping and finance, customer service, maintenance and groundskeeping, and public relations. For the past several years, beginning while I was still in high school and part-time throughout my college years, I have been involved in making decisions and advanced with the business as profits have increased yearly with 20% growth in the last five years.

I hope you will welcome my call soon to arrange a brief meeting at your convenience to discuss your current and future needs and how I might serve them. Thank you in advance for your time.

Sincerely yours,

Solomon Bissada

Alternate last paragraph:
I hope you will call or write me soon to suggest a time convenient for us to meet and discuss your current and future needs and how I might serve them. Thank you in advance for your time.

SOLOMON BISSADA

1110½ Hay Street, Fayetteville, NC 28305 • preppub@aol.com • (910) 483-6611

OBJECTIVE

To contribute to an organization through my education in biology as well as my experience related to small business management and exposure to such areas as public relations and customer service as well as financial and accounting operations.

EDUCATION

Bachelor's degree in Biology, Kent State University-Stark Campus, Canton, OH, December 2003. Studied Organic Chemistry, Eastern Tennessee State University, Johnson City, TN.

TRAINING

Completed more than 100 hours as a Lab Technician in the following two labs: chemistry lab and biology lab — Kent State University organic chemistry lab — Eastern Tennessee State University

EXPERIENCE

Gained experience in all phases of small business operations and made important contributions to the growth of a family-owned motel, the Family Inn, Canton, OH, in this track record of advancement:

MANAGER. (2003-present). Refined my managerial skills and learned to oversee the work of others while becoming familiar with the financial aspects of taking care of the company's bookkeeping activities.
- Quickly learned the details of handling financial activities and prepared the daily figures for the accountants and wrote checks to pay various operating expenses.
- Was praised for my decision-making skills and ability to develop ideas which led to increased profitability and smoother daily operations.
- Made suggestions which helped ease the transition to a new name after the motel had operated as the Florida Motor Inn for several years.
- Refined my interpersonal communication skills dealing with a wide range of customers and employees.
- Have been recognized as a key figure in the motel's record of annual increases in income — over the past five years the business has seen a 20% increase.

DESK CLERK and **REPAIRMAN.** (2001-03). Advanced to take on a more active role in day-to-day operations of the hotel as a front-desk clerk responsible for providing helpful and courteous service to customers and handling large sums of money.
- Maintained the swimming pool which included seeing that the proper chemical balances were reached and that the pool was clean and safe to use.
- Demonstrated my versatility by doing painting, roofing, and minor electrical repairs on air conditioning systems and TVs which resulted in extending the life of many appliances and reduced the need for outside repairs.

MAINTENANCE WORKER/GROUNDSKEEPER. (1999-2001). While still in high school, began helping with building maintenance, minor repairs, and lawn maintenance.
- Became aware of the importance of seeing that buildings and lawns were in good repair and that preventive maintenance could reduce the need for future repairs.
- Learned that customers are appreciative and that return business depends on the physical upkeep as well as quality of customer service provided.

LANGUAGES

As a native of Egypt who came to the U.S. as a young teenager, can speak, read, and write in English, Egyptian, and Arabic. Also have basic knowledge of French.

PERSONAL

Lived in three countries and attended 15 schools while growing up: always adapted to new cultures and ways of life and earned the respect of those around me.

CAREER CHANGE

Date

Exact Name of Person
Exact Title
Exact Name of Company
Address
City, State, Zip

**HOTEL RESTAURANT
MANAGER**

seeks to return to the
hospitality industry

Dear Exact Name of Person (or Dear Sir or Madam if answering a blind ad):

With the enclosed resume, I would like to make you aware of my desire to explore employment opportunities within your organization in some capacity in which you could utilize my strong management, customer service, and financial management skills.

As you will see from my resume, I have excelled in jobs which involved managing people, finances, schedules, and personnel. In my most recent job as General Manager, I managed three people in a store which was named Regional Store of the Month for two straight months. Through my skill in collections and my strong management skills, I was able to raise revenue volume by 20%.

In earlier jobs in the hospitality industry, I excelled as Banquet Manager, Restaurant Manager, Dining Room Supervisor, and Bartender. In those jobs I refined my customer service and public relations skills, and I developed a reputation as a professional who emphasized courtesy, team work, and concern for customers at all times.

Although I have enjoyed my current position related to credit management, I have a desire to return to the hospitality industry. If you can use a polished young professional who offers a proven ability to impact the bottom line positively while providing the kind of service that keeps customers coming back, I hope you will contact me to suggest a time when we might meet to discuss your needs. I can provide excellent references at the appropriate time.

Sincerely,

Darrell Sykes, Jr.

DARRELL WILLIAM SYKES, JR.

1110½ Hay Street, Fayetteville, NC 28305　•　preppub@aol.com　•　(910) 483-6611

OBJECTIVE

To offer my management and customer service skills to an organization that can use a dynamic young professional with an aggressive bottom-line orientation as well as a strong desire to provide the finest experience for customers by emphasizing courtesy and team work.

EDUCATION & TRAINING

Completed extensive college-level course work with an emphasis on Hotel and Restaurant Management, English, and Early Childhood Education, Temple University, Philadelphia, PA. Earned certifications from Southwestern Virginia Community College, Richlands, VA.

EXPERIENCE

GENERAL MANAGER. Cross Country Credit, Richmond, VA (2003-present). Manage three people and handle collections while excelling in all aspects of debt control, collections, and financial management.
- Manage a branch named *Regional Store of the Month* for two straight months, and increased its revenue volume by 20%. Recruit, train, and manage all staff.

RESTAURANT MANAGER & FRONT DESK CLERK. Howard Johnson Hotel and Restaurant, I-95 Richmond, VA (2001-02). Began as Front Desk Clerk and handled a wide range of daily activities which included guest services and hospitality as well as administrative and clerical duties; then was asked to take over as Restaurant Manager when the hotel opened a restaurant within the facility.

BANQUET MANAGER. Sheraton Suites West, Allentown, PA (2000-01). Set up meeting and banquet rooms for a variety of functions such as wedding receptions and birthday celebrations.
- Acted as the Bartender; prepared staff schedules and supervised other staff members.
- Assisted guests in making decisions on what food would be served and how to decorate.
- Processed payments and decorated according to the type of event taking place.

DINING ROOM SUPERVISOR. Sugarleaf Restaurant, Quality Inn, Allentown, PA (1998-2000). Prepared schedules for hosts, hostesses, and servers and solved any problems guests might have. Made dinner reservations; set up entrees and assisted in the kitchen.
- Checked with guests to ensure they were satisfied with the food and the service.
- Promoted weekly specialties; set up and conducted interviews for new personnel.

BARTENDER and **WAITER.** McArthur's, Norfolk, VA (1996-98). Was known for my friendly and personable manner of dealing with customers in this popular gathering place.
- Seated guests and took orders; served appetizers, entrees, and desserts to guests.
- Made more than 50 different house drinks to the customers' order as well as coffee drinks and frozen drinks along with well, premium, and top-shelf drinks; took drink orders and prepared specialty drinks as well as frozen drinks and cordials.

SERVER. DeSha's, Philadelphia, PA (1991-95). Became adept at "upselling" and provided outstanding customer service in this fine dining restaurant.
- Took guests' orders; showed the dessert tray to customers at the end of their meal.
- Accepted cash payments and processed credit card payments.
- Greeted guests with a smile and helpful manner within a minute of their being seated.

PERSONAL

One of my strongest personal goals is to show every customer that they are special and to treat everyone I meet and serve with respect and professionalism. Excellent references.

Exact Name of Person
Title or Position
Name of Company
Address (no., street)
Address (city, state, zip)

KITCHEN MANAGER

in a privately owned
restaurant

Dear Exact Name of Person: (or Dear Sir or Madam if answering a blind ad):

I would appreciate an opportunity to talk with you soon about how I could contribute to your organization through my supervisory and managerial experience along with my reputation as a dedicated, hardworking, and personable professional.

As you will see by my resume, for about eight years I have worked for a succession of owners in a popular restaurant location. After starting as the Head Cook, I advanced into positions with ever-increasing amounts of responsibility for all aspects of operational activities from inventory control, to training and motivating employees, to guaranteeing customer satisfaction through great customer service.

Among my major personal strengths are my enthusiasm, my willingness to do whatever is necessary to ensure the job is done right, and my motivational skills. I am very patient and willing to take the time to train employees so that they are inspired to provide quality performance in their jobs. With my optimistic attitude and ability to get along with everyone I meet, I can quickly adapt to a new work environment and rapidly make valuable contributions to an organization that seeks a professional with these qualities.

I hope you will welcome my call soon to arrange a brief meeting at your convenience to discuss your current and future needs and how I might serve them. Thank you in advance for your time.

Sincerely yours,

Marvin D. Hodges

Alternate last paragraph:
I hope you will call or write me soon to suggest a time convenient for us to meet and discuss your current and future needs and how I might serve them. Thank you in advance for your time.

MARVIN D. HODGES

1110½ Hay Street, Fayetteville, NC 28305 • preppub@aol.com • (910) 483-6611

OBJECTIVE

To offer my supervisory and managerial skills to an employer in need of a hardworking and dedicated professional who is known for an enthusiastic and friendly personality, ability to get along with others, and optimism.

EXPERIENCE

Advanced into managerial roles in a situation where there were three changes of ownership over an eight-year period and each successive owner requested that I remain in supervisory and managerial roles with their organization, Star Valley, ID.

KITCHEN MANAGER. The Spud House (2003-present). Based on my reputation for reliability, a strong work ethic, and knowledge, was aggressively recruited by the new owners to oversee the transition period including the restaurant's grand opening under new ownership.

- In a job usually filled by two full-time employees, handle a large volume of business and provide customer service which has led to a strong repeat customer base.
- Apply problem-solving skills in situations where business is unusually heavy or when supplies do not arrive when promised.
- Handle day-to-day activities ranging from helping unload supplies from trucks, to checking invoices to be sure proper items are being delivered, to stocking the shelves.

ASSISTANT MANAGER and **KITCHEN MANAGER.** Bob and Sue's Steak Stop (2000-02). Constantly praised for my reliability and thorough knowledge of all areas of activity in the business, supervised a 10-person staff and managed the entire kitchen operation.

- Controlled inventory from making decisions on what to order, to ordering, to accepting deliveries, to stocking, to completing necessary paperwork.
- Made the decisions on hiring and firing of employees; trained new personnel.
- Developed ideas for menu items and procedural changes which eliminated waste by using all parts of the meat products on hand.

HEAD COOK. Sizzler Family Steak House (1995-2000). Honored as "Employee of the Year" for three consecutive years, was consistently praised for my ability to efficiently and productively handle multiple tasks simultaneously.

- Gained experience in areas of responsibility including:
    Submitting complete and accurate paperwork for ordering supplies
    Scheduling employees so that all positions were filled for all shifts
    Ensuring the facility was cleaned and closed at the end of the day
- Remained upbeat and positive at all times and motivated employees to display this type of attitude which ensured a high quality of customer service and satisfaction.

EDUCATION & TRAINING

Completed two years of college coursework with a major in Physical Education and a minor in History, University of Nebraska-Lincoln.

Selected to attend a Sizzler corporate management training program, received training and guidance on company policies in the areas of inventory control, profit, and supervision.

ATHLETIC HONORS

Displayed a strong personal drive for success and dedication while earning honors for athletic skills: broke county and state records in three sports—football, wrestling, and track.

PERSONAL

Am very physically fit, strong, and not afraid of hard work. Motivate those around me to accomplish a lot through my patience and outgoing personality.

CAREER CHANGE

Date

Exact Name of Person
Title or Position
Name of Company
Address (no., street)
Address (city, state, zip)

MANAGER-IN-TRAINING
for a fine dining restaurant
seeks a faster pace.

Dear Exact Name of Person: (or Dear Sir or Madam if answering a blind ad)

I am sending my resume in response to the advertisement you recently placed in *The Star Tribune* for a General Manager.

As you will see from my resume, I have skills and abilities that could make me a valuable part of your team. In addition, I feel certain that you would find me to be a hardworking and reliable professional who prides myself on doing any job to the best of my ability. I can provide excellent personal and professional references.

I am currently being groomed for management at a restaurant known as "the" fine dining spot in town. While I find it enjoyable, I feel that my skills are not being used to their potential. I enjoy the challenge of senior level management and have a proven track record of success in past positions.

I hope you will call or write me soon to suggest a time convenient for us to meet and discuss your current and future needs and how I might serve them. Thank you in advance for your time.

Sincerely yours,

R. Andrew Parks

R. ANDREW PARKS

1110½ Hay Street, Fayetteville, NC 28305   •   preppub@aol.com   •   (910) 483-6611

OBJECTIVE

To contribute to an organization that can use a highly skilled professional manager who offers experience as an area manager along with a reputation as a hard worker who combines strong customer service and communication skills with an aggressive approach to maximizing profit, controlling costs, and streamlining all internal functions.

EDUCATION & TRAINING

Studied Business Administration for 1 1/2 years at night while excelling in my full-time job, Itwamba Community College, Fulton, MS, 1997-99.

Completed extensive formal and hands-on training in numerous aspects of restaurant management related to restaurant sanitation and computer software programs for controlling restaurant operations.

HONORS

Won awards for producing the highest increase in restaurant sales and for maintaining the lowest food and labor costs in the chain.

EXPERIENCE

MANAGER-IN-TRAINING. Bravo's, Hattiesburg, MS (2003-present). Am being groomed for management in a fine dining establishment at a restaurant known as the top dining spot in the city.

Was promoted in this track record by CiCi's Pizza (1999-2003):
AREA SUPERVISOR. Meridian, Mississippi, and surrounding area (2002-03). Was promoted to supervise an area with six stores located in Meridian, Ellisville, Senatobia, Clinton, and Perkinston; in consultation with the franchise owner, handled all hiring and firing of store management personnel.
- Coordinated all advertising and developed personal relationships with radio, television, and print media personnel in six cities.
- Developed and implemented marketing, promotion, and publicity plans.
- Increased sales at five out of six stores and transformed two unprofitable stores into profitable operations.

STORE MANAGER. Village Green Shopping Center, Ellisville, MS (2000-02). Became aware of the importance of a good product and excellent customer service in the highly competitive restaurant business.
- Managed 30 employees daily while directing all aspects of store operations including:

inventory purchasing and control	overhead and variable costs
sanitation and maintenance	budgeting and payroll
employee hiring and training	sales and customer service

- Increased sales at this store from $12,000 weekly to $25,000 through a campaign based on creative advertising backed up by superb product and service.
- Achieved and maintained the highest sales volume of any store in the chain; won company awards for producing the highest increase in sales while also maintaining food and labor costs at the most efficient level.

ASSISTANT MANAGER. Clinton, MS (1997-2000). Assisted the store manager in the daily operations of the store; directed shifts on the manager's days off and learned to prepare all paperwork required of restaurants.

PERSONAL

Am a highly motivated individual who offers a talent for motivating others. Customers and fellow workers regard me as congenial, professional, and very hard working. Am a single young professional with a talent for developing unique marketing strategies.

Date

Exact Name of Person
Exact Title
Exact Name of Company
Address
City, State, Zip

**MULTIUNIT DIRECTOR
OF OPERATIONS**

for Arby's Restaurants

Dear Exact Name of Person (or Dear Sir or Madam if answering a blind ad):

Can you use a results-oriented manager who has established a track record of rapid promotion based on outstanding results while earning a reputation as a talented motivator and supervisor?

Although I am held in very high regard by my current employer and have achieved excellent results in my almost nine years with Stauffer's Restaurants (Arby's) in the Decatur, GA region, I am selectively and confidentially exploring opportunities at other fine companies. I ask that you treat my interest in your organization with confidence as I explore the possibility of making a change.

With Arby's, I am excelling in applying my managerial, leadership, and training skills in developing personnel at all levels of the organization while aggressively increasing sales. My efforts have resulted in numerous accomplishments; for example, half of the 18 locations in the region have received certification as "training stores," which is a distinction given to only 5% of the chain's stores worldwide! As I have advanced rapidly in managerial responsibilities, I have taken numerous strong initiatives which have played a key role in increasing sales, including an overall monthly 6% increase in sales in the district.

My background has included experience in all aspects of store operations from hiring, training, scheduling, and supervising employees, to controlling expenses and costs, to ordering supplies and controlling inventories. I also have prepared annual budgets and various types of weekly, monthly, and annual reports and graphs.

If you can use a versatile and adaptable management professional with well-developed leadership abilities, I hope you will call or write me soon to suggest a time when we might have a brief discussion of how I could contribute to your organization. I can provide excellent professional and personal references at the appropriate time.

Sincerely,

Juanita Macias

JUANITA MACIAS

1110½ Hay Street, Fayetteville, NC 28305 • preppub@aol.com • (910) 483-6611

OBJECTIVE

To offer an organization my aggressive bottom-line orientation along with strong management, motivational, communication, and planning skills which have led to increased profitability, employee satisfaction, and quality customer service for my current employer.

EDUCATION & MANAGEMENT TRAINING

Completed two years of college-level work in general studies.

Attend regular management training courses, DeVry Institute of Technology, Decatur, GA; programs have included: Conflict Resolution, Interpretation of Financial Statements, Human Behavior, Legal Rights in Hiring and Firing, and Tools for Managers.

EXPERIENCE

Have advanced to increasingly higher managerial levels with Stauffer's Restaurants, Inc. (Arby's) in the Decatur, GA, region:

DIRECTOR OF OPERATIONS. (2002-present). Was specially selected and promoted ahead of three other District Managers for this job; oversee all phases of store operations for 18 locations, each with four or five managers supervising up to 35 crew members.

- Guide training efforts which have resulted in nine of the 18 stores being certified as "training stores," a designation given to only 5% of all Arby's restaurants worldwide.
- Am increasing overall regional sales 5% to 6% each month through improvements in training methods and operational procedures.

DISTRICT MANAGER. (2000-02). Earned rapid promotion from General Manager of one of the region's 18 locations to become one of the three people at this level: controlled budgets and supervised as many as five managers per store.

- Increased sales 10% over the previous year's figures while providing oversight for a total of eight stores in Americus, Dalton, Tifton, Rome, and Decatur.
- Handled the preparations which led to the certification of the oldest store in the region as a "training store." Mentored personnel including two General Managers.

GENERAL MANAGER. (1999-2000). Supervised four managers and approximately 30 employees while overseeing a wide range of operational activities on a shift which covered breakfast and lunch (7 a.m. to 2 p.m.).

- Motivated employees to achieve a 6 to 7% increase in monthly sales over the previous year's figures to $19,000 weekly from $14,500 in my first two months.
- Oversaw day-to-day operations including ordering and inventory control as well as budgeting and the preparation of financial reports and graphs.
- Excelled in motivating personnel and in building teams of employees who worked together to ensure customer satisfaction. Hired, trained, motivated, and fired employees.

OFFICE MANAGER. (1999). Earned rapid advancement based on my outstanding results in supervising a two-person office staff and assisting in budget forecasting and preparations.

CO-MANAGER. (1998-99). Originally assigned as Assistant Manager, soon earned advancement based on my dedication and hard work; supervised up to 16 employees.

Highlights of earlier experience with Stauffer's Restaurants (Arby's):

As **Administrative Assistant to the Director of Operations (1998),** handled an executive's schedule and met with media representatives to arrange radio, TV, and ads.

As **Office Manager (1997-98),** supervised two people; oversaw weekly cost reports; processed accounts payable, payroll, and expenses for the Decatur regional office.

As a **Crew Member (1995-97),** learned the value of team work and attention to detail.

Exact Name of Person
Exact Title
Exact Name of Company
Address
City, State, Zip

**MULTIUNIT GENERAL
MANAGER**

in the food industry

Dear Exact Name of Person (or Dear Sir or Madam if answering a blind ad):

With the enclosed resume, I would like to make you aware of my background as an accomplished food industry professional who has achieved a track record of success in managing single and multiunit operations through a results-oriented management style focused on customer satisfaction and bottom-line profitability.

I am permanently relocating to the Westfield area to be near family, and I am interested in selectively exploring opportunities with firms in that region. I can provide excellent references at the appropriate time and I trust that you will hold my inquiry in the strictest confidence until after we have had a chance to meet.

Currently as General Manager of Benson Service Company in Brookline, I manage all aspects of a diversified regional food service company including the supervision of multiunit, cafeteria, catering, and vending operations with annual sales of more than $4.2 million. In addition to supervising 75 employees in the Brookline location, I oversee the operation of a branch office in Quincy, MA. While ensuring the retention of existing accounts through exceptional customer service, I aggressively sell our products and services to new customers, with the result that our market share and client base have both increased substantially. By focusing on the bottom line, I reduced food costs district-wide by three percent, dramatically increasing profitability without sacrificing customer service.

Earlier with American Industries, I oversaw district-wide operation of 27 full-service business and industrial cafeterias, many of which supported vending operations, while simultaneously serving as on-site manager of a commissary which served more than 2,100 meals daily and functioned as a catering service. In previous positions in the food industry, I have managed multiunit vending and cafeteria operations as well as full-service restaurants in locations statewide.

If you can use an accomplished and motivated food service professional who offers expertise in single and multiunit operations management and sales, then I look forward to hearing from you soon. I assure you in advance that I have an excellent reputation and could quickly become an asset to your organization.

Sincerely,

Theodore Joseph Rivers

THEODORE JOSEPH RIVERS

1110½ Hay Street, Fayetteville, NC 28305 • preppub@aol.com • (910) 483-6611

OBJECTIVE

To benefit an organization that can use a food industry professional with strong communication skills who offers a strong bottom-line orientation and a background in sales and management of multiunit operations in cafeteria and vending services.

EXPERIENCE

GENERAL MANAGER. Benson Service Company, Brookline, MA (2002-present). Supervise all aspects of multiunit cafeteria and vending operations for this regional food service company with annual sales of more than $4.2 million.
- Supervise 75 employees in the Brookline location as well as overseeing the operation of the branch office in Quincy, MA. Service existing accounts, from full service cafeterias with catering operations to full-line vending customers.
- Aggressively present products and services to new and potential customers, resulting in substantial increases in market share and a growing base of satisfied clients.
- Prepare and develop long- and short-term financial plans, analyzing existing data to prepare forecasts and managing capital requisitions for the branch.
- Coordinate and implement the servicing of eight delivery routes for vending customers as well as numerous on-site locations.
- Reduced food costs district-wide by 3%, dramatically increasing bottom-line profitability.

DISTRICT FOOD SERVICE DIRECTOR. American Industries, Quincy, MA (1996-01). Oversaw district-wide operations of 27 full service business/industrial cafeterias which also supported vending operations, including on-site management of a commissary which served 2,100 meals daily and functioned additionally as a catering service.
- Supervised and directed the training and development of 160 personnel, including 15 salaried employees and 145 hourly associates.
- Developed and sustained strong relationships with existing customers as well as building new business to ensure long-term stability of the company's client base.

INDEPENDENT FOOD SERVICE CONSULTANT. Self-employed, Worcester, MA (1994-95). Provided consultation to troubled food service operations, offering process reengineering and staff development suggestions to improve operational efficiency.
- Analyzed existing procedures, developing new concepts to improve customer service and efficiency; modified existing operations to ensure profitability.

DIRECTOR OF CASH OPERATIONS, FOOD SERVICE. Rogers Food Service Management, Inc., Westfield, MA (1993-94). Directed multiunit food service business for the Bean Street operation at the Westfield State College.
- Managed nine separate profit points as well as five independent satellite units, a full-service cafeteria, and a catering department. Served as many as 5,000 customers daily, generating cash sales of $2.3 million annually, including $545,000 per year from catering.

Highlights of earlier experience: **RESTAURANT MANAGER.** Lowry Foods Co., Worcester, MA. Oversaw all aspects of the operation of a local independent cafeteria, including planning and developing the concept, conducting lease negotiations, and financial responsibility for approximately $860,000 in annual sales.

EDUCATION

Completed college courses in Professional Food Service Management and Management Leadership and Development at the New England Culinary Institute and Westfield College.

PERSONAL

Outstanding personal and professional references are available upon request.

Date

Exact Name of Person
Title or Position
Name of Company
Address (number and street)
Address (city, state, and zip)

MULTIUNIT MANAGER
for a restaurant group

Dear Exact Name of Person: (or Sir or Madam if answering a blind ad)

With the enclosed resume, I would like to make you aware of my interest in joining your management team in some capacity which could utilize my proven skills in strategic planning, operations management, new venture startup, and troubled unit turnaround.

I am currently working as a Multi-Unit Manager with the Sanders Restaurant Group in northern Louisiana where I have made dramatic improvements in lowering food costs while increasing unit controllable income, boosting unit net income, and strengthening customer service. In addition to retraining employees and developing three new General Managers who are excelling in their jobs, I have led the company in producing the highest gross profit margin.

As you will see from my resume, I worked in the Netherlands for ten years. My wife is Dutch and I speak Dutch proficiently. While working for EJH Consulting in Rotterdam, I earned a reputation as a creative and resourceful management consultant. I enjoyed helping business executives make wise investments in the Dutch market and I trained numerous area supervisors in effective management techniques. Projects in which I was involved included establishing a 47-unit restaurant facility in Maastricht; developing the strategic plan for an $11 million restaurant; and transforming a downtown bus station in Amsterdam into a 32-floor Marriot Hotel with restaurants on nine different floors. I helped Kentucky Fried Chicken establish its first 35 restaurants in the Dutch and Austrian markets. In that position I oversaw a 450-person work force which was only 5% American.

With a reputation as a dynamic and creative manager with unlimited personal initiative and superior problem-solving skills, I am confident that I could become a valuable addition to your outstanding management team. If you can use a top performer with the proven ability to positively impact the bottom line, I hope you will contact me to suggest a time when we might meet to discuss your goals and how I might help you achieve them. I can provide outstanding personal and professional references at the appropriate time.

Sincerely,

Caleb D. Williams

CALEB D. WILLIAMS

1110½ Hay Street, Fayetteville, NC 28305   •   preppub@aol.com   •   (910) 483-6611

OBJECTIVE

To contribute to an organization that can use a vivacious and enthusiastic problem solver who has excelled in both management consulting and line management positions internationally while helping companies in the hospitality industry to improve their sales, customer service, quality assurance, profitability, market share, and cost control.

EXPERIENCE

MULTIUNIT MANAGER. Sanders Restaurant Group, Northern Louisiana (2003-present). For this 1100-unit restaurant concern, have combined my leadership skills and technical expertise in producing the following results in six units in northern LA.
- Reduced food costs by 6% ($120,000 yearly); lowered food costs from 29% to 23.02%.
- Raised average sales ticket by 15%; increased unit controllable income by 4% ($245,000 yearly) and boosted net unit income by 15% ($150,000) annually.
- Produced the highest gross profit in the company (73.15% versus 65% industry standard).

OPERATIONS CONSULTANT. EJH Consulting, Rotterdam, Netherlands (2002-03). As a management consultant for this international consulting group, played a key role in helping business executives make wise investments in the Dutch market while also training area supervisors to utilize effective management styles; was involved in these and other areas:

Concept adaptation from English to Dutch	Service operations training
Multi-Unit management training	Project management
New venture start-ups	Turning around unprofitable units
Market analysis, sales, and pricing decisions	Profitability management

- Played a key role in establishing a new 47-unit restaurant facility in Maastricht.
- For the Dutch Railroad, Inc., helped develop the strategic plan for an $11 million restaurant called "Depot Cafe" which achieved $11 million in sales annually (this restaurant serves only two meals a day with a modest capacity of 290 seats!)
- From the concept stage to operational reality, provided leadership in transforming a main downtown bus station in Amsterdam into a 32-floor Marriot Hotel with restaurants on nine different floors.

MULTIUNIT RESTAURANT MANAGER. Department of Transportation, the Netherlands (1996-2002). In this international environment, managed 15 restaurants as well as six school cafeterias. Hired, trained, managed, and continuously developed 450 employees in a work force which was only 5% American.
- Helped Kentucky Fried Chicken establish its first 35 restaurants in the Dutch/Austrian market, and functioned as a consultant in helping KFC maximize profitability.
- In Maastricht, opened the largest food court ever located in a shopping mall in the country; with 18,000 sq. ft., the facility produced $8 million in annual sales.

RESTAURANT MANAGER. Chippers, Rotterdam, The Netherlands (1993-95). Worked as the Kitchen Manager and Restaurant Manager for this popular local "American" restaurant.

CHEF & FULL-SERVICE COOK. Stella's, Monroe, LA (1987-93). Began working for this full-service restaurant when I was 14 years old; in my junior year, helped the company establish its second restaurant in Lafayette, LA; became a Chef upon high school graduation.

EDUCATION

Extensive executive development training sponsored by organizations including Kentucky Fried Chicken, EJH Consulting, and other organizations.

PERSONAL

Excellent references. I am married to a Dutch wife and speak Dutch proficiently.

GWENDOLYN M. JARVIS

1110½ Hay Street, Fayetteville, NC 28305   •   preppub@aol.com   •   (910) 483-6611

NUTRITIONIST

in a public health department

GOAL

I would like to be accepted for an internship in dietetics at Belmont University; my long-term goal is to make significant contributions to the field through combining my strong communication skills, solid educational background, and creativity, while working toward my ultimate goal of becoming a clinical dietitian in a pediatrics setting.

RESEARCH INTEREST

Have a strong research interest in the nutritional status of high-risk children, and have had some experience in working with children; intend to pursue a master's degree in the future so that I can be even better equipped to play a role in reducing infant mortality.

PUBLICATIONS

Designed and drafted a brochure detailing the importance of the vitamin folate in the diets of women during childbearing age.
Created a brochure and designed a lesson plan to inform people about lactose intolerance which is used by the Florence County Health Department; the brochure gives tips for easing symptoms of lactose intolerance and provides examples of calcium-rich foods that contain little or no lactose.

PHILOSOPHY OF DIETETICS

Believe that the field of dietetics is the vital component in preventive medicine, and am excited about the prospect of making professional contributions in the area of maternal and child care services; believe strongly that prevention is the best medicine.

HONOR

Was nominated Chairperson of National Nutrition Month (March 2002), and organized memorable activities based on the theme "Nutrition Fuels Fitness."
- Organized activities to educate employees and clients of the Davis County Health Department about National Nutrition Month.
- Created a weight loss contest among employees which offered prizes of free memberships at local health clubs.
- Provided weekly educational materials about nutrition and fitness for clients and employees.

EXPERIENCE

NUTRITIONIST II and **WIC SITE SUPERVISOR.** Florence County Health Department; Women, Infants, and Children (WIC) Clinic, Florence, SC (2003-present). At the local Health Department, have been promoted to supervise five staff members who include three clerks, a Nutritionist I, and a medical assistant; simultaneously manage a caseload of 2500 participants in this prevention/wellness/nutrition program.
- Designed internal office procedures including the scheduling of appointments.
- Counsel high-risk clients and make referrals to medical and social services agencies.

NUTRITIONIST I. Florence County Health Department, WIC at FCHD, Florence, SC (2002-03). Was promoted to the job above because of my hard work and excellent performance in this job; on my own initiative, designed a brochure about lactose intolerance which eliminated confusion about the difference between lactose intolerance and milk allergies.

- Made clients more aware of the lactose intolerance food packages offered by WIC.
- Provided nutritional counseling to WIC participants on various nutrition and health-related topics.
- Learned how to manage a WIC office which was outside the health department.
- Was trained to collect blood for hematocrits in the absence of the nurse.

NUTRITIONIST I. Davis County Health Department, Aiken, SC (2001-02). Became aware of the importance of rural public health services while working in one of the state's poorest areas.

- Collected medical histories as well as anthropometric and biochemical data while evaluating dietary recalls necessary to certify patients for the WIC Program.
- Provided nutrition counseling and education materials to clients.
- Designed individual care plans and food packages for clients.
- Referred clients to various medical and social agencies.
- Member of the Mobile WIC Satellite Team.

Other experience:
In order to finance my college education, worked in these jobs related to nutrition, food service, dietetic research, and human relations.
FOOD SERVICE TECHNICIAN. USC-Clinical Research Unit at USC Hospitals, Columbia, SC (2001). Assisted the dietitians and food service staff members while also preparing and delivering food trays to patients, delivering menus to patients, and analyzing patients' food consumption after meals; stripped trays.

FIT STOP VOLUNTEER. USC Wellness Center, Columbia, SC (2000-01). Performed anthropometric measurements and other fitness tests on UNC students and employees; then analyzed and explained test results to clients and suggested improvements in the areas in which they scored below average.

- This job was the one which "opened my eyes" to the general public's need for well-written and well-researched nutrition and health education materials.

HABILITATION SUPERVISOR. Helping Hands Residential Services, Columbia, SC (2000). Developed a patient attitude while working with five mentally retarded residents of the group home; supervised two staff members.

- Administered medications to residents at scheduled times.

PHARMACY VOLUNTEER. St. Joseph Hospital, Florence, SC (1998). Volunteered in the St. Joseph Hospital Pharmacy at a point when I was considering becoming a pharmacist.

EDUCATION

Earned a **Bachelor of Science in Public Health,** University of South Carolina; majored in Nutrition with a minor in Chemistry; Columbia, SC, 2001.
Have completed continuing education courses at Francis Marion University and Florence-Darlington Technical College; courses included Spanish, computer operations, abnormal psychology, as well as two chemistry courses to upgrade my previous course grades.

AFFILIATIONS

American Dietetic Association
University of South Carolina General Alumni Association

PERSONAL

Read numerous magazines and journals to keep abreast of nutrition topics and developments in dietetics. Read monthly ADA journals, NCDA newsletters, and Dietetic newsletters.

CAREER CHANGE

Date

Exact Name of Person
Title or Position
Name of Company
Address (number and street)
Address (city, state, and ZIP)

OPERATIONS MANAGER
for a small restaurant. This
individual seeks a career
change back into the law
enforcement field.

Dear Exact Name of Person: (or Dear Sir or Madam if answering a blind ad)

I would appreciate an opportunity to talk with you soon about how I could contribute to your organization through my experience and reputation for effectiveness in prioritizing and organizing activities, maximizing human as well as material and fiscal resources, and dealing with others effectively.

As you will see from my enclosed resume, I offer a history of success in positions that require the ability to think and react quickly as well as those in which organizational, managerial, and customer service skills are required. Both as a security/law enforcement professional and in my present position, I have built a clean driving record while familiarizing myself with the geographical layout and locations throughout the city and county.

In addition to strong computer skills, I can provide an employer with a dependable, honest, and assertive professional who can make a difference through a strong customer-service orientation.

I hope you will welcome my call soon to arrange a brief meeting at your convenience to discuss your current and future needs and how I might serve them. Thank you in advance for your time.

Sincerely yours.

Daniel J. Pope

Alternate last paragraph:
I hope you will call or write me soon to suggest a time convenient for us to meet and discuss your current and future needs and how I might serve them. Thank you in advance for your time.

DANIEL JEREMY POPE

1110½ Hay Street, Fayetteville, NC 28305　　•　　preppub@aol.com　　•　　(910) 483-6611

OBJECTIVE

To offer my experience and reputation for reliability, honesty, and dependability to an organization that can use a mature professional who offers a clean driving record, knowledge of the city and county, and a history of effectiveness with the public and coworkers.

EXPERIENCE

OPERATIONS MANAGER. Billy's BBQ, Austin, TX (2003-present). Refined my managerial abilities while handling a wide range of administrative functions in this busy family-owned restaurant:

accounting — handle payroll and daily sales journals

inventory control — make decisions on what is needed and order food including perishable/nonperishable food as well as supplies

planning — make arrangements for parties and various catered events

driving and making deliveries — unload stock and drive company vehicles in order to make deliveries as well as pick up supplies

dealing with others — consult with vendors, supervise employees, and deal regularly with members of the public

financing — handle the store's finances and business dealings

- Have gained further experience in the areas of time management, prioritizing and organizing multiple activities, and scheduling.

DESK SERGEANT and **DEPUTY SHERIFF.** Jefferson County Sheriff's Department, Austin, TX (1999-2003). Handled a wide range of activities including using computers on a regular basis to prepare reports and maintain records, responding to complaints, and making decisions on how to respond to situations as they arose.

- Built a "clean" driving record while becoming familiar with the county and city's streets and geographical locations.
- As a Desk Sergeant, made daily briefings to personnel on activities and events they needed to have knowledge of.
- Earned a reputation as a patient and understanding person and good listener.
- Became effective in prioritizing demands on limited human resources and in organizing responses in order to get the most out of personnel.

SECURITY OFFICER and **COLLEGE STUDENT.** Austin Community College (ACC), Austin, TX (1993-99). Juggled the demands of attending college and working part time for the ACC campus security office.

EDUCATION

A.A., Law and Criminal Justice, Austin Community College, Austin, TX, 1999.
Studied Business Management at the University of Texas-Austin.

- While attending both schools, completed specialized coursework including the following subjects:
  business management — organizing and prioritizing activities and maximizing human resources; accounting; stress management and human behavior; use and applications for PCs; and First Aid/First Responder training for Emergency Medical Technicians
- Am proficient in using Apple and IBM-compatible computers.

PERSONAL

Am proud of my reputation as a persistent and determined person who will not rest until the job is done. Always give 100% and believe in striving for one's personal best. Am dependable, punctual, and reliable.

Date

Exact Name of Person
Title or Position
Name of Company
Address (number and street)
Address (city, state, and ZIP)

OWNER/OPERATOR
of a restaurant business. After taking a break from the hospitality industry, this individual seeks to return to the restaurant business.

Dear Exact Name of Person: (or Dear Sir or Madam if answering a blind as.)

With the enclosed resume, I would like to make you aware of my background as an experienced hospitality industry manager who offers proven supervisory and guest services skills and a track record of success as Owner/Operator and General Manager of a number of local establishments. I am responding to your recent advertisement for General Manager of a restaurant serving the Missoula Golf and Tennis Club.

In one position in the hospitality industry, I purchased a 150-seat restaurant and 50-seat lounge from a large chain. I changed the restaurant's name and developed a new, expanded menu while implementing higher levels of guest service. I directed the work of the front end, bar, and kitchen managers, overseeing a staff of 25 employees. Previously at George's Restaurant and Tavern, we dealt with a large client base of repeat customers, arranging reservations at local golf courses as well as serving their dining needs.

For the past year, I have excelled as Business Manager of Seller's Paint, helping my brother to set up his commercial paint contracting business. Now that his business is up and running, I am very interested in returning to the hospitality industry, and my wife and I are considering relocation to the Missoula area. I feel that my strong management background and proven skills in customer service, staff development, and training would make me a valuable addition to your operation.

When we meet in person, you will see that I am a friendly and personable professional with a lifelong interest in golf and practical experience in operations management that could make me an ideal candidate for this position. I can assure you in advance that I have an outstanding reputation and would quickly become a valuable asset to your organization.

Yours sincerely,

George Martin Moore

GEORGE MARTIN MOORE

1110½ Hay Street, Fayetteville, NC 28305 • preppub@aol.com • (910) 483-6611

OBJECTIVE

To benefit an organization that can use an experienced hospitality industry professional with exceptional communication and customer service skills who offers a track record of accomplishment in facility management.

EDUCATION

Studied biology and general college courses at the University of Montana-Missoula. Graduated from Helena Senior High School, Helena, MT, 1978.

EXPERIENCE

BUSINESS MANAGER. Seller's Paint, Bozeman, MT (2003-present). Co-responsible for all aspects of the operation of this successful painting contractor; developed relationships with a number of business accounts in Montana, building a strong client base for the company.
- Serviced a number of convenience store accounts including SuperAmerica, Exxon, and Gas 'N' Sip; painted and refurbished stores throughout the chain.
- Built a rapport with building contractors and construction companies, providing painting services for new construction and existing structures.

OWNER/OPERATOR. George's Restaurant and Tavern, Helena, MT (1990-2003). Purchased this 150-seat restaurant and 50-seat lounge from the Western Steer chain, developing a slightly different menu and service style.
- Oversaw managers and a kitchen, host, and wait staff totaling 25 employees.
- Directed managers in performance of daily operations, including food and beverage orders and menu planning.
- Sold the restaurant to a competitor.

GENERAL MANAGER. Friendly's, Bozeman, MT (1988-90).
Supervised 110 employees at this restaurant at a busy mall location.

GENERAL MANAGER. Big Sky Grill, Bozeman, MT (1985-87).
As general manager, supervised a kitchen and wait staff of 22 employees.

OWNER/OPERATOR. George's Deli, Missoula, MT (1984-85).
Controlled all daily operations and supervised 15 employees.

GENERAL MANAGER. Friendly's, Missoula, MT (1983-84).
Set up equipment, hired staff, and managed 125 employees.

Rapidly progressed in this "Track Record" with Western Steer, 1979-83:
GENERAL MANAGER. Was promoted from Assistant Manager after only five months in the Missoula, MT, location to General Manager supervising up to 35 employees at the Bozeman, Billings, and then Helena, MT locations.
- Helped set up equipment and hired the startup crew for the Bozeman, Billings, and Helena restaurants.

PERSONAL

Excellent personal and professional references are available upon request.

CAREER CHANGE

Exact Name of Person
Title or Position
Name of Company
Address (no., street)
Address (city, state, zip)

PACKAGE HANDLER

Although this individual has restaurant experience, he is moving in a different career direction. He seeks to make a career in the automotive industry, and he has used his restaurant industry experience to gain customer service skills.

Dear Exact Name of Person: (or Dear Sir or Madam if answering a blind ad)

I am sending you the enclosed resume to express my interest in joining your organization. You will see that I have recently completed the Autobody Repair Course at Scott Community College.

Currently I am working with the Food Lion grocery chain as a package handler loading trucks, sorting packages, and performing a variety of jobs related to keeping the warehouse clean and organized. Previously, I held a position with Connor Farms in Bettendorf, IA for several years. I began working on the farm at a young age and gained vast experience in operating, repairing and maintaining an expensive inventory of farm equipment as well as planting and cropping tobacco and grains. I offer exceptionally strong mechanical and technical problem-solving skills.

I hope you will call or write soon to suggest a time convenient for us to meet and discuss your current and future needs and how I might serve them. Thank you in advance for your time.

Sincerely yours,

Marcus D. Stevenson

MARCUS D. STEVENSON

1110½ Hay Street, Fayetteville, NC 28305 • preppub@aol.com • (910) 483-6611

OBJECTIVE   I want to benefit an organization that can use a dedicated and hardworking young professional with excellent sales and customer service skills.

EDUCATION   Completed Autobody Repair Course, Scott Community College, Bettendorf, IA, 2003. Received high school diploma from Scott Community College, Bettendorf, IA, 2001.

EXPERIENCE   **PACKAGE HANDLER.** Food Lion Packing, Fort Dodge, IA (2002-present). Stock refrigerated road trucks with boxed food and produce and ensure that packages are located correctly in the warehouse for stocking into proper trucks.
  - Perform numerous jobs in the warehouse related to keeping the warehouse in an organized and clean condition.
  - Sort packages coming off the conveyor belt.
  - Handle labeling, scanning, and taping.
  - Have worked in this full-time job while completing the Autobody Repair Course.

FARM LABORER & EQUIPMENT OPERATOR. Connor Farms, Bettendorf, IA (1997-2002). Began work on this family farm when I was 14 years old, and gained vast experience in operating, repairing, and maintaining an expensive inventory of farm equipment which included tractors, combines, light trucks, grain trucks, and other equipment.
  - Drove tractor and was recognized for my safe driving habits.
  - Participated in all phases of planting and landscaping.
  - Repaired wood slats and other equipment and fixtures related to farm property.
  - Cropped and topped tobacco.
  - Helped unload grain from combine into grain truck.
  - Performed preventive maintenance on equipment, vehicles, and machinery.

DISHWASHER & COOK. Roger's Grille, Bettendorf, IA (2002). For a six-month period of time, became a valuable employee of this restaurant, and learned to perform nearly every job related to food preparation.
  - Acted as Prep Cook; stocked the refrigerator, freezer, and pantry.
  - Participated in all aspects of maintaining the restaurant in a sanitary and clean condition.
  - Washed dishes, stocked dishes on the line, cleaned cooking equipment, sanitized cooking service, made sauces, and picked up supplies.

DISHWASHER & COOK. Darryl's Restaurant, Bettendorf, IA (2000-01). While earning my high school degree, worked at this popular family restaurant.
  - Earned a reputation as a reliable, hardworking, and dependable employee

PERSONAL   Interests include college and professional football, motor sports, reading, and collecting knives. Can provide outstanding personal and professional references.

Date

Exact Name of Person
Exact Title
Exact Name of Company
Address
City, State, Zip

PASTRY CHEF

with administrative skills
wants full-time
employment as a pastry
chef.

Dear Exact Name of Person (or Dear Sir or Madam if answering a blind ad):

With the enclosed resume, I would like to express my interest in exploring employment opportunities with your organization. I will be relocating to the Chicago area in the near future and would like to meet to discuss your organization's needs.

As you will see from my resume, I have specialized in the food service field. While developing excellent culinary and food service management skills, I have gained experience as a Purchasing Manager, Pastry Chef, Night Shift Supervisor, and Shift Manager. I have won gold, silver, and bronze medals in international competitions testing my skills in 4-plated desserts, petit fours, and 5-course meals.

I have also excelled in and received multiple other awards for my skills in catering, creating banquets, and servicing special ceremonies. I have been continually singled out for my "positive attitude" and "tireless ability to take charge."

Most recently I have succeeded in a position in which I manage the purchasing of perishable and   semi-perishable food items for the daily needs of twenty-seven restaurants located in the "food court" area of the Rio Hotel and Casino in Las Vegas, NV. This is a fast paced and extremely popular eating spot for both locals and tourists and requires the utmost care and attention to detail to ensure smooth operation.

If you can use a versatile food service professional who is an accomplished chef, I encourage you to contact me to suggest a time when we might talk about your needs. I can provide outstanding references at the appropriate time.

Yours sincerely,

Derek R. Truesdale

DEREK RILEY TRUESDALE

1110½ Hay Street, Fayetteville, NC 28305 • preppub@aol.com • (910) 483-6611

OBJECTIVE   To pursue a position with an organization that can use an award-winning chef who offers expert skills in the culinary arts; along with experience in food service management and customer service.

HONORS   Selected for the Rio Hotel and Casino Culinary Arts Team which competed in a nationwide competition held in Las Vegas.
- Won a **Gold, Silver and Bronze Medal** in a culinary arts competition in Reno, NV, 2000.
- Received **Best in Show** award in a culinary arts show in San Francisco, CA, 1999.
- Named **Junior Chef of the Year, National Culinary Arts Convention,** Chicago, 1995.

TRAINING   Culinary Principles I & II, Culinary Institute of America, Hyde Park, NY, 1994.
Menu Planning, Culinary Institute of America, Hyde Park, NY, 1994.
ServSafe Food Protection Manager course, Culinary Institute of America, Hyde Park, NY, 1994.
Food Service Specialist Course, Genesee Community College, Batavia, NY, 1993.

EXPERIENCE   **ADMINISTRATIVE SUPERVISOR.** Food Court, Rio Hotel and Casino, Las Vegas, NV (2003-present). Involved in purchasing and other administrative activities related to providing food service for the 27 restaurants in the food court area of this popular casino and hotel.
- Used UNIX based system to track account status and expenditure reports.

PURCHASING MANAGER. Food Court, Rio Hotel and Casino, Las Vegas, NV (2002-03). Handled the purchasing and receiving of perishable and nonperishable food needed to stock the kitchens of 27 different restaurants in the food court area of this popular casino and restaurant.
- Reorganized the stock control system to decrease inventory size by 12%.

SHIFT MANAGER. Vincenzo's, Rio Hotel and Casino, Las Vegas, NV (2000-01). Managed a shift of eight cooks involved in the preparation of main entrees, short order items, and salads in a fine Italian restaurant located inside a popular hotel and casino.
- Assigned work and scheduled employees to ensure appropriate coverage and control labor hours. Increased shift productivity through job specialization.
- Placed orders and conducted regular inventories to maintain adequate stock levels.

PASTRY CHEF & NIGHT SHIFT SUPERVISOR. Gold Coast Casino, Las Vegas, NV (1999-2000). Supervised seven bakers in the preparation and production of bread, pastries, cakes, and yeast dough. Catered banquets and buffets for ceremonies and conventions.

PASTRY CHEF. Le Matin Bakery, San Francisco, CA (1997-99). Served as a chef in a four-person crew responsible for baking various pastries to include fruit tortes and numerous French specialties. Created new dessert menu which was instrumental in increasing business by 10% for two consecutive years.

LINE COOK. Rialto Restaurant, San Francisco, CA (1994-97). Gained expertise in preparing all types of soups, salads, and appetizers in this fine dining establishment.
- Learned about the importance of presentation. At the National Culinary Arts Convention competition in Chicago, I was named Junior Chef of the Year, 1995.

CAREER CHANGE

Date

Exact Name of Person
Title or Position
Name of Company
Address (no., street)
Address (city, state, zip)

RESTAURANT CONSULTANT

with startup experience seeks her first management job in the restaurant field. So far this individual has had more success finding employment in retail than in restaurant environments.

Dear Exact Name of Person: (or Dear Sir or Madam if answering a blind ad)

I am interested in gaining employment with your organization and would like to ask you to consider my qualifications based upon my enclosed resume. I am a creative, innovative, and results-oriented professional who offers knowledge, education, and experience related to the food and hospitality industry along with a strong background in sales and marketing.

You will see from my enclosed resume that I graduated with honors from the Culinary Arts Program of Tacoma Community College in Tacoma, WA, where I was named to the President's Honor Roll. While attending this school, I displayed organizational, time management, and planning skills while simultaneously excelling in a sales and consulting job in the art field, developing an effective business plan for a new restaurant, working as a chef's apprentice, and working in a college catering division.

My education in menu design, kitchen design, and restaurant management allowed me to develop a proposal for a restaurant. My plans received approval and my partner and I gained loans from two major banks. As a result, the Hamlet Café opened in Olympia, WA, and is an effective ongoing business.

As an Apprentice Chef for Tacoma Community College, I gained experience in a profit-making food service business which served 500 people daily with breakfast and lunch while also catering numerous banquets and buffet meals. During one six-month period, I assisted a chef in a wide range of food preparation, cooking, and serving dinners, banquets, and buffet meals for various community and college events.

If you can use a versatile, adaptable, and mature professional with a reputation as an innovative and creative individual, I hope you will contact me soon to suggest a time when we might have a brief discussion of how I could contribute to your organization. I can provide excellent professional and personal references at the appropriate time.

Sincerely,

Miranda C. Turner

MIRANDA C. TURNER

1110½ Hay Street, Fayetteville, NC 28305   •   preppub@aol.com   •   (910) 483-6611

OBJECTIVE   To offer my experience in the food and hospitality industry as well as my strong sales and marketing skills to an organization that can use a creative and artistic professional known for possessing "an eye for detail" along with a commitment to aggressive bottom-line results.

EDUCATION   **A.A.S., Culinary Arts,** Tacoma Community College, Tacoma, WA, 2003.
- Maintained a 3.98 GPA and was named to the President's Honor Roll; refined my time management skills working simultaneously in sales and food service jobs.
- Was an Apprentice for six months to the chef in the school catering division.

AFFILIATION   Member, American Culinary Federation and National Restaurant Association.

EXPERIENCE   **ASSISTANT MANAGER.** Lerner, Inc., Tacoma, WA (2003-present). Provide support for the store manager in all phases of operations of a high-end retail clothing store which averages $2 million in annual sales.
- Trained and now supervise and motivate three sales associates: the store has increased sales over the previous year's figures. Coordinate planograms and merchandise displays.
- Made recommendations which reduced loss and shrinkage.

APPRENTICE CHEF. Tacoma Community College, Tacoma, WA (2000-03). Refined my culinary arts skills in a profit-making cafeteria while rotating through stations to prep, cook, and serve breakfast and lunch menus for 500 people daily while also providing lunch for 35 children in the school's child development center.
- Mentored new students in baking, soups and sauces, and the prep line.
- As a **Catering Representative,** worked with chefs while planning, preparing food for, and catering special events including a sit-down graduation dinner for 150 people.

SALES REPRESENTATIVE & ART CONSULTANT (Part-Time, Saturdays & Sundays). Green Forest Trading Post, Tacoma, WA (2000-03). While attending college and working full-time in the job above as an Apprentice Chef, also worked part-time at a large trading post attraction, applied my expertise in Southwestern and Native American art; educated clients and attracted new clients to this gallery visited by thousands weekly.
- Developed relationships with artists; bought and displayed high-quality merchandise.
- Sold high-dollar art, including custom paper art, worth thousands of dollars in this gallery which was ranked number one for the region of Star Company merchandise.

ASSISTANT TO THE PLANT MANAGER. Fowler's Uniform Service, Olympia, WA (1997-99). Handled a wide range of duties as Assistant to the Plant Manager: Was the buyer for contracted services, supervised assembly workers, negotiated with vendors, controlled inventory, advised sales personnel of contractual matters, and operated computers.

OUTSIDE SALES REPRESENTATIVE. Advantage Advertising, Olympia, WA (1996-97). Refined my communication, marketing, and sales skills while assessing customer needs, making cold calls, creating sales promotions, and attending trade shows.

Highlights of earlier experience: As **Sales Manager** for the cosmetics department of Nordstrom's Department Store in Seattle, WA, consistently ranked in the top three in fragrance launches for the company as a whole.

PERSONAL   Excellent references upon request.

Exact Name of Person
Title or Position
Name of Company
Address (number and street)
Address (city, state, and zip)

RESTAURANT GENERAL MANAGER

for a Joe's Crab Shack franchise

Dear Exact Name of Person: (or Sir or Madam if answering a blind ad)

I would appreciate an opportunity to talk with you soon about how I could contribute to your "bottom line" through my proven management abilities and outstanding motivational and communication skills as well as my knowledge of inventory control and budgeting.

As you will see from my resume, I am presently the General Manager of a Joe's Crab Shack franchise and have been successful in increasing sales from 10 to 15% over the previous year's figures. I have been effective in managing a 74-person operation while ensuring complete and accurate record keeping, controlling inventory, and ensuring compliance with sanitation standards.

Earlier I advanced from Assistant Manager to Store Manager overseeing 15 employees while becoming knowledgeable of all aspects of restaurant functions.

I am certain that I could contribute through my reputation as a well-rounded manager with outstanding organizational, planning, and motivational abilities.

I hope you will call or write soon to suggest a time convenient for us to meet and discuss your current and future needs and how I might serve them. Thank you in advance for your time.

Sincerely yours,

Gregory Terrence Yates

GREGORY TERRENCE YATES

1110½ Hay Street, Fayetteville, NC 28305　•　preppub@aol.com　•　(910) 483-6611

OBJECTIVE	To contribute my management experience as well as my knowledge of operations including inventory control, budgeting, and sales to an organization in need of a skilled communicator, motivator, and supervisor.
EXPERIENCE	**GENERAL MANAGER**. Joe's Crab Shack, Mobile, AL. (2003-present). Supervise 74 employees while overseeing operational areas including controlling inventory, labor, costs, and compliance with health and safety regulations.

- Earned recognition for my efforts which resulted in increasing sales figures approximately 10 to 15% over those of the previous year.
- Maintain all records from food ordering and purchasing to cost controls and payroll information on the Norand computer system.
- Excel in managing employees and training them to achieve effective increases in profitability and customer satisfaction.
- Was officially commended for achieving the franchise's second highest sales record.

Earned advancement in management roles with Waffle House, Inc., Dothan, AL:
RESTAURANT MANAGER. (2001-03). Was promoted from Assistant Manager to oversee all functional areas in a food service operation with approximately 15 employees.

- Refined my skills in numerous areas including inventory, labor, and cost control.

ASSISTANT MANAGER. (1998-2000). Increased my knowledge of restaurant management operations while handling all functional areas from inventory control to hiring/training/firing employees.

- Learned to communicate effectively and tactfully with customers and employees.

RESTAURANT WORKER. Maury's Restaurant, Muscle Shoals, AL (1997). Earned a reputation as a hardworking and dependable employee as a "bus boy" in a busy family restaurant.

Other experience: Applied my abilities in planning and organizing production while printing textiles as a Screen Printer, L.D. Fields, Muscle Shoals, AL.

TRAINING	Completed 32 hours of **"Food Service and Sanitation"** training, Bishop State Community College, Mobile, AL. Received almost 100 hours of corporate-sponsored management training.
EDUCATION	Completed Computer Operations courses at Northwest Shoals Community College, Muscle Shoals, AL.
PERSONAL	Am known for my ability to motivate employees and encourage them to put forth their best efforts. Offer a background of expertise in handling finances and records. Will relocate.

Exact Name of Person
Title or Position
Name of Company
Address (no., street)
Address (city, state, zip)

RESTAURANT GENERAL MANAGER

for Shoney's Restaurant

Dear Exact Name of Person: (or Dear Sir or Madam if answering a blind ad)

I would appreciate an opportunity to talk with you soon about how I could contribute to your organization through my thorough knowledge of food service management and my outstanding abilities related to training, developing teams, and maximizing human resources.

You will notice from my resume that I intended to spend my working life in academic environments, and I taught English as a College Professor. Subsequently I became interested in the restaurant business and earned a Master's degree in Nutrition and Food Service Management. Subsequently I worked in both cafeteria and restaurant environments.

I enjoy the challenge of working in a high-volume food service establishment and, as you will see from my resume, I offer skills in training, supervision, and management. I am quite experienced in the areas of preparing menus, using progressive cooking techniques to avoid waste, and in making attractive and creative food offerings using high quality ingredients.

My reputation as a creative manager has been established in situations where I have increased sales, reduced waste and food costs, virtually eliminated turnover and overtime, and trained skilled employees.

I hope you will welcome my call soon to arrange a brief meeting at your convenience to discuss your current and future needs and how I might serve them. Thank you in advance for your time.

Sincerely yours,

Scott Nathaniel Spencer

Alternate last paragraph:
I hope you will call or write soon to suggest a time convenient for us to meet and discuss your current and future needs and how I might serve them. Thank you in advance for your time.

1110½ Hay Street, Fayetteville, NC 28305   •   preppub@aol.com   •   (910) 483-6611

OBJECTIVE	To apply my talent for developing productive teams of employees and making the most effective use of available human resources as well as my thorough knowledge of service operations management and inventory control.
EXPERIENCE	**GENERAL MANAGER.** Shoney's Restaurant (formerly Golden Family Restaurant), Austin, TX (2001-present). Began with this company as a cook and was rapidly promoted into management in the following "track record" of assignments:

- When the company went through a name change and corporate reorganization in 2002, was handpicked as **General Manager** because of my proven ability to implement new ideas and instill in employees a sense of pride in performing quality work; excel in controlling costs, building sales, improving internal communication, and creating effective menus.
- As **Operations Manager** of Golden Family Restaurant in 2002, trained and supervised 60 employees while handling all hiring, firing, and training for this restaurant; developed a new "team spirit" that led to a dramatic decrease in employee turnover while also instituting careful rotation of stock to reduce waste and assure freshness.
- As **Assistant Manager** of Golden Family Restaurant from 2001-02, decreased overtime 90%, increased sales 10%, and reduced food costs 3%.
- Began as a **Cook** in 2001 and frequently cooked all three meals daily while working from 4 am past 6 pm; reorganized cooking operations in order to reduce waste and maximize time efficiencies.

OPERATIONS MANAGER. Morrison's Cafeteria, locations throughout TX (1996-2001). Played a key role in setting up new restaurant operations "from scratch" while working in more than 10 different locations; earned a reputation as a creative troubleshooter and problem solver while hiring, training, and supervising dining room and serving line employees.

COLLEGE INSTRUCTOR. Middlebury College, Middlebury, VT (1990-91).
Taught college English courses, including freshman grammar and literature.

Other experience: Extensively traveled and worked throughout Europe prior to enrolling in my Master's degree program in 1994.

EDUCATION	**Master's degree in Nutrition and Food Service Management,** the University of Texas at Austin, 1996.

- Major area of study was **nutrition and food service management**.

B.A. in Journalism, Temple University, Philadelphia, PA, 1987.
B.A. in Business, Rhode Island College, Providence, Rhode Island, 1983.
Studied Creative Writing and Literature, University of Alberta, Edmonton, Canada, 1988-89.

TECHNICAL SKILLS	Extensive knowledge of computerized systems for inventory control and spreadsheet analysis. Knowledgeable of commercial food preparation equipment such as: deep fryers, steamers, convection ovens, flat-top grills, and steam tables.
PERSONAL	Am a creative professional with an ability to motivate employees to do their best. Offer a strong "bottom-line" orientation; am skilled in cutting costs.

Exact Name of Person
Title or Position
Name of Company
Address (no., street)
Address (city, state, zip)

**RESTAURANT GENERAL
MANAGER**

with a chic cafe

Dear Exact Name of Person: (or Dear Sir or Madam if answering a blind ad)

I would appreciate an opportunity to talk with you soon about how I could contribute to your organization through my thorough knowledge of food service management and my outstanding abilities related to training teams, developing marketing and promotional programs, and increasing profits.

As you will see from my resume, I offer experience in managing both a fine dining local restaurant as well as a large national chain. I am quite experienced in the areas of planning, human resources management, and marketing support. I recently negotiated a three-year contract with the local coliseum that has already proved highly successful for the restaurant.

Before I entered the hospitality industry I excelled in various sales and marketing positions in the radio industry in Tallahassee. I believe that this background coupled with my Bachelor's of Science degree in Communications has enabled me to become a valuable asset to any organization.

I hope you will welcome my call soon to arrange a brief meeting at your convenience to discuss your current and future needs and how I might serve them. Thank you in advance for your time.

Sincerely yours,

Reuben Wright

Alternate last paragraph:
I hope you will call or write soon to suggest a time convenient for us to meet and discuss your current and future needs and how I might serve them. Thank you in advance for your time.

REUBEN WRIGHT

1110½ Hay Street, Fayetteville, NC 28305   •   preppub@aol.com   •   (910) 483-6611

OBJECTIVE

To benefit an organization that can use an articulate communicator with exceptional motivational and training skills who offers a versatile background in marketing and sales, operations management, and human resources in the hospitality and advertising industries.

EXPERIENCE

GENERAL MANAGER. Markethouse Square Cafe, Coral Gables, FL (2003-present). Provided planning, human resources management, and marketing support for the opening of this popular local restaurant; currently manage all aspects of daily operation.

- Supervise up to 25 employees, directing the kitchen, host, and wait staff.
- Perform all interviewing, hiring, and training for new and existing staff members; known as a talented trainer, exceptional motivator, and articulate communicator.
- Oversee the creation and implementation of innovative and effective marketing programs; heavily involved in the development of all print and radio advertisements.
- Negotiated a three-year contract with the local coliseum, launching a marketing program that includes signage for the restaurant at all coliseum events, ticket giveaways, joint contests, and other promotions.
- Was a key player in the opening of the restaurant, directing equipment purchasing and setup for the kitchen, developing marketing and promotions for the opening, and interviewing, hiring, and training the initial staff.

GENERAL MANAGER. Domino's Pizza, Panama City, FL (1998-2003). Oversaw all operational aspects for this busy branch of the national pizza restaurant chain, including human resources, quality assurance, training, and profitability.

- Supervised as many as 45 employees, including assistant managers, shift managers, and wait, kitchen, and delivery staff.
- Interviewed, hired, and trained all employees; developed, updated, and modified employee schedules to ensure maximum profitability by controlling labor costs.
- Prepared Profit and Loss statements, monitored food ordering and local store vendors, oversaw all payroll, as well as C.O.S., and C.O.L. administration.
- Earned numerous awards given for both food quality and customer satisfaction awareness. Exceeded previous yearly sales for three consecutive years; ran a controllable profit of 43% at a startup unit after only three months, along with the highest profit analysis for two different units within my 13-unit area.

Highlights of earlier experience:
Before entering the hospitality industry, excelled in previous sales and marketing positions as a **SALES MANAGER** and **ACCOUNT EXECUTIVE** in the radio industry at several different stations in the Tallahassee market.

- While putting myself through school, served as **SALES MANAGER** at WTAL in Tallahassee; supervised a team of four Account Executives, servicing an established list of 40 accounts as well as developing new accounts.
- As an **ACCOUNT EXECUTIVE**, personally serviced as many as 25 new accounts while calling on local companies to cultivate new business.

EDUCATION

Bachelor of Science degree in **Communications** with a minor in **Business Administration**, Florida State University, Tallahassee, FL, 1995.

PERSONAL

Am a positive and optimistic professional who offers energy and enthusiasm along with an outgoing personality. Enjoy participating in community events, teamwork, and seeing both employees and customer benefit from a well-run unit. Work well under pressure.

CAREER CHANGE

Date

Exact Name of Person
Title or Position
Name of Company
Address (number and street)
Address (city, state, and zip)

RESTAURANT GENERAL MANAGER

seeks career in international affairs. This individual has gained many skills by working in the restaurant business, but she now seeks to establish a career which will utilize her International Studies degree.

Dear Exact Name of Person: (or Sir or Madam if answering a blind ad)

I would appreciate an opportunity to talk with you soon about how I could contribute to your organization through my versatile experience, education, and the application of my office operations and clerical skills.

As you will see from my enclosed resume, I attend the City University of New York at Buffalo, where I am pursuing a B.S. in International Studies and already have earned an associate's degree with a concentration in Biology. I am an excellent manager of time who has attended college and worked in often simultaneous jobs to finance my education. I am experienced in using Microsoft Word and many other popular software programs.

I have worked in restaurant management as well as in other jobs which have called for strong organizational, supervisory, and managerial skills. My versatile experience includes answering phones and handling general office responsibilities as well as inventory control, merchandising, employee training and supervision, and financial management of small businesses.

I am an enthusiastic, energetic, and outgoing individual who is known for my attention to detail and my ability to quickly learn new procedures to improve bottom-line profitability and the quality of customer service provided.

I hope you will call or write me soon to suggest a time convenient for us to meet and discuss your current and future needs and how I might serve them. Thank you in advance for your time.

Sincerely,

Yolanda P. Stewart

YOLANDA P. STEWART

1110½ Hay Street, Fayetteville, NC 28305 • preppub@aol.com • (910) 483-6611

OBJECTIVE   To offer a well-rounded background in environments where strong customer-service, organizational, supervisory, and managerial abilities are required to a business that can use a detail-oriented young professional with a knack for mathematics.

EDUCATION   Currently completing **B.S. degree with a concentration in International Studies,** City University of New York at Buffalo (CUNYB), Buffalo, NY.
Earned **Associate's degree with a concentration in Biology,** CUNYB, 2003.
Studied Biology at Kean University, Union, NJ.

SPECIAL SKILLS   Through experience and training, offer knowledge and skills which include:
Computers and word processing: type 40 wpm and am experienced in using Word.
Customer service: answering phones, providing information, and routing calls to the proper person; ability to get along with others; skill in working toward team and corporate goals; attention to detail; talent for creatively finding ways to increase productivity and bottom-line results

EXPERIENCE   *Am refining my time management as well as my business and supervisory skills while financing my education in these part-time and sometimes simultaneous jobs:*
GENERAL MANAGER. The Blue Oyster, Buffalo, NY (2002-present). Was credited with increasing overall business income as much as 60% during my work shifts because of my strong service orientation and genuine concern that diners enjoyed their visits.
- Apply my creativity to develop frequent menu changes and promotional ideas which have impacted the level of sales.
- Conduct weekly inventories of food items and supplies and coordinate the process of ordering from three separate retail sources. Train and supervise employees; prepare work schedules. Manage business accounting and financial support services while controlling the operating budget.
- Brought about an increase in revenues from large groups by actively marketing the restaurant as a place for business dinners and parties.
- Organize functions for as many as 100 people in a restaurant where one large party could easily equal the average daily income.
- Am relied on for my common-sense approach and ability to cement strong working relations as well as customer relations which lead to increased repeat business.
- Implemented a cost-saving idea which reduced expenses nearly $700 a year.

ASSISTANT MANAGER. Yat's, Union, NJ (2001-02). Had the opportunity to expand my knowledge of small business operations while handling day-to-day activities ranging from supervising a subordinate, to preparing the store for operations, to making food items for sale to customer's orders.

CUSTOMER SERVICE AND TRAINING SPECIALIST. Ye Olde Taverne and Grille, Newark, NJ (1998-2001). Provided high quality service in a large-volume restaurant which seated as many as 600 people and was selected to supervise and train new employees.

RECEPTIONIST. Gai Mode Beauty Salon, Newark, NJ (1995-1997). Gained practical experience in office operations, customer service, and clerical procedures for an exclusive upscale hair salon.

LANGUAGES   Have a working knowledge of the French and Italian languages.

Exact Name of Person
Title or Position
Name of Company
Address (no., street)
Address (city, state, zip)

RESTAURANT MANAGER
with a Radisson Hotel

Dear Exact Name of Person: (or Dear Sir or Madam if answering a blind ad.)

I would appreciate an opportunity to talk with you soon about how I could contribute to your organization through my talents as a restaurant manager with excellent financial and cost management skills as well as expertise in marketing, training, and customer relations.

In addition to 12 years of management experience, I have completed two years of formal education in food hygiene, quality control, stock control, purchasing, and food storage. I hold an Associate of Science degree.

With an outstanding ability to take a concept and make it work, I have boosted profits everywhere I have worked. For example, I have helped my current employer achieve a 46% growth in sales this year! In addition, I have a talent for designing menus that are both appealing and cost-effective.

I hope you will welcome my call soon to arrange a brief meeting at your convenience to discuss your current and future needs and how I might serve them. Thank you in advance for your consideration.

Sincerely yours,

Gene Holifield

Alternate last paragraph:
I hope you will call or write me soon to suggest a time convenient for us to meet and discuss your current and future needs and how I might best serve them. Thank you in advance for your time.

GENE HOLIFIELD

1110½ Hay Street, Fayetteville, NC 28305   •   preppub@aol.com   •   (910) 483-6611

OBJECTIVE   To benefit the restaurant industry through my formal education and track record of accomplishments as a manager who has earned a reputation directing food and beverage establishments in the United States and England.

ACHIEVEMENTS
- 2003: Within eight months, transformed an establishment losing money to achieve a 46% growth in sales.
- 1998: Started up a high-volume restaurant that continues to operate successfully in the Charlotte area.
- 1993: Developed a menu for an exclusive leisure complex in Manchester, England, that became a favorite of the clientele.

EXPERIENCE   **FOOD AND BEVERAGE DIRECTOR**. Radisson Hotel, Charlotte, NC (2003-present). Have introduced new setups for buffets and dining rooms to enhance aesthetics and traffic flow while excelling in a variety of roles because of my versatile management skills.
- *Employee training and supervision*: Oversee hiring, training, and scheduling while reducing labor costs.
- *Inventory control*: Cost-effectively manage the purchasing, receipt, and utilization of an inventory of perishable and nonperishable items.
- *Cost management*: Have reduced the cost of sales in beverage by 20%.
- *Customer service*: Continue to build a loyal clientele of regular, repeat business.
- *Sales and profitability*: Increased sales to 46% above the preceding year in only eight months.
- *Marketing/Advertising*: Advise sales personnel on menu setup and pricing; promote the restaurant through radio, newspaper, and TV advertisements.

GENERAL MANAGER. Kenny Rogers Roasters, Charlotte, NC (1998-00). Directed all aspects of the startup and operation of this new restaurant chain.
- *Operations management*: Through persistence and hard work, built this business "from scratch" to a successful first-year sales of $1.1 million.
- *Coordination*: Acquired skills in every aspect of unit operations management including sales/profit control, hiring/training, scheduling, and food cost control/ordering.

RESTAURANT MANAGER. La Fonte Restaurant, Raleigh, NC (1994-97). Directed the day-to-day operations of this 175-seat family restaurant, including employee hiring and training, cash handling, cost controls, stock control, monthly profit-and-loss statements, customer service, and purchasing.

FOOD AND BEVERAGE DIRECTOR. Herriots Leisure Complex, Ltd., Manchester, England (1990-1993). Advanced from Banquet Manager to direct all food and beverage departments at this leisure complex designed and built around the Roman baths in England.
- Coordinated operations of a full silver-service restaurant, a disco and cocktail lounge, and all banquet facilities. Wrote the restaurant's menu.

EDUCATION   Associate of Science degree in Electronics Engineering, Salford College of Technology, Manchester, England.
Continuing education courses in food hygiene, quality control, stock control, purchasing, and food storage, Openshaw Technical College, Catering Department, Manchester, England.

PERSONAL   Am a skilled trainer, creative organizer, and innovative problem-solver.

Date

Exact Name of Person
Exact Title
Exact Name of Company
Address
City, State, Zip

SALES MANAGER
with background as a
microbrewery entrepreneur

Dear Exact Name of Person (or Dear Sir or Madam if answering a blind ad):

With the enclosed resume, I would like to introduce you to my background and make you aware of my interest in exploring employment opportunities with your organization.

As you will see from my enclosed resume, for the past several years I have been involved in cofounding and co-managing a successful new restaurant and microbrewery. I used my strong sales, marketing, and communication skills to raise $2 million in startup funds, and then I applied those skills in motivating employees, communicating with vendors, and establishing strong business relationships. Once the restaurant and microbrewery were operational, I established an internal beer distribution business for the company and set up all channels of distribution in cities throughout Tennessee, West Virginia, and North and South Carolina. I have thoroughly enjoyed being the sales manager and "marketing arm" of the organization, and after much soul-searching, I have decided to leave the company I cofounded to embark upon a full-time career in sales.

Prior to my most recent entrepreneurial and management endeavor, I excelled in a track record of promotion to District Manager in a convenience store chain. As District Manager in charge of 10 stores, I boosted sales 16% and profits 19% while overseeing annual sales of $8 million. While overseeing 42 employees, I became known as a "hands-on" manager because of my personal style of interacting closely with all store managers and maintaining strong relationships with employees, vendors, and customers.

I am confident that my outgoing personality and effective sales style could become valuable assets for your organization, and I would enjoy an opportunity to talk with you about your needs and goals. A loyal team player, I tremendously enjoy the challenge of working with other committed individuals to produce outstanding bottom-line results. I can assure you that I am respected for my business ethics and can provide strong business, credit, personal, and professional references.

If my background and skills interest you, I hope you will contact me to suggest a time when we could meet in person to discuss your needs. Thank you in advance for your professional courtesies.

Yours sincerely,

Kevin P. Bell

KEVIN PATRICK BELL

1110½ Hay Street, Fayetteville, NC 28305　　•　　preppub@aol.com　　•　　(910) 483-6611

OBJECTIVE

To join an organization that can use an accomplished sales professional and operations manager with strong motivational and communication skills who offers experience in food and beverage sales and distribution, restaurant and microbrewery operations, as well as multiunit convenience store sales and management.

EXPERIENCE

ENTREPRENEUR, GENERAL MANAGER, & SALES MANAGER. Smoky Mountain Brewing Co., Asheville, NC (2002-present). As one of two founders of a 300-seat restaurant and microbrewery operation, was involved in all aspects of the company's startup, from the construction phase through the development of systems related to human resources, accounting and payroll, as well as marketing and sales.
- Used my strong sales, marketing, and communication skills to raise $2 million in startup funds; subsequently use those same skills to motivate employees, communicate with vendors, and establish strong business relationships.
- After launching a successful microbrewery, established an internal beer distribution business and set up all channels of distribution which included grocery stores, convenience stores, and other outlets in cities including Charlotte, Knoxville, Huntington, Spartansburg, as well as Gatlinburg. The microbrewery's beer is ranked best in town and barrel production broke the "top ten" among Southern brewpubs.
- Design point-of-sale items which included stickers, t-shirts, labels, and other tools.

DISTRICT SUPERVISOR (promoted from **Store Manager)**. Dairy Mart Convenience Stores, 10 locations, Cookeville, TN (1995-2001). After excelling as a Store Manager from 1995-96, was promoted to District Manager. As District Manager, boosted sales 16% and profits 19% while overseeing annual sales of $8 million in 10 stores. Took the initiative to computerize many operations.
- Oversaw 42 employees; made strategic decisions about opening new stores and closing unprofitable locations. Visited all stores to interact with staff and perform quality control "spot checks" on the chain's control systems related to labor practices, merchandising methods, cash control, inventory control, and customer service.
- Negotiated contracts with vendors and maintained liaison with prime vendor accounts.
- Solved problems related to pilferage; determined the inventory mix for maximum customer satisfaction and profitability; chose new store sites and their product mix.
- During my employment as Store Manager of Store #31, increased sales 27% while managing four employees. Coordinated with vendors, controlled cash, and oversaw product mix.

AFFILIATIONS

Former member, Board of Directors for Bele Chere Festival; member of the fundraising event. Served as President, Cookeville Academy Alumni Council.

EDUCATION

Majored in **Business and Psychology**, B.S. Program, *University of North Carolina at Asheville*, Asheville, NC. Previously attended Western Carolina University and Cookeville College.
Completed numerous executive development programs and technical training seminar.
Completed American Craft Brewers Academy, Denver, CO; studied leasing and finance, government regulation, flow of operations, beer styles, equipment selection, product formulas, and the management of brewing business and microbrewery operations.

PERSONAL

Reputation for business ethics. Outstanding business, credit, and professional references.

Date

Exact Name of Person
Exact Title
Exact Name of Company
Address
City, State, Zip

SALES MANAGER
for convention bookings at
a Radisson Hotel

Dear Exact Name of Person (or Dear Sir or Madam if answering a blind ad):

With the enclosed resume, I would like to make you aware of my background as a detail-oriented professional with exceptional communication, time management, and customer service skills in sales, retail, and management situations.

In my current position as Sales Manager for the Radisson Plaza Hotel in Cincinnati, I sell convention meeting space and hotel accommodations to corporations and associations throughout Ohio. Previously, after one year of experience as an Assistant Manager at Sandlin's Shoes, I was moved out of state to help build up a location with sagging sales. There I supervised approximately 20 employees, prepared payroll figures, oversaw inventory control, and gained experience in developing attractive displays.

I have thoroughly enjoyed becoming a part of the hospitality industry in my current job, and with my years of experience in management positions and customer relations, I have developed exceptionally strong sales skills and a proven ability to motivate others throughout and beyond training. I feel that these qualities would make me a valuable asset to any organization in the industry.

If you can use a self-motivated and flexible "go-getter" to benefit your company in countless ways, I hope you will contact me soon to arrange a time when we might meet to discuss your needs. I can provide excellent references upon request.

Sincerely,

Teresa Maria Enrique

TERESA MARIA ENRIQUE

1110½ Hay Street, Fayetteville, NC 28305 • preppub@aol.com • (910) 483-6611

OBJECTIVE

To contribute my managerial, sales, training, and motivational abilities in a position where my experience in high-volume retail sales environments will be beneficial to a company that can use a flexible "go-getter" who adapts easily to new situations.

EXPERIENCE

SALES MANAGER. Radisson Plaza Hotel, Cincinnati, OH (2003-present). Sell convention meeting space and hotel accommodations to corporations and associations throughout Ohio.
- Refined my telemarketing and interpersonal communication skills.

ASSISTANT MANAGER. Tiny Town, Cincinnati, OH (1999-03). Was moved from the Covington, KY location in 2000 to help build up a store with "sagging" sales; applied my skills and knowledge in areas including training and supervising employees in a high-quality shoe store.
- Sold an average of $3,000 in merchandise a week in a store which has reached a one-million dollar level in annual sales.
- Supervised approximately 20 employees with additional time spent in preparing payroll figures and overseeing inventory control activities.
- Gained experience in developing and setting up attractive merchandise displays.
- At the store in Covington, KY, from 1999-2000, handled operations including making bank deposits, opening and closing the store, and preparing payroll for 10 employees in children's wear.
- Contributed to repeat sales through my highly refined selling skills.
- Used creativity and an understanding of merchandising to prepare displays.

DEPARTMENTAL SUPERVISOR. Dawahare's Department Store, Louisville, KY (1998-99). Polished time management skills while overseeing operations and supervising and preparing time cards for about 20 employees in four departments.
- Gained knowledge of inventory control procedures while accepting and in-processing shipments of new merchandise.
- Received additional experience in floor management as well as merchandising.
- Was invited to share my knowledge as a sponsor for high school students who were members of the Distributive Education Clubs of America (DECA).

CO-MANAGER. Lane Bryant, Louisville, KY (1997-98). As co-manager, shared the supervision and managerial responsibilities in a 15-employee women's specialty apparel location.

ASSISTANT MANAGER and **SALES ASSOCIATE.** Lazarus Department Store, Louisville, KY (1995-97). Displayed my adaptability while progressing from a sales position to assist the manager of the intimate apparel and children's departments.
- Was selected to run the specialty Christmas Shop for the 1997 season which gave me increased opportunities to create attractive displays.

EDUCATION & TRAINING

Studied Business Management, University of Louisville, Louisville, KY.
Completed corporate training programs emphasizing developing customer relations and management techniques.

PERSONAL

Am very effective in training employees and helping them develop their own abilities.

Date

Exact Name of Person
Exact Title
Exact Name of Company
Address
City, State, Zip

Dear Exact Name of Person: (or Dear Sir or Madam if answering a blind ad):

With the enclosed resume, I would like to express my interest in offering my background and accomplishments to a facility that can benefit from my knowledge and experience related to food processing sanitation and production operations.

As you will see from my enclosed resume, I am presently a Production Foreman and the Sanitation Department Manager at Bellemeade Farms in Lansing, Michigan. In my time with Bellemeade I have been credited with reducing the rates of absenteeism and turnover for the Sanitation Department through my leadership and the example I set. Because I am fully bilingual in Spanish and English, I am able to communicate with the company's many non-English speaking employees and assist them in learning procedures and becoming a part of a productive team. I have received training in hazardous materials handling as well as in First Aid and CPR.

With a reputation as an intelligent, articulate, and creative professional, I have excelled in motivating and instructing others in prior jobs in fast food management and as a Foreign Language Instructor of Spanish. Throughout my career I have been singled out for praise by senior personnel for my ability to achieve results with limited resources, increase productivity and efficiency, and motivate others to learn and work together as a team while exceeding expected goals.

If you can use an experienced manager with specialized knowledge and training in sanitation and production operations, I hope you will call me soon to discuss how I might contribute to your organization. Thank you for your consideration of my qualifications and skills.

Sincerely,

Norman Ellerbe

NORMAN ELLERBE

1110½ Hay Street, Fayetteville, NC 28305　　•　　preppub@aol.com　　•　　(910) 483-6611

OBJECTIVE

To offer my specialized knowledge, experience, and qualifications in sanitation management within the food production industry to a facility which can benefit from my exceptional motivational, planning, and leadership abilities as well as from my Spanish language skills.

EDUCATION

Received company-sponsored training which has included:
- Situational Leadership II, Richard Bowden Company, 2003
- Hazardous Material Handling, Lansing Community College, Lansing, MI, 2003.

Completed American Heart Association programs: First Aid, CPR, and Heart Saver Plus, 2003.
Studied Accounting, Rivier College, Nashua, NH.
Graduated from Manchester Preparatory School for Boys, Manchester, NH.

LANGUAGE SKILLS

Fully bilingual in English and Spanish.
Have used my language skills to translate employee handbooks and other written materials.

EXPERIENCE

PRODUCTION FOREMAN and **SANITATION DEPARTMENT MANAGER.** Bellemeade Farms, Lansing, MI (2003-present). As foreman for shift deboning operations at this poultry processing plant, oversee daily operation of eight production lines for deboning and five lines for wing disjointing while also gaining experience in overseeing all operations of the sanitation department.
- Through my emphasis on safety, have reduced the number of reportable accidents an impressive 68% for the most recent one-year period.
- Provide leadership while emphasizing safety, quality control, and reaching production levels. Am setting an example of professionalism and dedication to quality standards which has resulted in reducing the absenteeism rate to 2.1% and turnover to 1.5%.

OPERATIONS AND TRAINING MANAGER. Boston Market Restaurants, Lansing, MI (2001-03). Worked closely with a co-manager while overseeing daily activities with an emphasis on training and supervising employees in order to ensure courteous service.

At colleges in Lansing, MI, and Manchester, NH, became known as a proficient and highly effective FOREIGN LANGUAGE INSTRUCTOR in the following positions which earned me a reputation as an articulate speaker who was skilled in helping others improve their knowledge of the Spanish language:
Lansing Community College (1998-2001). Trained students interested in refreshing their Spanish skills; developed instructional materials.
- Achieved excellent results in a six-week refresher course which saw 75% of my students improve overall test scores and obtain expected standards as a result of my teaching

*Manchester Community Colleg*e (1995-98). Provided instruction in Spanish while also developing course materials and lesson plans.
- Was credited with making contributions which allowed the language program to be rated by the New Hampshire Community College Board as "the best in the state."

OPERATIONS MANAGER. Church's Chicken, Lansing, MI and Manchester, NH (1993-95). Gained knowledge of management responsibilities such as training, and supervision of employees and of fiscal management while advancing from co-manager to store manager.

PERSONAL

Am detail oriented and extremely capable of performing multiple simultaneous tasks. Enjoy the challenge of motivating and leading others to achieve goals and exceed expected standards.

Date

Exact Name of Person
Exact Title
Exact Name of Company
Address
City, State, Zip

Dear Exact Name of Person (or Dear Sir or Madam if answering a blind ad):

Can you use an adaptable, articulate, and innovative manager who offers more than 20 years in the food service industry along with experience as an instructor who works well with people from all backgrounds and skill levels?

As you will see from my enclosed resume, I am an adaptable and versatile professional who offers experience ranging from food service preparation and management, to training and instructing courses, to hotel management, to inspecting food and housing operations. During my current career at the Anterrabae Boarding School in Standish, Maine, I have been singled out for vital and highly visible roles and have always exceeded expected standards of service and support.

I am a creative and innovative thinker who has been effective in finding ways to reduce costs, eliminate waste, and improve the quality of services in every position I have held. I am familiar with budget preparation and control, inventory control and procurement, the use of standard commercial kitchen equipment, and all phases of menu planning for healthy, nutritious, and attractive meals for large groups.

If you can use an experienced manager who has been recognized several times for superior performance and exceptional skills and knowledge, please contact me to suggest a time when we might meet to discuss your needs. I can assure you in advance that I could rapidly become an asset to your organization.

Sincerely,

Roger M. Noble

ROGER MAURICE NOBLE

1110½ Hay Street, Fayetteville, NC 28305   •   preppub@aol.com   •   (910) 483-6611

OBJECTIVE

To contribute to an organization through my demonstrated expertise in the hospitality industry as well as through my abilities as an instructor and manager who is known and respected for creativity, vision, innovation, and a positive style of motivating and leading.

TRAINING & SPECIALIZED KNOWLEDGE

Completed training which included courses in housing management, instructional techniques, sanitation inspection procedures, advanced food preparation, Total Quality Leadership, healthy choice menu planning, and customer service.

Operate most food service equipment (broilers, griddles, ovens, mixing machines, deep fat fryers, and steamers); am skilled in a wide variety of food cookery and preparation.

EXPERIENCE

Have advanced in managerial roles at Anterrabae Boarding School in Standish, ME:
SENIOR FOOD SERVICE MANAGEMENT SPECIALIST. (2003-present). Have been credited with developing innovative ideas which have made the food service for up to 1,100 boarders more supportive, healthy, and efficient.
- Managed an $120,000 quarterly budget while supervising as many as 30 employees.
- Created and then implemented a 35-day menu cycle which simplified planning.
- Directed a renovation project which included the kitchen and preparation areas.
- Was recognized for my expertise while planning and carrying out food services for a week-long conference in which 300 people (both selected staff and students) from other schools stayed and ate at the school.
- Displayed initiative and expert knowledge as planner/manager of a formal VIP reception which was carried out "flawlessly" and earned praise from more than 60 dignitaries.

FOOD SERVICE MANAGER. (1999-2003). Supervised as many as 25 employees while directing the preparation of meals and sanitation of food preparation areas for a dining facility with service ranging from 350 to 2,000 people.
- Controlled a quarterly food budget which averaged approximately $80,000.
- Located sources for food service equipment used to replace aging equipment.
- Supported 1,500 guests and 57 dignitaries attending a school ceremony.
- Provided "flawless" management for a project during which dining facilities received new tile, paint, and laminated table tops as well as new equipment.
- Led the food service team to excellent and outstanding scores in supply management assessments and was honored as the school's "Cook of the Quarter" in 2001.

SENIOR INSTRUCTOR. (1996-99). Oversaw operation of a program which trained "student quarters" managers for boarding schools nationwide and graduated 200 managers annually.

HOUSING FACILITIES ASSISTANT MANAGER. (1992-96). Arranged student living quarters and acted as "second-in-command" and front desk supervisor for a complex housing up to 1,500 people. Managed the complete renovation of 66 rooms and the front desk area as well as implementing a new key control system which replaced more than 600 locks.

Highlights of earlier experience: Managed four people while planning menus, ordering supplies, and overseeing preparation of meals at Applebee's Restaurant; was Cook/Baker for two hotel restaurants; was Supervisory Cook for a corrections center and police school.

PERSONAL

Possess exceptional skills in introducing innovative techniques, ensuring smooth service in a high-volume kitchen, and demonstrated leadership ability. Excellent references.

CAREER CHANGE

Date

Exact Name of Person
Title or Position
Name of Company
Address (number and street)
Address (city, state, and ZIP)

SHIFT MANAGER
with technical
electronics
background.
At first glance, this
individual looks out of
place in a book
containing people
with restaurant, food
service, and hotel
experience. However,
this individual seeks
to work in a hotel
environment in a
technical capacity
where he would be
involved in
maintaining power
generation equipment
and telephone
equipment for guests
at luxurious resorts
or on cruise ships.

Dear Exact Name of Person: (or Sir or Madam if answering a blind ad)

I would appreciate an opportunity to talk with you soon about how I could contribute to your organization through my well-developed skills and technical proficiency with telecommunications systems along with my outstanding motivational, supervisory, and managerial abilities. It is my desire to utilize my technical expertise to benefit a company in the hospitality industry.

You will see from my enclosed resume that I worked with Turner Telecommunications for almost five years as a Supervisory Telecommunications Specialist. I was widely recognized as the most technically proficient and skilled troubleshooter and operator in my department while installing, troubleshooting, operating, and supervising others in the operation of the Mobile Subscriber Equipment Network Switching System. My knowledge and expertise with this state-of-the-art system allowed me to advance ahead of my peers and earn three promotions within one 18-month period.

In addition to my demonstrated technical skills, I have excelled in positions where I trained and supervised others while ensuring high levels of customer satisfaction. In my present job as a Shift Manager with The Princess Hotel, I have already reduced operating costs approximately 4%.

You would find me in person to be an articulate young professional who enjoys the challenge of learning new systems and equipment. I am a fast learner who can easily absorb new information and put it to use.

I hope you will welcome my call soon to arrange a brief meeting to discuss your current and future needs and how I might serve them. Thank you in advance for your time.

Sincerely,

Kenneth R. Hicks

Alternate last paragraph:
I hope you will call or write me soon to suggest a time convenient for us to meet and discuss your current and future needs and how I might serve them. Thank you in advance for your time.

KENNETH R. HICKS

1110½ Hay Street, Fayetteville, NC 28305   •   preppub@aol.com   •   (910) 483-6611

OBJECTIVE

To offer my technical proficiency in the telecommunications field as well as my reputation as a creative thinker and a talented leader and motivator who can be counted on for innovative ideas which lead to higher levels of efficiency and productivity.

TECHNICAL SKILLS

Through training and four years of experience with Turner Telecommunications, developed and refined skills related to troubleshooting, installing, operating, and supervising others in the operation of telecommunications equipment with emphasis on the Mobile Subscriber Equipment Network Switching System.

- Installed, operated, supervised, and performed unit-level maintenance on the systems control center, node center switch, extension node switches, associated multiplexing, net radio interface equipment, communications security devices, and remote transmission radios.
- Troubleshoot to the board level using digital multimeters, computer terminals with diagnostic readouts, and board-level LEDs and configuration switches.
- Handled operational duties including initializing and loading databases along with positioning, assembling, and interconnecting equipment components.
- Interpreted and used operating instructions, database information, and system diagrams.
- Established and maintained network connectivity.
- Received and input information which was transmitted to the system control center as well as receiving operating directives and database input and output.
- Interpreted computer printouts to troubleshoot, repair, or replace faulty line-replaceable parts.
- Coordinated with system operators and managers in order to resolve difficulties.
- Placed spare equipment into operation on any occasion when on-line equipment failed.

EXPERIENCE

SHIFT MANAGER. The Princess Hotel, Boulder, CO (2003-present). Provide leadership while overseeing all phases of operations in this elegant 5-star hotel to include supervising 30 employees and ensuring a high level of customer service and satisfaction.

- Reduced operating costs on one shift and kept them within corporate guidelines.

SUPERVISORY TELECOMMUNICATIONS SPECIALIST. Turner Telecommunications, Atlanta, GA (1998-2003). Earned rapid advancement ahead of my peers including three promotions in one 18-month period while refining my technical, supervisory, and managerial abilities.

- Singled out for my skills and accomplishments, was widely recognized as the most technically proficient and skilled operator and troubleshooter in my department.
- Was awarded for my contributions as the senior telecommunications operator during a training session while my supervisor was absent.

TRAINING SPECIALIST. Taco Bell, Kirtland, OH (1996-98). Was responsible for training new employees in areas such as customer service standards, food preparation procedures, and handling money, including how to properly make change.

EDUCATION

Earned Associate of Science in Electronics Engineering, Atlanta College, Atlanta, GA, 2002.

PERSONAL

Am highly skilled in motivating and supervising others while setting the performance standard for them to follow. Excellent references available upon request.

Date

Exact Name of Person
Title or Position
Name of Company
Address (number and street)
Address (city, state, and ZIP)

SHIFT MANAGER
at Long John Silver's.

Dear Exact Name of Person: (or Dear Sir or Madam if answering a blind ad)

I would appreciate an opportunity to talk with you soon about how I could contribute to your organization through my experience related to bookkeeping, office management, and customer service in the manufacturing and hospitality industry environments.

As you will see from my enclosed resume, I offer a history of success in positions that require the ability to think and react quickly as well as those in which organizational, managerial, and customer service skills are required. I began my working career in the textile industry with Fairweather Textiles in Jersey City, NJ. From an entry-level position, I quickly advanced into positions of increasing responsibility throughout the facility. I was soon excelling in handling accounts receivable, accounts payable, cash disbursements, payroll and benefits, and general ledger accounting as well as performing customer services.

In addition to my exceptional business management skills, I can provide an employer with a dependable, enthusiastic, and hardworking professional who can make a difference through a strong customer-service orientation.

I hope you will welcome my call soon to arrange a brief meeting at your convenience to discuss your current and future needs and how I might serve them. Thank you in advance for your time.

Sincerely yours,

Allison Critchfield

Alternate last paragraph:
I hope you will call or write me soon to suggest a time convenient for us to meet and discuss your current and future needs and how I might serve them. Thank you in advance for your time.

ALLISON CRITCHFIELD

1110½ Hay Street, Fayetteville, NC 28305 • preppub@aol.com • (910) 483-6611

OBJECTIVE
To benefit an organization that can use an enthusiastic, hardworking professional with exceptional organizational skills who offers a background in bookkeeping, office management, and customer service in manufacturing and hospitality industry environments.

EXPERIENCE
SHIFT MANAGER. Long John Silver's, Cedar Rapids, IA (2003-present). Perform a variety of supervisory, administrative, customer service, and scheduling tasks for this busy local branch of the national fast food company.
- Provide managerial oversight and training to employees on my shift.
- Assign work and schedule employees according to customer traffic to ensure appropriate coverage and control labor hours.
- Conduct regular inventories to maintain adequate stock levels and facilitate ordering.
- Monitor the performance of associates, ensuring the highest possible levels of food quality, sanitation, and customer service.

BARTENDER. Texas Roadhouse, Cedar Rapids, IA (2002-03). Served as daytime Bartender at this popular local establishment, providing exceptional customer service to patrons as well as performing daily restocking and weekly inventories. Handled all telephone and takeout orders and performed hostess duties.

MANAGER. Diamond Dog's, Cedar Rapids, IA (2000-01). Managed all operational aspects for this popular local establishment, to include bookkeeping, inventory control, human resources, and events coordination.
- Interviewed, hired, and trained all employees; wrote weekly employee schedules and daily shift assignments according to traffic.
- Performed accounts payable, accounts receivable, and cash disbursements; processed weekly payroll for all employees.
- Planned and implemented promotions and other special events, coordinating entertainment and advertising as well as scheduling additional staff for the event.
- Conducted regular inventories to ensure adequate stores were on hand; ordered bar stock, paper products, cleaning supplies, etc. as needed.

SERVER. Johnson's Fishmarket, Norfolk, VA (1999-2000). Provided exceptional customer service to patrons of this local seafood restaurant, as well as assisting with light food preparation, closing the restaurant, cleaning assigned areas, and ensuring that everything was stocked up, cleaned, and ready for the next day's business.

Other experience: Excelled in a number of positions in the textile industry requiring attention to detail and the ability to work in a fast-paced, challenging environment.
PRODUCTION CONVERTER. Repro Depot Manufacturing, Trenton, NJ. Recorded incoming orders from customers, determining pounds of yarn needed and developing production schedules based on type of fabric and number of yards ordered.

ASSISTANT CONTROLLER. Fairweather Textiles, Jersey City, NJ. Started with Fairweather as an Order Processor, and quickly advanced into positions of increasing responsibility throughout the facility. Performed customer service, accounts receivable, accounts payable, cash disbursements, payroll and benefits, and general ledger accounting.

PERSONAL
Excellent personal and professional references are available upon request.

CAREER CHANGE

Date

Exact Name of Person
Title or Position
Name of Company
Address (no., street)
Address (city, state, zip)

STORE MANAGER
with Burger King. This
individual seeks a change
from restaurant work to
another field.

Dear Exact Name of Person: (or Dear Sir or Madam if answering a blind ad)

Can you use an enthusiastic, dedicated, and talented young professional who offers a strong background in management and office administration?

As you will see from my enclosed resume, I offer a background of success both in city government and a major international food service business. I am accustomed to working long hours and thrive on hard work, deadlines, and pressure.

In my most recent position as a Store Manager with the Burger King corporation, I reached this level in only one year in a career progression usually requiring twice the time. Although I am successful in handling the personnel, financial, and planning aspects of store operations, I have come to realize that this is not the environment in which I wish to make my permanent career home.

I am selectively exploring opportunities in an organization that can use my skills related to financial management, customer service and sales, and office administration.

I hope you will welcome my call soon to arrange a brief meeting at your convenience to discuss your current and future needs and how I might serve them. Thank you in advance for your time.

Sincerely yours,

Deborah Matlock

Alternate last paragraph:
I hope you will call or write me soon to suggest a time convenient for us to meet and discuss your current and future needs and how I might serve them. Thank you in advance for your time.

DEBORAH MATLOCK

1110½ Hay Street, Fayetteville, NC 28305   •   preppub@aol.com   •   (910) 483-6611

OBJECTIVE

To offer well-developed managerial abilities and thorough knowledge of office operations and administration to an organization that can use an adaptable young professional who could make valuable contributions through hard work and dedication to quality results.

EXPERIENCE

Advanced in the following track record of accomplishments with the international food service giant Burger King, Inc., Terre Haute, IN:
STORE MANAGER. (2003-present). In a progression usually taking two years, advanced from Management Trainee, to Second Assistant, to First Assistant, to Store Manager in only one year with the corporation.
- Gained experience in activities ranging from overseeing Quality Service Cleanliness (QSC) levels at all times, to holding controllable P&L items within budget, to insuring the accuracy of monthly reports for submission to the Owner-Operator.
- Supervise the staff and Swing Managers, including holding overall responsibility for the Management Development Program.
- Verify that deposits are received and processed by the bank.
- Create long-term objectives and action plans for QSC, sales, profit, and personnel development.

Gained valuable experience in office management and administrative support, Lexington-Fayette County Urban Government (L-FCUG), Lexington, KY:
ADMINISTRATIVE SUPERVISOR. (2000-02). Handled the daily administrative work flow and office management for the city's Community Service Branch as well as the responsibilities of Acting Director in her absence.
- Faxed and copied various memos and letters; posted and filed official documents.
- Answered phones, scheduled appointments, and met with clients.
- Processed and distributed mail.
- Organized the 2002 City Emergency Relief campaign which raised over $11,000, a higher-than-average level of contributions.
- Selected to conduct Teen Leadership group activities, was active as a leader/chaperone.

ADMINISTRATIVE SPECIALIST. (1999-2000). Was responsible for the safety, storage, and processing of materials used by couriers delivering classified information and secure communications back and forth between the city's government offices along with taking care of day-to-day clerical and office administration duties.
- Maintained a 100% accuracy rate on personnel actions for a ten-month period and continuously kept 100% accountability of supplies and equipment.
- Wrote new standard operating procedures for supply and administrative activities.

ADMINISTRATIVE SUPERVISOR. (1990-98). Supervised an administrative staff to ensure their compliance with assigned responsibilities and operations standards while also coordinating activities between a group of senior executives and managers.
- Ensured that annual employee performance reports were accurate and on time.
- Was officially commended for my sound judgment, decision-making skills, maturity, and planning abilities.

EDUCATION & TRAINING

A.A. degree, General Studies, Indiana State University, Terre Haute, IN, 1990.
Excelled in Burger King's management/supervisory skills program, Indianapolis, IN, 2003.

PERSONAL

Coach youth T-ball, soccer, and basketball teams. President of my neighborhood association.

Date

Exact Name of Person
Exact Title
Exact Name of Company
Address
City, State, Zip

Dear Exact Name of Person (or Dear Sir or Madam if answering a blind ad):

With the enclosed resume, I would like to make you aware of my background in food service and inventory control management as well as my skills as an instructor, supervisor, and leader.

A Certified Dietary Manager, I earned this distinction after being one of only two people at the Sandpiper Resort to pass the credentialing exam. I am presently assigned as a Subsistence and Supply Operations Manager at the Club Med Sandpiper Resort in Florida. In this capacity I have become recognized as an expert on computer ordering systems and was named the key player during the successful implementation of the resort's first Florida-based automated ordering and receiving systems. I traveled throughout the state while training and counseling personnel at various sites as they implemented the system at their own facilities. I also worked at the Club Med resort in Ibiza, Spain, for almost three years, during which time I became skilled at communicating with many local vendors.

Prior jobs in the nutritional services field have included training and supervising food preparation specialists, managing procurement and forecasting activities, ensuring compliance with sanitation and safety standards, and teaching courses in nutrition and in food sanitation. During my years of employment with Club Med International, I have consistently advanced and been commended in recognition of my professionalism and leadership skills.

If you can use an experienced professional who offers computer knowledge along with experience in food service and inventory control, I hope you will contact me to suggest a time when we might meet to discuss your needs. I can assure you in advance that I could rapidly become an asset to your organization.

Sincerely,

Curtis P. Eichbaum

CURTIS P. EICHBAUM

1110½ Hay Street, Fayetteville, NC 28305 • preppub@aol.com • (910) 483-6611

OBJECTIVE

To offer experience with an emphasis in inventory control/purchasing and food service operations management to an organization that can benefit from my reputation for leadership and motivational skills as well as my ability to promote teamwork and cohesion.

EDUCATION & TRAINING

Have completed 86 credit hours with a concentration in Hospitality Management, Rollins College, Winter Park, FL.

Attended numerous advanced courses with an emphasis on food service operations, dietary counseling, and restaurant sanitation as well as leadership and supervision.

CERTIFICATION

Passed the credentialing examination and became a Certified Dietary Manager (CDM), 2000.

EXPERIENCE

Have advanced to managerial/supervisory roles ahead of my peers with Club Med International:

SUPPLY OPERATIONS MANAGER. Club Med's Sandpiper Resort, FL (2000-present). Have become known as an expert in computer ordering systems and as a bottom-line-oriented professional while overseeing supply operations for the main dining facility of the resort.

- Control and manage a $500,000 budget while developing forecasts of food requirements.
- Oversee requisitioning, receipt, transportation, inspection, storage, security, issuing, and maintenance of funds related to the organization's subsistence and supply accounts.
- Developed cost-saving and efficient changes in procedures which reduced the physical subsistence inventory 35% and the number of assigned personnel 50%.
- Negotiate contracts with vendors.
- Was credited as the driving force behind the successful implementation of the resort's first Florida-based automated ordering and receiving system; trained and counseled personnel from sites throughout Florida as the system was implemented at their facilities.
- Was one of only two people at the Sandpiper Resort to pass the examination and become a CDM.
- Achieved a 100% certification rate after providing all employees with training in the National Restaurant Association's Applied Food Service Sanitation Course.

NUTRITION CARE DIVISION SHIFT SUPERVISOR. Club Med's Sandpiper Resort, FL (1998-00). Trained and supervised 15 people involved in preparing and serving regular and modified diets to resort visitors and staff members.

- Emphasized the importance of customer service and satisfaction as well as insisting on compliance with strict sanitation and safety guidelines.

SUPERVISOR FOR PRODUCTION AND SERVICES. Club Med, Ibiza, SPAIN (1995-99). Managed diverse activities which included subsistence procurement and issue, food production, and the preparation and servicing of both regular and modified diet meals.

- Trained and supervised kitchen staff while maintaining awareness of factors such as food costs, availability, and popularity as well as labor costs and individual skill levels.

COOK and **DIETARY TECHNICIAN.** St. Joseph Hospital, Pensacola, FL (1997-98). Selected to fill two separate positions within the same community hospital, worked as a Cook and as a Dietary Technician (1998) which involved assessing dietary needs.

PERSONAL

Offer computer skills with Windows, Microsoft Excel and Word, and several computer ordering programs. Excellent references upon request.

CAREER CHANGE

Exact Name of Person
Title or Position
Name of Company
Address (no., street)
Address (city, state, zip)

TRAINING MANAGER
for Boston Backyard
Burgers seeks transition
to retail

Dear Exact Name of Person: (or Dear Sir or Madam if answering a blind ad)

I would appreciate an opportunity to talk with you soon about how I could contribute to the Lerner management team through my well-rounded background, experience, and track record of success in roles calling for financial expertise, effective training and personnel management, and my bottom-line orientation.

As you will see from my enclosed resume, I am presently excelling as General Manager/Training Manager for two Boston Backyard Burgers' restaurants. With full responsibility for profit and loss, I have reduced food costs 5% and cut employee turnover in half. Heavily involved in training, I interview and make hiring decisions. Then I provide new-employee orientation and training for both locations which have a total of approximately 50 employees.

With proven organizational abilities, an eye for the bottom line, and a strong customer service orientation, I am confident that I have a great deal to offer any organization needing an experienced manager. I pride myself on my ability to creatively solve problems, be decisive in making decisions, and ensure that employees are working to their highest personal levels.

I hope after reviewing my resume you will be interested in setting up a brief meeting to discuss my qualifications for a managerial role with your organization. I look forward to talking with you soon to discuss your current and future needs and how I might serve them. Thank you in advance for your time.

Sincerely,

Rebecca J. Carver

REBECCA JENNIFER CARVER

1110½ Hay Street, Fayetteville, NC 28305   •   preppub@aol.com   •   (910) 483-6611

OBJECTIVE

To contribute to an organization that can use a mature, honest professional who offers financial expertise, strong interpersonal skills, and experience in developing and carrying out effective training and personnel development programs.

EXPERIENCE

GENERAL MANAGER/TRAINING MANAGER. Backyard Burgers, Boston, MA (2003-present). Was recruited for a trainee position by a church acquaintance and advanced quickly into management. Now direct all phases of activities which impact on the restaurant's profitability for two locations with a total of 50 employees. Increased average daily customer transactions and amounts spent per customer through the development of more focused local marketing campaigns.

- Refined the ability to read people and make decisions on their suitability for employment while interviewing and hiring new employees. Deal with corporate executives on a regular basis while keeping them informed of store operations and also interact with vendor representatives.
- Develop orientation programs for new hires and train them on corporate policies and activities which impact on them.
- Reduced food costs 5% through the development of improvements to the purchasing and inventory control procedures.
- Cut employee turnover **in half** in an industry where rapid turnover is the norm: make employees aware of the level of performance I expect from them and am known for treating people in a fair but firm manner.
- Oversee administrative activities including the development of monthly budgets, ordering of food and other supplies, and facility maintenance. Prepare profit and loss reports.

BRANCH OPERATIONS SUPERVISOR. Boston Public Library, Braintree and Dorchester branches, Boston, MA (1999-2002). Relocated to Boston because of my husband's promotion and decided to work outside the nursing field. Demonstrated versatile skills while overseeing areas including public relations, circulation, patron services, training and program management, and collection development for two geographically separate branches of the public library system.

- Established standards of accuracy and consistency in cataloging and shelving materials.
- Maintained 80,000 books, tapes, and videos and prepared regular reports on library utilization figures.
- Explained and interpreted regulations and procedures to members of the public as well as being called on to assist other staff members.

SUBSTANCE ABUSE PROGRAM COUNSELOR/NURSE. Charter Ridge, Jamaica Plains, MA (1997-98). Coordinated, monitored, and assessed activities in a 25-bed adolescent substance abuse unit while making certain that everything was being done to ensure the safety and security of the patients physically, medically, and psychologically.

**EDUCATION
&
TRAINING**

B.S., Nursing, Boston University, Boston, MA, 1996.
Studied Psychology at the University of Massachusetts, Boston, MA.
Completed training programs which emphasized the prevention of sex discrimination and elimination of sexual harassment in the workplace.

PERSONAL

Apply innovative, creative ideas while solving problems and making decisions. Am a proven leader with the ability to motivate employees to their highest level of productivity.

Date

Exact Name of Person
Title or Position
Name of Company
Address (no., street)
Address (city, state, zip)

WAITRESS

seeks promotion into
management.

Dear Exact Name of Person: (or Dear Sir or Madam if answering a blind ad)

I would appreciate an opportunity to talk with you soon about how I could contribute to your organization through my management experience as well as through my personal drive and ambition to succeed. I was very interested in your ad which stated that you are looking for management personnel for your Tony Roma's restaurant here in Anchorage and am enclosing my resume for your consideration.

I earned my B.S. degree in Business Administration recently from the University of Alaska-Anchorage. One of my greatest accomplishments was that I completed my degree while working full time in a variety of different jobs.

I believe I offer the type of track record in management that you are seeking. I consistently earned rapid advancement based on my abilities, skills, and knowledge. At UA-A I participated in a work-study program and after eight months was promoted to a full-time job supervising the 12 work-study students in the university's Financial Aid Department. Success in revitalizing this program and providing outstanding customer service led to my selection as the Veterans Affairs Coordinator.

As you will also see from my resume, I am highly experienced in customer service and sales and very skilled in organizing my priorities so that time is used wisely and most productively. I offer practical office administration experience including the ability to type 50 wpm, use 10-key adding machines, and operate computer systems for word processing and spreadsheet functions.

Certain that I offer experience and an educational background which give me a broad base on which to build, I also offer personal qualities of persistence and dependability. A proven team player, I work well independently or as a leader contributing to group efforts with a high level of success.

I hope you will call or write me soon to suggest a time convenient for us to meet and discuss your current and future needs and how I might serve them. Thank you in advance for your time.

Sincerely yours,

Valerie S. Epstein

VALERIE SUSANNE EPSTEIN

1110½ Hay Street, Fayetteville, NC 28305   •   preppub@aol.com   •   (

OBJECTIVE	To offer my managerial abilities to an organization that can benefit through the app of my ability to handle multiple tasks simultaneously while guaranteeing that each de taken care of and each customer receives the best and most courteous service possible.
EDUCATION	**B.S., Business Administration,** University of Alaska-Anchorage, 2002. • Earned my degree while working full time.
EXPERIENCE	**WAITRESS.** Loose Moose Cafe and Billiards and Keeper's Grill, Anchorage, AK (2003-present). Have become very adept at maximizing limited time while working at these two popular restaurants simultaneously: contribute my efforts in operational areas including serving customers, maintaining supplies at wait stations, and assisting in cleaning. • Refined my ability to read people and quickly decide how to respond to them in order to see that they are satisfied with the food and service.

ASSISTANT ATHLETIC TRAINER. University of Alaska-Anchorage (2002-03). Provided a variety of support services to the college's athletic departments by assisting the head trainer in the evaluation, diagnosis, and rehabilitation of sports injuries; was responsible for the upkeep of training room supplies and equipment.
- Learned to be patient with athletes who were sometimes uncooperative in helping with their own rehabilitation and often frustrated with the progress of their recovery.
- Applied my organizational skills while acting as secretary for a professional association.

VETERANS AFFAIRS COORDINATOR. University of Alaska-Anchorage (2001-02). Singled out for this position in the Veterans Affairs Office on the basis of my demonstrated organizational and communication skills, supervised four work-study students processing the paperwork for more than $250,000 a year in educational benefits for military veterans.
- Applied my organizational skills while coordinating the department director's schedule and handling the supporting paperwork for financial aid to veterans.
- Advised clients on the availability of financial aid and in making decisions on course work and scheduling.

ADMINISTRATIVE ASSISTANT, FINANCIAL AID DEPARTMENT. University of Alaska-Anchorage (1998-2000). After approximately eight months as a work-study student, was singled out for my skills and maturity and given a permanent position as the supervisor of 12 work-study students.
- Counseled students and their parents on the different choices available to them for financing their college education.

MANAGER. Snowy Ridge Exxon, Anchorage, AK (1996-98). Began working as a Cashier at another location (Cedar Creek Exxon) and was quickly singled out for the manager's job and promoted.
- Applied organizational abilities and attention to detail while ensuring paperwork was reconciled at the end of each shift as well as monthly inventory reports.

SPECIAL KNOWLEDGE	Offer computer skills in working with the following operating systems and software: Windows, Word, Microsoft Works, other software.
PERSONAL	Hold CPR certification. Am very people-oriented and strive to always ensure total customer satisfaction. Can handle multiple tasks simultaneously.

910) 483-6611

lication
tail is

ABOUT THE EDITOR

Anne McKinney holds an MBA from the Harvard Business School and a BA in English from the University of North Carolina at Chapel Hill. A noted public speaker, writer, and teacher, she is the senior editor for PREP's business and career imprint, which bears her name. Early titles in the Anne McKinney Career Series (now called the Real-Resumes Series) published by PREP include: *Resumes and Cover Letters That Have Worked, Resumes and Cover Letters That Have Worked for Military Professionals, Government Job Applications and Federal Resumes, Cover Letters That Blow Doors Open,* and *Letters for Special Situations.* Her career titles and how-to resume-and-cover-letter books are based on the expertise she has acquired in 20 years of working with job hunters. Her valuable career insights have appeared in publications of the "Wall Street Journal" and other prominent newspapers and magazines.

PREP Publishing Order Form

You may purchase any of our titles from your favorite bookseller! Or send a check or money order or your credit card number for the total amount*, plus $4.00 postage and handling, to PREP, 1110 1/2 Hay Street, Fayetteville, NC 28305. You may also order our titles on our website at www.prep-pub.com and feel free to e-mail us at preppub@aol.com or call 910-483-6611 with your questions or concerns.

Name: _____

Phone #:_____

Address: _____

E-mail address:_____

Payment Type: ☐ Check/Money Order   ☐ Visa   ☐ MasterCard

Credit Card Number: _____ Expiration Date: _____

Put a check beside the items you are ordering:

- ☐ Free—Packet describing PREP's professional writing and editing services
- ☐ $16.95—REAL-RESUMES FOR RESTAURANT, FOOD SERVICE & HOTEL JOBS. Anne McKinney, Editor
- ☐ $16.95—REAL-RESUMES FOR MEDIA, NEWSPAPER, BROADCASTING & PUBLIC AFFAIRS JOBS. Anne McKinney
- ☐ $16.95—REAL-RESUMES FOR RETAILING, MODELING, FASHION & BEAUTY JOBS. Anne McKinney, Editor
- ☐ $16.95—REAL-RESUMES FOR HUMAN RESOURCES & PERSONNEL JOBS. Anne McKinney, Editor
- ☐ $16.95—REAL-RESUMES FOR MANUFACTURING JOBS. Anne McKinney, Editor
- ☐ $16.95—REAL-RESUMES FOR AVIATION & TRAVEL JOBS. Anne McKinney, Editor
- ☐ $16.95—REAL-RESUMES FOR POLICE, LAW ENFORCEMENT & SECURITY JOBS. Anne McKinney, Editor
- ☐ $16.95—REAL-RESUMES FOR SOCIAL WORK & COUNSELING JOBS. Anne McKinney, Editor
- ☐ $16.95—REAL-RESUMES FOR CONSTRUCTION JOBS. Anne McKinney, Editor
- ☐ $16.95—REAL-RESUMES FOR FINANCIAL JOBS. Anne McKinney, Editor
- ☐ $16.95—REAL-RESUMES FOR COMPUTER JOBS. Anne McKinney, Editor
- ☐ $16.95—REAL-RESUMES FOR MEDICAL JOBS. Anne McKinney, Editor
- ☐ $16.95—REAL-RESUMES FOR TEACHERS. Anne McKinney, Editor
- ☐ $16.95—REAL-RESUMES FOR CAREER CHANGERS. Anne McKinney, Editor
- ☐ $16.95—REAL-RESUMES FOR STUDENTS. Anne McKinney, Editor
- ☐ $16.95—REAL-RESUMES FOR SALES. Anne McKinney, Editor
- ☐ $16.95—REAL ESSAYS FOR COLLEGE AND GRAD SCHOOL. Anne McKinney, Editor
- ☐ $25.00—RESUMES AND COVER LETTERS THAT HAVE WORKED. McKinney. Editor
- ☐ $25.00—RESUMES AND COVER LETTERS THAT HAVE WORKED FOR MILITARY PROFESSIONALS. McKinney, Ed.
- ☐ $25.00—RESUMES AND COVER LETTERS FOR MANAGERS. McKinney, Editor
- ☐ $25.00—GOVERNMENT JOB APPLICATIONS AND FEDERAL RESUMES: Federal Resumes, KSAs, Forms 171 and 612, and Postal Applications. McKinney, Editor
- ☐ $25.00—COVER LETTERS THAT BLOW DOORS OPEN. McKinney, Editor
- ☐ $25.00—LETTERS FOR SPECIAL SITUATIONS. McKinney, Editor
- ☐ $16.00—BACK IN TIME. Patty Sleem
- ☐ $17.00—(trade paperback) SECOND TIME AROUND. Patty Sleem
- ☐ $25.00—(hardcover) SECOND TIME AROUND. Patty Sleem
- ☐ $18.00—A GENTLE BREEZE FROM GOSSAMER WINGS. Gordon Beld
- ☐ $18.00—BIBLE STORIES FROM THE OLD TESTAMENT. Katherine Whaley
- ☐ $14.95—WHAT THE BIBLE SAYS ABOUT... *Words that can lead to success and happiness* (large print edition) Patty Sleem

_____ **TOTAL ORDERED**

_____ **(add $4.00 for shipping and handling)**

_____ **TOTAL INCLUDING SHIPPING**

PREP offers volume discounts on large orders. Call us at (910) 483-6611 for more information.

Would you like to explore the possibility of having PREP's writing
team create a resume for you similar to the ones in this book?

For a brief free consultation, call 910-483-6611
or send $4.00 to receive our Job Change Packet to
PREP, 1110 1/2 Hay Street, Fayetteville, NC 28305. Visit our
website to find valuable career resources: www.prep-pub.com!

QUESTIONS OR COMMENTS? E-MAIL US AT PREPPUB@AOL.COM